DATE DUE

11-13-18	

THE STATE
AND
GLOBAL CHANGE

The Political Economy of Transition in the Middle East and North Africa

Edited by

Hassan Hakimian

and

Ziba Moshaver

CURZON

First Published in 2001
by Curzon Press
Richmond, Surrey
http://www.curzonpress.co.uk

Editorial Matter © 2001 Hassan Hakimian and Ziba Moshaver

Designed and Typeset in Sabon by LaserScript Ltd, Mitcham, Surrey
Printed and bound in Great Britain by
Biddles Ltd, Guildford and King's Lynn

British Library Cataloguing in Publication Data
A catalogue record of this book is available from the British Library

Library of Congress Cataloguing in Publication Data
A catalogue record for this book has been requested

ISBN 0–7007–1365–4 (Hbk)
ISBN 0–7007–1366–2 (Pbk)

To Our Sons
Bijan and Babak (HH)
and
Cyrus (ZM)

Contents

Contents

Preface

Economic liberalization and reform are widely considered as the favoured remedies for the declining economic fortunes of the Middle Eastern and North African states in the past two decades. International economic institutions have been among the main advocates of transition to market-led economies in the region and a force contributing to its realization. This has placed the state at the centre of the proposed transformations, acting both as an instrument of, and an obstacle to, change.

With attempts at liberalization worldwide spanning over twenty years, the time was considered ripe for a re-evaluation of its premises and outcome. This was the principal reason behind the Middle East and North Africa Region Division of the World Bank to propose a conference to enlarge the debate on the role of the state in this region. This initiative resulted in a World Bank sponsored conference on 'The Changing Role of the State in the Middle East and North Africa' held on 6th May 1998 at the School of Oriental and African Studies (SOAS), University of London. The conference was organized by the Centre of Near and Middle East Studies (CNMES) at SOAS.

Most of the contributions to this volume originated in this conference and reflect closely its multidisciplinary approach. The conference was pioneering in two respects. First, it provided an opportunity for a unique gathering of experts from the World Bank and academics from the region, the UK and the United States to debate their views on the political economy of transition and reforms in the region. Second, the contributions to the conference drew from interdisciplinary approaches and outlooks involving international, regional and national levels of analysis.

ix

The outcome of the debate is presented in this volume in three distinct, yet interrelated, parts that go beyond providing a balance sheet and invite a re-thinking of the main issues involved in the political economy of transformation in the region. The re-thinking revolves around three themes: the rationale and strategies for reform, the processes and outcomes, and, finally, the nature of the state in a changing global setting.

We thank the World Bank for generous funding of the conference and the CNMES at SOAS for organizing it. The project owes a great deal to various individuals at the World Bank for direct initiative, support and encouragement throughout. Among them special thanks are due to: Dr Kemal Derviş, Vice-President, Middle East and North Africa Region, Dr A. Bouhabib, Regional Communication Advisor, Andew Rogerson, Special Representative at the Bank's London office, and Keiko Itoh also of the World Bank in London.

While benefiting from their full support and generosity, we were left to our own devices in putting together this volume as we wished. We are also grateful to various colleagues at SOAS, especially Massoud Karshenas and Charles Tripp for their support and inspiration, and to the staff of CNMES, especially its coordinators, Dr Sarah Stewart and Regina Miesle for their help at different stages of our work. Thanks are also owed to Katharine Pulvermacher, who provided meticulous research and editorial assistance, and to Malcolm Campbell of the Curzon Press for his encouragement and patience with the manuscript. The views expressed and any errors contained in individual contributions are the responsibility of the authors and not of their respective institutions or any other party.

H. Hakimian and Z. Moshaver

Notes on the Contributors

Mustapha Kamel Al-Sayyid is Professor of Political Science and Director of the Centre for the Study of Developing Countries, Cairo University. [rucsdc@rusys.cg.net]

Linda Van Gelder is Senior Economist in the Middle East and North Africa Region of the World Bank, Washington, D.C. [Lvangelder@worldbank.org]

Hassan Hakimian is Senior Lecturer in Economics at the School of Oriental and African Studies (SOAS), University of London. [H.Hakimian@soas.ac.uk]

Raymond Hinnebusch is Professor of International Relations and Middle East Politics at the University of St. Andrews, Scotland. [rh10@st-andrews.ac.uk]

Massoud Karshenas is Reader in Economics at the School of Oriental and African Studies (SOAS), University of London. [mk@soas.ac.uk]

Ziba Moshaver is Research Associate at the International Institute for Strategic Studies (IISS), London, and at the Centre of Near and Middle Eastern Studies (CNMES) in the School of Oriental and African Studies (SOAS), University of London. [zm@clara.net]

Emma C. Murphy is Lecturer in Middle East Politics at the Centre for Middle Eastern and Islamic Studies, University of Durham. [emma.murphy@durham.ac.uk]

Roger Owen is Professor of Middle East History at the Centre for Middle Eastern Studies, Harvard University. [rowen@mideast.fas.harvard.edu]

John Page is Director, Poverty Reduction Strategy, at the World Bank, Washington, D.C. [Jpage@worldbank.org]

Charles Tripp is Head of the Department of Political Studies and Senior Lecturer in Middle East Politics at the School of Oriental and African Studies (SOAS), University of London. [ct2@soas.ac.uk]

Oktar Türel is Professor of Economics at the Middle East Technical University (METU), Ankara. [oturel@metu.edu.tr]

Chapter One

Introduction

Interest in the role of state has been at the centre of a growing body of literature dealing with transition and reform in developing countries in the past few decades. This interest has been intensified in recent years by the rising trend of globalization and its impact on various regions, territories and states around the world.

This book is concerned with the changing role of the state in the Middle East and North Africa (MENA) region in the past two decades. It addresses the rationale, context and impact of reform on those states in the region that have already initiated structural adjustment and liberalization programmes, and examines the challenges facing those that are yet to follow this path.

The slow pace and limited scale of reforms in the MENA region have received special attention in a wide range of recent literature. With transition to market-oriented policies intensifying in many parts of the developing world, the states in the MENA region have come under greater scrutiny for their apparent reluctance to institute such reforms. This has led to frustration by international development agencies and financial institutions on one hand, and scholarly explanations, on the other, seeking its reasons in various political and socio-cultural attributes of the region (see Waterbury 1998).

Two interrelated considerations have underlined the case for strong prescriptions in favour of transition to market-led reforms in MENA: the region's faltering growth trend in recent decades, on the one hand, and its failure to take advantage of increasing global opportunities, on the other. As far as the former is concerned, MENA's economic performance after the oil-boom prosperity of the 1970s has been characterized by comparative decline and a deterioration in its

1

position compared to other regions and its own potential. This trend is supported by a variety of indicators (real per capita GDP, oil revenues and investment trends) all highlighting the need for action to halt, and reverse, this trend and to revive MENA's economic fortunes.

It is in this setting – described by some as the 'growth crisis' of the 1980s (Page 1998) – that the latter consideration, i.e. bygone global opportunities, acquires special significance in the MENA context. Here, too, similar concerns have pointed to the high opportunity cost for the region of 'being left behind' on a world stage characterized by a larger number of poorer nations benefiting form globalization. Before the international economic arena was rocked by the Asian financial crisis, upbeat accounts of the future of globalization in the MENA region abounded, making success largely a function of 'the choice of appropriate policies' alone. While the lessons of the crisis in Asia may have helped moderate this type of overt optimism, interest in MENA's integration into the global economy remains keen and is likely to be intensified with a number of regional integration initiatives involving principally the EU and the Mediterranean region (Shafik 1998; Diwan *et al.* 1998; Hoekman 1998).

On both these accounts – internal imperatives and external opportunities – therefore, the policies favoured by the 'Washington consensus' are likely to remain firmly on the agenda for the MENA region in the coming years. A battery of recent literature has thus made a strong case for reforming MENA states' political and economic systems and for transition to market-oriented regimes including domestic economic liberalization and a more open approach to the international economy (see, for instance, World Bank 1995; Shafik 1998; Handoussa 1997).

But if the economic logic of reform is so manifestly simple and almost universally understood, how can one comprehend – let alone explain – the MENA states' low propensity to respond? As Page and Van Gelder rhetorically put it in their contribution to this book: '*Some economists in the development policy business have begun to ask, "If our advice is so good, why don't more people take it, and why don't those who take it do better?"*'

Almost all contributors to this book engage directly or indirectly with different aspects of these two questions. Some are invariably concerned with the *rationale* for transformation; others with its *process* in specific circumstances and countries; yet others with actual *outcomes* (some are of course concerned with more than one aspect). But as the contributions demonstrate, the answer to these questions lie as much in the specificity of the MENA context as in the nature of the transition project itself, which has now been articulated and prescribed by the Washington consensus for the last two decades.

The structure of the book and the order of presentation of different chapters in it reflect these questions. In Part I, chapters by Page and Van Gelder, Karshenas and Hakimian, respectively, grapple with various aspects of the *logic* for and strategies of state transformation. This does not necessarily mean that they accept or reject wholly the rationale for reforms, but address aspects of the transition process that impinge on its logic and various strategies needed for achieving optimum outcomes.

In Part 2, the contributors focus on the *process* of transformation in selected countries and examine its *outcomes*. Here, Hinnebusch offers a comparative study of the politics of liberalization in Egypt and Syria; Murphy examines Tunisian reforms since the late 1960s; Al-Sayyid addresses the international and regional environments influencing reform and transition in Jordan, Tunisia and Egypt; and Türel offers a comprehensive assessment of the restructuring of the public sector in Turkey – arguably one of the most 'transformed' states of the region.

The division between 'logic and process' – or 'rationale and outcome' – should not be overstated. Several of the chapters address more than one aspect of the transformation process. For instance, in examining the process of the changing role of state in case studies in Part 2, several authors also take up, directly or indirectly, the question of strategies and rationale for reforms. Likewise, the contributions in Part 1 are simultaneously concerned with outcomes. Nevertheless, the division imposed between these parts is based on the central focus and principal concerns of each contribution.

Finally, in Part 3, three contributions (by Owen, Tripp and Moshaver, respectively), offer a fresh assessment of the transition experience by advocating a 'rethinking' of the role of state. The first two take a critical look at the methodological problems of studying the 'changing role of state', and scrutinize the notion of the 'state' and what constitutes the 'state apparatus' in the transition process. The latter addresses the challenges of globalization questioning its impact on individual states in light of changing structures of international political and economic relations. These three contributions, as we shall see, draw together various aspects touched upon earlier by other contributions in the volume.

In what follows, a summary of different chapters is presented.

3

In Chapter 2, John Page and Linda Van Gelder search the 'missing link' between 'the chain running from policy reform to accelerated growth'. They address directly the question highlighted earlier – why advice from 'Washington consensus' (presuming it is good advice) has failed to be heeded universally and even when it has been taken up, why its success rate has been disappointing. They verify that there is a strong, and statistically significant, positive correlation between 'institutional capability' – defined as the state's ability to perform critical institutional functions – and economic growth. They thus establish a 'virtuous circle' between institutional reform, policy reform, and growth. Their statistical analysis is further supported by evidence from the MENA region showing that even during the contraction days of 1985–95 those economies with reformist policies and better than average institutions avoided negative growth. On the contrary, weak institutional capability and organizations impeded policy reforms and ultimately, growth prospects. This leads Page and Van Gelder to conclude that, ultimately, the quality of public administration in MENA will need to change if these states are to forge the missing link between policy reform and sustained growth.

In Chapter 3, Massoud Karshenas too starts with similar concerns about the slow pace of economic reforms and lack of supply response to them in the MENA region. He recognizes the 'urgent need for the MENA economies to diversify their export base' in order to take advantage of the new opportunities provided by the global economy. Yet he diverges from the 'Washington consensus' and its approach to the experience of globalization in the region in two important ways. First, he concentrates on what he considers the 'fundamental structural features' of the MENA economies as the possible causes for the sluggishness of economic reform and adjustment. Second, he argues that economic development is essentially 'a path dependent' process. This means that 'the past experience of development limits the set of choices available to societies at any point in time.' Translated into the MENA context, this implies the MENA economies seem to have been 'locked' into social institutions and skill patterns that are inappropriate in the context of new technological realities and the prevailing trends for primary commodity prices in the global economy. A prominent feature of the MENA economies, inherited from the past experience of development, is the low stock of skills and human capital compared to other countries with similar levels of per capita income. This feature of the MENA economies, which is reflected in relatively low human skill/natural

4

resource ratios by international standards, has proved particularly inimical to export diversification at a time when the new automated technologies demand high levels of general skills and education. This feature is likely to act as a major obstacle to competitiveness in manufacturing and processing activities in the MENA region. Karshenas's main conclusion is that in addition to the usual liberalization policies, which are aimed at improving the efficiency of resource use, it is also imperative for MENA countries to develop specific strategies to address their serious educational and human skills gaps in order to ensure a successful outcome of their globalization experience.

Chapter 4 by Hassan Hakimian takes up the question of 'lessons' of globalization after the Asian crisis. According to Hakimian, East Asia's impressive economic successes in the past had led to an optimistic paradigm in development that emphasized the link between 'sound' development policies and successful performance outcome. In recent years, in particular, there has been growing expectation that inferior economic performance in LDCs, in general, and in the MENA region, in particular, can be remedied solely through adoption of 'appropriate economic policies'.

Whilst not negating the case for the outward-oriented model of development, the tumultuous Asian crisis has helped highlight the hitherto discounted risks and challenges *en route* to the glory associated with globalization (e.g., risks due to capital account liberalization, or an unprecedented integration between the local, regional and international assets, equity and currency markets).

As far as MENA countries (or other LDCs) are concerned, the risks stemming from globalization now need to be understood, and carefully set against its promises. This experience can thus help restore some balance to claims and counterclaims about what *can* or *cannot* be achieved through open door policies in practice, and it can only be hoped that the MENA countries can positively learn from it in designing their strategy for participation in the globalization 'project'.

As stated above, the chapters in Part 2 focus on the processes behind state transformation in selected MENA countries and examine their outcomes. In Chapter 5, Raymond Hinnebusch questions the absence of a political 'logic' or 'strategy' in the economists' conceptualization of the liberalization process. The 'Washington consensus' views liberalization as 'an inevitable response to economic crisis'. Accordingly, there is one rational objective formula for economic success: failure to pursue it in the Middle East is viewed as a function of political irrationality. Hinnebusch develops an interesting analytical framework to examine the *political* logic of reform in Egypt and Syria in a comparative context and uses it to explain their different experiences. His analysis involves an examination of the impact of multiple variables – the international context, the balance of social forces (classes and groups), and elite strategies. He shows that at each and every level, the process and outcome of the Egyptian reforms have gone beyond those of the Syrian ones.

Despite intense external pressures, both Egypt and Syria have successfully insisted that the pace and scope of economic reform be compatible with political stability. Hinnebusch maintains that this emanated from 'a rational balancing of external and indigenous pressures and opportunities and was far from being the product of an economically irrational political culture.' Another sensitive area – so often ignored by international economic institutions – was the social class implications of economic policies. These considerations lead Hinnebusch to conclude that the Egyptian and Syrian cases suggest that incremental liberalization is wiser and helps avoid political instability.

A similar concern with the political logic and rationale of economic reforms characterizes the study of state transformation in Tunisia in Chapter 6 by Emma Murphy. Murphy examines in some detail the transformation of state in Tunisia – one of the region's most successful, and early, liberalizers. Although the country abandoned socialism in favour of a gradual process of reform as early as 1969, the real transformation shaped up in earnest after the coming to power of President Ben Ali in 1987. In the absence of a strong private-sector industrial class, the regime has acted as the spearhead of economic liberalization, usually pre-empting rather than responding to demands of external actors such as the World Bank or IMF. Murphy shows that the regime has been driven by its own needs to reconstruct a power-base following the failures of populist and socialist policies in the post-independence era.

One of the main contentions of this chapter is that the state is not a monolithic actor (a theme to which we return below), but comprises a variety of interests which may find themselves at odds with one another during economic transition (such as conflicts of interest between the bureaucracy and party officials). She shows that, through careful political manoeuvrings, the regime has succeeded in transforming Bourguiba's old corporatist state into a new multi-party version of corporatism that allows the regime to act with relative autonomy from both its own party and the bureaucracy. As a result, an ongoing process of 'stage-managed' democratization has concealed the reality of a retreat into an authoritarian mode of government, giving the regime the ability to implement economic liberalization and compensating for the consequent loss of direct economic control by increasing its political powers through a re-structured state apparatus.

In Chapter 7, Mustapha Al-Sayyid draws examples from three Arab countries of Egypt, Tunisia and Jordan to examine those external political influences that have helped shape their economic policy choices since the 1970s. He argues that both the international and regional environments have contributed in several ways to a reduction in the role of state as a direct producer and provider in the economic sphere in these countries: by offering inducements; by highlighting success stories; or even by placing constraints on the implementation of certain development strategies. The analysis also suggests that both these environments contributed to the adoption of the state-led model of development in the 1950s and 1960s, but reversed their directions after the mid-1980s in favour of the neo-liberal model.

Al-Sayyid argues that the shift of emphasis towards market-led policies is part of a broader, pragmatic process of adaptation in many countries of the South, which is best understood by the state elites' attempt to maximize the political power of the state and preserve social and political stability – rather than by any rigid adherence to ideology. This puts the current 'commitment' to a free-market economy, or to a liberal political order, in perspective – suggesting that it will always be a highly qualified one.

In the final chapter of Part 2 (Chapter 8), Oktar Türel turns to Turkey for a comprehensive and detailed assessment of the process of restructuring of her public sector. He shows that the far-reaching transformation of the economic role of state has been intertwined with a remarkable reshaping of the political landscape – as seen in a notable convergence of the economic platforms of diverse political parties in the April 1999 elections.

But while a wide ranging and extensive commitment to 'market-friendly' economic policies may suggest the ultimate triumph of the 'Washington consensus' in Turkey, Türel remains doubtful about the social and political feasibility and sustainability of further reforms in the public sector. First, further cuts in public spending and/or the commercialization of public services can erode both the legitimacy of governments and the credibility of the formal political system. They can encourage the impoverished segments of society to seek refuge in communal clusters of kinship, neighbourhood, ethnicity and religion rather than in established and formal social safety nets.

Second, the prevailing practice of 'management by crisis' can result in a loss of trust in, and credibility of, public administration, leading to widespread resistance and cynicism against all reform proposals – irrespective of their aims and instruments and whether benevolent or not.

Several of the studies in Parts 1 and 2 highlight methodological and philosophical difficulties of studying the role of state in general and those in the MENA region, in particular. This is why two of the contributions in the final section of the book (Part 3) are mainly concerned with the need to 'rethink' the state and its role in the broader political economy context.

In Chapter 9, Charles Tripp questions two widely-held theses: first, that the project to transform the economic role of state leads necessarily to its 'enfeeblement'; and second, that economic resources and the structures which allow for their exploitation and distribution play a primary or determining role in the transformation process. For Tripp, the essence lies in the 'competition for the power conferred by control of the resources', and it is here that the struggle is at its fiercest and where the logic of state maintenance has its tightest grip. This in turn implies a methodological differentiation partly rooted in emphasis on the *political* logic of reform (so neglected by economists – as mentioned earlier in this Introduction), and partly an understanding of the state as a multi-function, multifaceted, 'imaginative and resilient' phenomenon.

Thus – like Hinnebusch, Murphy and others in this volume – Tripp departs from the dominant, monolithic, view of state, which sees it as a singular, and uni-dimensional phenomenon. He highlights three functions of state: state as community, as hierarchy and as coercive apparatus. This enables him to 'rethink' the state in terms of the struggles of those 'who rule as well as the aspirations of their challengers' – and less about the state's role in the economy. Hence, just as the initiation of the reforms implied by economic restructuring may only be possible because of the ambitions of elites who see this as a manageable strategic asset in their struggle for survival, so the consequences may be sealed by the unforeseen outcome of those struggles.

This is also the theme that Roger Owen develops further in Chapter 10. For him, the principal difficulty and challenge in the study of the changing role of the state is conceptual. He examines two notions of the state: one as a 'single entity', another disaggregated and multidimensional. The former, widely in vogue in the literature, depicts change as a unilinear movement and is useful in studying change between different situations. However, this notion cannot capture a host of important processes such as 'the initial shift in state direction, the changing relationship with economy and society and, above all, the play of internal politics dictating the course of change'. More significantly perhaps, it fails to provide insight into a process which is best understood as one of 'repositioning, of reshaping vis-à-vis the society, and of taking on some new tasks while abandoning some old ones'. This, Owen argues, requires a disaggregated notion of the state, one which allows us to see the transformation of the Middle Eastern states not merely in terms of the quantitative diminution of their power and control over various aspects of the economy – retreat – but in terms of ongoing internal 'reorganization' and 'restructuring'.

For Owen – as with several other contributors to the volume – this underscores the *resilience* and *durability* of the state (caught up even, or especially, in the throes of change and restructuring) and emphasizes the importance of appreciating the *political logic* of transformation and transition.

In the final Chapter, Ziba Moshaver casts doubts over the widely accepted, and supposedly universal, benefits of globalization for developing countries. She does this by addressing how global changes influence state autonomy and state capacity in developing regions in general and in the MENA region, in particular. She takes issue with the very rationale of the 'Washington consensus' by highlighting two of its shortcomings: its failure to understand the way in which global forces influence internal forces (or the 'inside' – in her words) in the developing states, and its neglect of regional differentiation (North-South as well as South-South). Moshaver argues that, contrary to commonly-held views, global processes of change put considerable pressure on developing areas with opportunities that large parts of the South would not be able to exploit. Moreover, global forces with multiple sources of authority may challenge territorial states and their autonomy, but this is not necessarily at the expense of the survival of the 'state'. With some exceptions, the states in the Third World, especially in the MENA region, have held on and are not being reduced to 'empty shells'.

Moreover, the weakening of the states in LDCs may not necessarily be desirable as long as their internal political, social, economic and institutional weaknesses remain unchanged. Rather, the end result is that the gap, both socio-economic as well as political, between the North and South is likely to persist and widen. Global change has contributed to the political marginalization of many developing areas implying that the poorer and the less economically significant a state, the more marginalized is it likely to become as an actor in international politics. This seems even true of the MENA region with its unique geo-strategic location and financial resources compared to other parts of the South.

Although our readers will be well-placed to draw their own conclusions from the book, a number of common themes emerge from the above brief synopsis of the chapters. These are highlighted briefly below.

First, is the notion of the 'state' and what commonly constitutes a singular, monolithic concept widely used in the economic policy discourses. As we have seen, the dominant, neo-liberal school views the state as a one-dimensional entity subject to universal rational choice and capable of 'picking' appropriate policy tools off the shelf. Yet, as many contributors have emphasized in this volume, the state may well be multi-faceted and multi-dimensional and subject to a variety of internal, and often conflicting, forces. It thus lacks the cohesion it is so widely assumed to have. This in turn leads to the second point, which pertains to the diversity of outcomes and experiences despite the supposedly 'universal logic' of transition. What may appear as paradoxically irrational from the point of view of the dominant perspective (such as slow response or reluctance to institute reforms) may yet be explained in terms of the political strategies of different and conflicting constituent elements within the state apparatus and essential to its long term survival and resilience.

A third and final point refers to the globalization debate and its supposed outcomes for the developing regions. While it is commonly agreed that international economic forces will continue to exert increasing influences over the policy direction and content of individual states, there is less agreement over the impact of international integration on these states and its implications for their future survival. In marked contrast to the positive outlook of the 'Washington consensus', most contributors to this volume favour a more cautious approach – one that is capable of differentiating between challenges and opportunities of globalization and can build duly on the basis of its genuine strengths.

Introduction

Ultimately, the justification for such a varied collection of contributions by subject experts from multiple disciplines rests in the depth and breadth of analysis and the wealth of insight they potentially have to offer. It is hoped that the current collection meets these criteria and that its publication can make a positive contribution to an understanding of the complex processes of change in the Middle East.

REFERENCES

Diwan, Ishac, Chang-Po Yang and Zhi Wang (1998) 'The Arab Economies, The Uruguay Round Predicament, and the European Union Wildcard', Ch. 3 in Shafik (1998).

Handoussa H. (ed., 1997) *Economic Transition in the Middle East – Global Challenges and Adjustment Strategies*, Cairo: The American University in Cairo Press.

Hoekman, B. (1998) 'The World Trade Organization, the European Union, and the Arab World: Trade Policy Priorities and Pitfalls,' ch. 4 in Shafik (1998).

Page, J. (1998) 'From Boom to Bust – and Back? The Crisis of Growth in the Middle East and North Africa,' in Shafik (1998).

Shafik, N. (ed., 1998) *Prospects for Middle Eastern and North African Economies – From Boom to Bust and Back?*, Basingstoke and London: Macmillan Press.

Waterbury, J. (1998) 'The State and Economic Transition in the Middle East and North Africa', in Shafik (1998), ch. 6: 159 177.

World Bank (1995) *Claiming the Future – Choosing Prosperity in the Middle East and North Africa'*, Washington, D.C.: The World Bank.

11

Part I

Logic of and Strategies for Transformation

Chapter Two

Missing Links: Institutional Capability, Policy Reform, and Growth in the Middle East and North Africa

*John Page and Linda Van Gelder**

INTRODUCTION

After half a century of experience with the theory and practice of economic development, economists and development practitioners confront the stark reality that, on average, the gap in per capita incomes between rich and poor nations is widening. Economists interested in public policy have sought explanations for this disappointing outcome in the choice of economic policies. The search for economic policy regimes that can promote rapid growth has relied primarily on cross-country econometric research, and case studies drawing extensively on the experience of the successful high performing Asian economies for positive lessons and on the economic crisis of the 1980s in Latin America for negative ones (World Bank 1991 and 1993; Edwards 1995).

From that work, an emerging consensus has developed that, at a minimum, governments need to put in place policy frameworks that result in macroeconomic stability, rapid accumulation of human capital, sustained high levels of private investment, effective and secure financial systems, and price signals which reflect economic costs and benefits. There is also a broadly held view that economies which have chosen to develop a high degree of integration with the world economy have grown faster than those which have failed to do so (World Bank 1996). These 'policy fundamentals' – often referred to

* The findings, interpretations, and conclusions expressed in this paper are entirely those of the authors. They do not represent views of the World Bank, its Executive Directors, or the countries they represent.

15

as the Washington consensus – are now part of the tool kit of virtually every economist and development agency in the business of advising governments in low and middle income countries.[1] They form the 'hardware' of development policy.

What is striking, however, is the difficulty that many governments and societies have had in changing policy regimes and the limited extent to which many countries have adhered effectively to 'policy fundamentals' over the long run (see, for example, World Bank 1998). Put more bluntly, some economists in the development policy business have begun to ask, 'If our advice is so good, why don't more people take it, and why don't those who take it do better?'

This question motivates our study of the relationship between institutions, policies and growth in the Middle East and North Africa (MENA). Throughout the MENA region, governments have moved in the last several years to change the basic economic policy framework from an inward-looking, statist model toward the policy directions outlined in the Washington consensus (surveys of the economic reform process in MENA include World Bank 1995a, and Shafik 1998a). Individual economies in the region have moved at quite different rates, however, in terms of the pace of reform and with differing outcomes in terms of economic growth. To some extent this reflects varying degrees of conviction in the benefits of policy reform to MENA societies and varying perceptions of the costs of transition from one policy regime to another. But, where governments in MENA have begun the process of economic reform, institutional capability has emerged as a major determinant of the pace of implementation of reforms, of their sustainability, and, ultimately, of the capacity of MENA economies to realize economic benefits from policy change.

INSTITUTIONAL FUNCTIONS, ORGANIZATIONS, AND INSTITUTIONAL CAPABILITY

Institutions make up the 'software' of economic development. That they matter for sustained economic growth is by now a widely shared view. But, while there is a growing literature on institutional development and institutional reform in developing countries, there is not yet a consensus on which institutional elements are critical to economic success (see The World Bank 1997a for a useful summary of the major issues). Indeed, even the definition of 'institutions' in the economic development literature shifts, depending on the purposes for which it is used and the disciplinary background of individual authors.

In this chapter we use an approach which focuses on institutional functions, rather than on the definition of institutions themselves (see Graham and Naim 1997, or World Bank 1997a). We can identify five broad types of institutional functions: (i) Making of rules and laws; (ii) Enforcement and adjudication of rules and laws; (iii) Provision of public services; (iv) Provision of public and quasi-public goods; and (v) Interventions to improve the functioning of markets.[2]

These functions reveal the substantial overlap between institutions and organizations. In many societies, organizations such as legislatures, ministries or special bodies are empowered to make laws and rules; courts and police authorities are charged with administration and enforcement; and bureaucracies are tasked with the provision of public services and public goods and with administration of programs designed to improve the functioning of markets. Private organizations may also perform these functions, either as a complement to or in competition with the public sector. A typology of institutional functions and their organizational counterparts is set out in Chart 1.

Measures of institutional capability tend also to reflect the substantial overlap between institutional functions and the organizations which perform them. In practice, they often attempt to estimate either: (i) the extent to which individual institutional functions are present in an economy (e.g., the existence of laws regulating contracts) or (ii) the capability of organizations to perform their institutional functions (e.g., the effectiveness of courts in resolving contract disputes). Three common techniques of institutional assessment are:

(i) *Surveys of economic agents* – usually foreign and domestic investors – in individual countries concerning the importance of the quality of institutional functions or organizations (for example, the predictability and transparency of rules and regulations, for their economic decisions).[3]

(ii) *Cross-country comparative evaluations of key institutional functions or public organizations* (for example, the 'level of corruption' or 'quality of the civil service') often carried out by organizations attempting to provide information to foreign investors.[4]

(iii) *Case studies of the functioning of public organizations* (such as agencies of the public bureaucracy), which attempt to assess their performance in fulfilling institutional functions (see Wade 1996 for a particularly useful study).

CHART 1: Institutional Functions and Organizations

Institutional Functions	Examples	Organizational Counterparts
Making Rules and Laws	Social and Criminal Codes Property Rights Regime Economic 'Rules' Commercial Codes	Legislatures Ministries Central Banks Local Authorities
Enforcing Rules and Laws	Judicial Systems Regulatory Regimes Control Boards Supervisory and Disclosure Rules	Courts Ministries Regulatory Bodies Supervisory Bodies
Providing Public Services	'Public' Utilities (Roads, Ports, Agricultural Extension) Bureaucratic Services (Investment Promotion)	Municipalities Authorities Ministries Private Providers
Providing Public and Quasi-Public Goods	Defense Environmental Protection Education, Health and Social Protection	Ministries Authorities Bureaucracies Private Providers
Improving the Functioning of Markets	Export Promotion Technology Policies Industrial Policies	Ministries Authorities Bureaucracies

Each of these measures is useful but limited. Investor surveys are often not comparable across countries either because of differing survey designs or sampling frames. Usually they do not permit cross-country comparisons. Cross-country evaluations focus on a limited number of variables – primarily to ensure greater consistency across countries – but still suffer from comparability problems as well as difficulties in the interpretation of the indices generated. Case studies are the most richly detailed, but unless they are undertaken in an explicitly comparative framework they often do not permit cross-country comparisons.

INSTITUTIONAL CAPABILITY, PUBLIC POLICIES, AND GROWTH

In the last decade the availability of consistent data on such important economic variables as GDP, investment, and educational attainment for a wide range of countries has spawned a cottage industry in the economics profession exploring the determinants of long run economic growth. Much of this work has been directed at attempting to specify the relationship between economic policies – such as macroeconomic stability, openness to international trade or the extent of domestic competition – and long run growth (see, for example, Barro 1997; Sachs and Warner 1995; or World Bank 1997a).

Recently some attention has been directed toward analyzing the impact of institutional capability on growth.[5] This literature relies primarily on cross-country measures of institutional capability, and attempts to use indices of the effectiveness of institutional functions or organizations to explain variations in long run growth or its determinants. The basic conclusions of that work – as summarized in World Bank (1997a) – are that, controlling for policies, economies with higher levels of institutional capability grow faster.

Institutions can affect growth in at least three ways. First, institutional capability (or perceptions of it) may directly affect the behavior of economic agents. For example, foreign investors may allocate investments among countries based on their assessment of the ability of economic management organizations (the central bank or ministry of finance) to maintain macroeconomic stability and on their perceptions of the transparency and modernity of the legal and administrative framework governing business activity.

Second, the capability of public organizations may affect the pace, sequencing, and sustainability of economic policy reforms. For example, the coherence of views of cabinet-level decision makers can affect the pace and sequencing of reforms of the international trade regime, privatization of public enterprises, or introduction of competition policies. Organizational performance can also affect the extent to which policy reforms, once enacted, are pursued in practice (reforms of customs laws, for example, can be undermined by inaction or subversion by the customs service).

Third, institutional capability can affect the ability of governments to act to improve the functioning of markets. Governments with limited capability in environmental protection, for example, will find it difficult to make polluters bear the social costs of their activities. Similarly, efforts to increase technological capacity in the economy through public interventions may fail if public organizations cannot fulfil their market-enhancing role.

19

Institutional Capability and Economic Growth

Economic theory suggests two channels by which the performance of institutions may affect growth. The first is through investment. Surveys of existing enterprises and potential investors consistently rank elements of institutional capability as among the major factors determining the attractiveness of developing economies for new private investment.[6] These surveys tend to focus on the first two institutional functions described above – making rules and laws, and enforcing rules and laws – often referred to in short hand as the 'investment climate'. Because the clients of international reporting agencies such as *Business International* or *Political Risk Services* – mainly large foreign investors – pay for that information to help make their investment decisions, we would expect that better institutional capability would be closely correlated with higher private investment.

Low levels of institutional capability may also lower the marginal returns to investment. This is the case, for example, when public (or private) organizations fail in providing public services or public goods that affect the cost structures of other firms. A common case, identified in investor surveys, is lack of adequate infrastructure (see Page 1998 for a survey of investors' perceptions of infrastructure adequacy in MENA). Frequently, this failure to provide public services reflects lack of the capability of public organizations – power companies, for example – to recover costs and generate sufficient surpluses to finance new investments. And often, the failure of public organizations is compounded by the lack of enforceable rules – such as an appropriate regulatory structure – defining the incentives for private organizations to provide the service efficiently.

Other than through investment, institutional capability can also affect economic performance through the allocation of resources. Providing public services, providing quasi-public or public goods, and intervening to improve the functioning of markets are all directly concerned with resource allocation. The simplest mechanism by which a lack of institutional capability might result in resource misallocation is through inefficient investment choices by the public sector (see, for example, Pritchett 1997). It is also possible that low institutional capability – and one of its manifestations, high levels of corruption – may lead to inefficient investment choices by the private sector. Finally, if lack of institutional capability leads to 'rent seeking' (Krueger 1974), societies may expend substantial resources not in productive activities but in attempting to capture rents.

20

High institutional capability on the other hand may actually improve resource allocation. As we noted above, public interventions to improve the functioning of markets can potentially improve the allocation of resources both statistically and over time. Indeed, much of the debate concerning the utility of industrial policy, especially in East Asia, reflects differing interpretations of the efficacy of public interventions to increase technological capability through changes in industrial structure.

These allocative effects of institutions are unlikely to be captured directly by the relationship between investment and institutional capability.[7] Rather, they should be reflected in variations in total factor productivity (TFP) – the overall efficiency with which productive factors are used in the economy. We would expect that, controlling for other factors, countries that score well in international comparisons of institutional functions or organizational competence, such as bureaucratic efficiency, would have higher TFP growth rates, while those that have high perceived levels of corruption would have lower TFP growth rates.

Institutional Capability and Policy Reform

In addition to its potential direct impact on investment and resource allocation, institutional capability can effect economic growth through the reform and implementation of economic policy. There is broad agreement among economists that some aspects of good economic management are essential for growth.[8] Macroeconomic stability for example – characterized by moderate and predictable inflation, fiscal discipline, and low volatility of real exchange rates – has been shown to be correlated with higher long run rates of economic growth in large cross-country samples (Fischer 1993). Similarly, the degree of integration of countries into the world economy appears to be positively correlated with long run growth (World Bank 1996).

Casual observation, case studies, and to a lesser degree cross-country empirical work show that institutional capability matters for economic policy reform and implementation. There is, for example, a rather large literature on the role of independent central banks in assuring macroeconomic stability (for a summary, see Cukierman, Webb and Neyapti 1992). Studies of OECD countries suggest that political systems characterized by multiple decision makers respond more slowly to fiscal shocks (Roubini and Sachs 1989). One widely held interpretation of the success of the rapidly growing East Asian economies was that each developed mechanisms by which competent bureaucracies were given substantial scope to implement growth-oriented macroeconomic and sectoral policies (World Bank 1993; Campos and Root 1996).[9] And a number of case studies have shown that institutional capability in export support services – promotion, finance and customs facilitation – was a critical element in the success of export-push trade strategies (World Bank 1993 and 1996; Rodrik 1993).

Success in policy reform may also matter for institutional reform. First stage economic reforms in developing countries tend to reduce the scope for discretionary decision making by entrenched interests in the public sector, allowing governments to implement a second set of reforms (Graham and Naim 1997). Moreover, there is some evidence from Latin America and Eastern Europe to suggest that countries that succeed in implementing economic policy reforms rapidly may achieve accelerated growth more quickly (see, for example, Bruno and Easterly 1996; and Aslund, Boon and Johnson 1996). Thus, rapid economic reform may set up a virtuous circle in which the reform process generates positive economic results that in turn provide the political momentum for further institutional reform. This is the process that characterized the formation of elite bureaucracies in Korea and Singapore, and that more recently has permitted governments in Argentina, Bolivia and Peru to implement such institutional reforms as setting up new organizations for macro-economic management and implementing tax and social security reform.[10] A recent study (Chong and Calderon 1997) using cross-country panel data finds – not surprisingly – that two-way causality exists between institutions and growth; better institutions lead to higher growth rates, but more rapid growth is also positively correlated with measures of performance on such institutional functions as enforceability of contracts and quality of infrastructure.

Economic policy reforms vary in terms of their demands on institutional capability. Some are organizationally simple to achieve, requiring decisions by a small number of actors, but may be critically dependent on communications and coalition building if they are to succeed in the long run. Changes in economic 'rules' – for example, opening the trade regime or increasing domestic competition – can be made by the executive in many countries, subject frequently to legislative review, but the changes usually affect the interests of small, influential and well-organized interest groups adversely. Without successful efforts to build coalitions of the beneficiaries – and better economic performance – it may be difficult to sustain rule-based policy changes in the long run. Reforms of economic rules, therefore, will generally have a timing, sequencing and pace that reflects the success of the economic leadership in building and maintaining coalitions for change, and the success at achieving accelerated rates of economic growth (for an interesting case study, see Naim 1993).

At the opposite extreme are changes in public organizations providing services or public goods, for example customs or tax administrations or investment (regulation or promotion) authorities. In these cases reform strategies are often fairly clearly prescribed, but require changing the values, work practices, and structures of large bureaucratic entities. Here, while public acquiescence is needed, the principal challenge is to change the incentives faced by and the behaviors of incumbent public servants. Where the public administration comprises a large proportion of the modern economy's labor force, as is the case in much of the Middle East and North Africa, this may be politically difficult. One option in these circumstances is to create islands of good performance within the public administration, even among very inefficient organizations, but the sustainability of such organizations without a broader reform of the public service may be problematic (see Campos and Root 1996, or Tendler 1997, for examples).

Reforms of public services in areas such as education, health and social security are particularly institutionally complex, because to succeed they require changes in rules, organizations, and behaviors, supported by effective mechanisms to obtain the feedback and participation of beneficiaries. These can also require both reform of existing public organizations as well as the elimination of public monopolies and the introduction of private competition. Decentralization of functions is one popular mechanism to make providers of these public services more accountable to users, but it cannot substitute for reform of organizational and incentives issues at the center. Indeed, in some cases, such as reform of the educational curriculum, decentralization cannot solve the problem of asymmetric information between users (students and their parents) and providers (teachers and educational administrators) regarding the relevance of skills taught, and may reduce the potential for successful reform.

Chart 2 presents a typology of economic reforms, classified by the type of institutional function to be changed and the organizational complexity of the task. The classification reflects our judgement that

23

CHART 2: **Institutional Capability and Policy Reform**

Policy Reform Area	Institutional Function	Organizational Complexity	Need for Consensus and Communication	Participation of Beneficiaries
Macroeconomic Stabilization	Rule Change	Low	High	Low
Trade Policy Reform	Rule Change Administration of Rules	Low Moderate	High Moderate	Low
Privatization	Rule Change Administration of Rules	Low Moderate	High Moderate	Moderate
Judicial and Regulatory Reform	Rule Change Administration of Rules	Low Moderate	High Moderate	Moderate
Public Expenditure Reform	Rule Change Administration of Rules Provision of Public Goods and Services	Moderate Moderate High	Moderate	High
Education and Health Reform	Provision of Public Goods and Services	High	High	High
Social Protection	Provisions of Public Services	High	High	High

rule changes – 'stroke of the pen' reforms – require less organizational change, and therefore less institutional capability, than enforcement of rules or reforms of organizations providing public services or public goods. Nonetheless, as we have noted, many 'stroke of the pen' rule changes require communications and coalition building to be sustainable. We regard reforms of social services, including education, health, and social protection, as the most institutionally challenging, combining elements of rule change, enforcement, organizational change, and client feedback.

Institutional Capability and Market Interventions

A primary function of markets is coordination of the production (and consumption) decisions of the firms (and individuals) that make up an economy. When markets are incomplete or missing they cannot perform this coordinating function, and there are great potential benefits to institutions designed to promote sharing information and coordinating action. Among firms in advanced economies, formal and informal sharing of information is common. In developing countries, information that is freely available in industrialized economies is often a source of economic advantage and is tightly held. Coordination is difficult because firms are willing to share information only as long as they do not lose by doing so. Thus, governments in developing countries can in theory improve economic performance by acting as brokers of information and facilitators of mutual learning and cooperation.

Cooperation raises several problems however. First, cooperation may become collusion, if firms act together to raise prices or seek other economic advantages. Second, cooperation may inhibit competition, leading to managerial slack or a more general loss of efficiency. Third, business-government cooperation may lead firms to seek special favors from government, expending scarce resources in non-productive 'rent seeking'. Numerous case studies of developing countries have shown that attempts by governments to solve coordination problems have, in practice, reduced national well-being. Indeed, it is conventional to contrast unfavorably the potential gains from correcting market failures with the costs of 'government failures' (World Bank 1991).

Whether or not governments can play a market enhancing role depends on their capacity to combine cooperative behavior – including sharing of information among firms and between the public and private sectors, coordination of investment plans and promotion of interdependent investments – with competition by firms to meet well-defined economic performance criteria. Elsewhere, we have called the institutional structures which combine cooperation with competition 'economic contests' (World Bank 1993).

Institutional capability is critical to contests. In the first place governments must be credibly committed to the objectives of the contest. Rewards must be substantial enough to elicit broad participation and energetic competition. Rules must be clear-cut so that contestants know which behavior will be rewarded and which will be punished. And competent, impartial referees are critical. Where contests have succeeded – as in the economies of northeast Asia – these three elements have all been in place (see World Bank 1993 for a summary of some of the contests employed by Asian governments). But as the history of unproductive subsidies in developing economies makes clear, rewards in the absence of rules and referees do not improve economic performance.

HOW GOOD IS INSTITUTIONAL CAPABILITY IN MENA?

In this section, we summarize institutional capability in MENA through two of the measures outlined above: (i) investor's perceptions of institutional capability drawn from sample surveys; and (ii) cross-country indices of institutional quality in order to place investor perceptions of institutional capability in a more comparative context, both across regions and over time.

Investor Perceptions

In surveys worldwide, investors say that institutions matter.[11] Clear-cut rules, adequate enforcement, and consistency of the institutional framework with a market-oriented economy are all important considerations in business investment decisions. While the 1980s brought significant improvements to the institutional setting offered to private investors in the MENA region, in the eyes of investors, significant shortfalls remain.

While investment frameworks and licensing procedures have improved during the last 15 years, the quality of the bureaucracy in implementing these changes is still seen as a major obstacle in many MENA countries. By the mid-1990s, Tunisia was relatively successful in creating an 'investor-friendly' investment code and a 'one-stop shop' for investors. But the efforts of Jordan, Egypt, and Morocco had been less so. In Jordan, bureaucratic discretion in the interpretation of the investment code continued to present problems. In Egypt, while procedures were streamlined on paper, investors were impeded by slow bureaucratic approvals. In Morocco, private investors found that both the potential for discretionary treatment (in part caused by ambiguity in the investment codes) and slow bureaucratic processing greatly increased their cost of doing business. Further, investors felt that, among public officials, the notion of providing services and facilities for businesses (such as water and telephone connections) had not completely replaced the past system of bureaucratic controls.

Another persistent pattern of investor perception in the MENA region stems from the often vaguely defined power and responsibilities of authorities within the bureaucracy. The resulting discretionary environment creates a great deal of uncertainty, and investors are forced to *negotiate* important agreements. Even after such negotiations, *agreements* continue to be subject to change. Such uncertainty – and lack of transparency – is particularly troublesome to private investors.

Investors also care greatly about both the adequacy of the legal framework and the reliability of the judiciary. In MENA, perceived weaknesses with respect to recognition of property rights and contract enforcement contribute to a sense of insecurity and arbitrariness, and thereby reduce investment. Throughout the region, the formal court systems are viewed as slow, but specific concerns vary by country. In Egypt, while the court system is slow, investors tend to rely on a fairly good commercial arbitration system. In Lebanon, the main problem is the shortage of judges. Investors in Morocco cite concerns about reliable legal recourse, particularly with respect to enforcement of government contracts. Investors also express concerns that there is inadequate protection of intellectual property rights in the region. While by the mid-1990s, Morocco and Tunisia had fairly good patent and trademark protection, protection of intellectual property rights was a serious concern for investors in Egypt, Jordan, Lebanon, and the Gulf Countries.

There are also two areas of investor concern that stand out with respect to institutional failure to provide crucial public goods and services. First, investors cite the lack of skilled workers at internationally competitive wages as a constraint to their operations. While countries in both the Mashreq and the Maghreb tout low cost labor as a selling point to potential investors, some businessmen find this low cost illusory since there is a shortage of workers with the appropriate skills. The lack of a highly skilled, adaptable workforce may reflect distorted educational expenditures that, in line with the interests of influential social groups, emphasize costly higher-level education even when enrolment rates for basic education and literacy levels are relatively low. In the second case, outside of the Gulf countries, investors complain about the lack of adequate infrastructure. Here, the breakdown is both with an institutional framework that does not align prices with costs and with the lack of an enabling environment that would permit (and entice) private provision.

When investors are uncertain about a country's economic and political stability, they take a wait and see attitude. In MENA, many investors still feel uncertain, and governments' market-oriented reforms have not always been strong and consistent enough to allay these fears. For example, despite changes that are now occurring, the public sector still occupies an important role in many MENA countries. Further, investors view privatization programs as hesitant with slow, spotty results. Investor perception is that while change is occurring, it is at times reluctant. Since there are powerful social groups that still resist change, investors are concerned about the chance of backsliding. Consequently, even though MENA countries have made progress in transforming their policy and institutional environment, the full extent of these changes often lacks visibility and/ or credibility. In the case of institutions – and the perceptions of institutions – history definitely matters.

Indices of Institutional Quality

Numerous proxies are available for institutional quality.[12] The indices used in this chapter (Political Risk Services, International Country Risk Guide; Easterly 1997) include measures of bureaucratic quality (IB), rule of law (IL), freedom from risk of expropriation (IE), and freedom from risk that government will break its contracts (IG).[13] An overall Institutional Quality Index (IQ) is calculated as the simple sum of the four component indices. While bureaucratic quality and rule of law are commonly used as measures of institutional quality, we feel that the latter two are also significant indicators. Freedom from the risk of expropriation approximates the extent to which the *rules of the game* are investor-friendly; freedom from the risk that a government will break its contracts is one indicator of the extent to which rules are kept and enforced.

Values for IB and IL range take integer values from 0–6, while IE and IG, also integers, range from 1–10. In all cases, the indices are arranged such that higher values represent 'better' institutions. This data set was selected for two main reasons: (i) there are data for two time periods (1982 and 1990) so that rudimentary aspects of the dynamics of institutional change can be considered; and (ii) representation of countries in the MENA region is highest (15 countries). The main disadvantages are that the indices are drawn from a single year (and therefore may bias results for a given country if it is experiencing a particularly strong abnormality during the single sample year), and that the smaller range of values (i.e., scores ranging from 0–6 for IB and IL rather than 1–10 in some other indices) reduces the dispersion of countries across the institutional quality index.

All four indices are available for 1982 and 1990 for a sample of 81 countries.[14] As expected, there is strong correlation across indices; however this relationship is less pronounced in 1990 compared to 1982 (Table 1). While the regression analysis in the following section utilizes the composite index IQ, it is also instructive to examine MENA's performance relative to other regions on some of the sub-indices.

During the 1980s, the index of bureaucratic quality in MENA countries improved dramatically (Figure 1). Despite lagging behind all regions in 1982, by 1990 MENA's performance was exceeded only by the OECD and East Asia countries. Looking across the MENA region, the Maghreb countries had significantly stronger bureaucratic quality than the Mashreq, with the Gulf countries falling in between the two.[15] While overall MENA had become 'competitive' with other developing countries by 1990, the persistence of relatively poor performance in the Mashreq – as well as relatively low levels compared to OECD countries – point to this as an area that should remain of key concern.

TABLE 1: Correlation Matrices

	1982					1990			
	IB	IL	IG	IE		IB	IL	IG	IE
IB	1				IB	1			
IL	.93	1			IL	.81	1		
IG	.91	.91	1		IG	.74	.81	1	
IE	.90	.91	.95	1	IE	.79	.86	.89	1

FIGURE 1: Measure of Bureaucratic Quality (0–6)

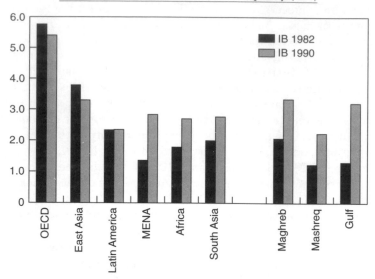

Similarly, in terms of rule of law, the MENA region began to close the gap during the 1980s. However, absolute performance on the rule of law indicator remained lower than OECD, Latin American and East Asian countries. Further, while perceived improvements in the Mashreq were quite significant, the absolute level remained well below that of its regional comparators (Figure 2).

The same trend is borne out when one looks at the composite index (IQ). MENA countries lagged behind the world in the early 1980s, but by 1990 had started to catch up. Performance in the Maghreb exceeded that in the Mashreq, while – because of strong performance on rule of law and freedom from risk of expropriation – the Gulf Countries had the highest IQ measure in the MENA region (Figure 3).

Looking more closely at the pace at which the IQ index improved, both Sub-Saharan Africa and MENA regions – starting from relatively low bases – made the largest gains. The portion of the 'gap' closed was highest in the Gulf countries (over 20 per cent of the gap to the maximum IQ score was closed), followed by the Maghreb (over 15 per cent) and then the Mashreq (over 10 per cent). Improvements to the IQ index closed about 5 per cent of the gap in both East Asia and Latin America, while the measure declined slightly in the OEDC and South Asia (Figure 4).

FIGURE 2: **Measure of Rule of Law (0–6)**

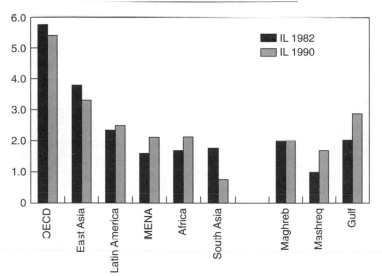

FIGURE 3: **Measure of Institutional Quality (2–32)**

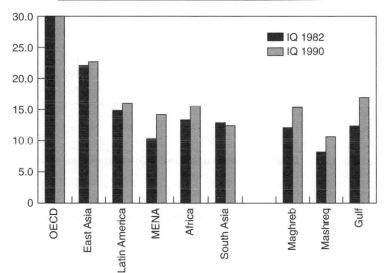

FIGURE 4: Change in Institutional Quality from 1982 to 1990

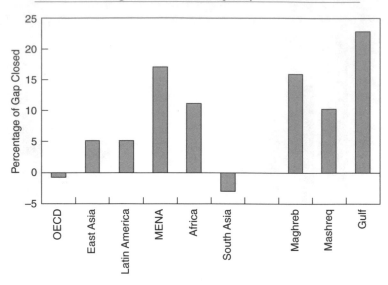

INSTITUTIONS AND GROWTH IN MENA –
EVIDENCE FROM CROSS-COUNTRY DATA

In this section, we estimate a cross-country regression using institutional capability to explain per capita income growth. The results allow us to focus on the relationship between institutions and growth in MENA. We use as our measure of institutional capability the composite Institutional Quality Index (IQ) described in the preceding section. Other economic variables used in the empirical work are described briefly below.

A Brief Description of the Economic Data

Except where otherwise noted, variables are based on the 1997 *World Development Indicators* (WDI). For MENA countries, when data available in the 1997 WDI were incomplete, we filled in data gaps to the extent possible (particularly on investment levels) based on the World Bank, Middle East North Africa Region database. With the exception of MENA, countries in the sample are those for which both the IQ index and other required variables were available.

Income growth is based on GDP per capita measured in constant 1987 prices. Average growth rates (for the periods 1980 to 1995, 1980 to 1987, and 1988 to 1995) were calculated using the least-square regression method. This method takes into account all available observations in a period, and hence the resulting growth rate reflects the general trend and is not unduly influenced by starting, ending, or extreme values.

The investment series is based on gross domestic investment as a percentage of GDP. Average investment as a percentage of GDP for a period was calculated as the geometric mean of the underlying yearly values. Private investment figures are drawn from IFC's *Trends in Private Investment in Developing Countries*. Education variables (gross enrolment rates at the primary and secondary levels, average years of schooling) are drawn from the World Bank's Education Statistics database. Other data used include the average population growth rate (1980 to 1995) and a trade openness indicator (the share of imports plus exports to GDP).

TFP estimates are from Bosworth, Collins, and Chen (1995) who assume a two-factor production function with human capital embodied in the stock of labor. Output elasticities of capital and labor are computed through the national accounts factor share method. As described above, the index of institutional quality comes from Political Risk Services.

Institutions and Growth – the Empirical Results.

Figure 5 is a scatter plot of per capita income in 1982 versus the Institutional Quality Index (IQ) in the same year. Figure 6 presents the same data for 1990. Both make a simple point; richer countries tend to have better institutions. The relationship between income and institutions is strongly statistically significant (at the one per cent level). Because the IQ variable is bounded, there is a concentration of observations of richer countries at the upper bound, with substantial variation in per capita income. This is consistent with our prior discussion of international comparisons of institutional capability in which the OECD – which had substantial variations in per capita income in 1982 – was ranked significantly better on institutional quality than all developing regions.

To establish an international benchmark we have fitted a non-linear regression to the data.[16] Several of the MENA countries depart quite substantially from the pattern. The GCC economies – Saudi Arabia,

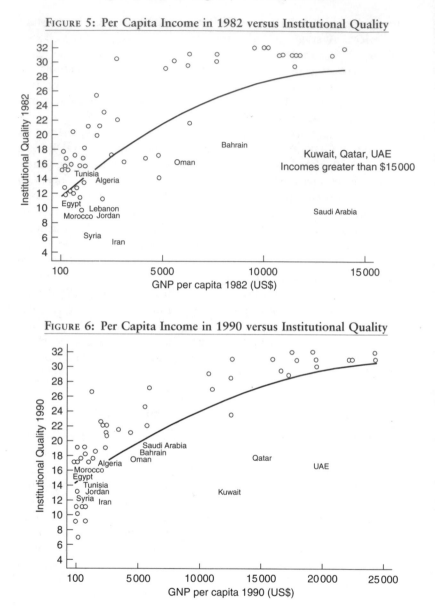

FIGURE 5: Per Capita Income in 1982 versus Institutional Quality

FIGURE 6: Per Capita Income in 1990 versus Institutional Quality

Qatar, Kuwait, Bahrain and Oman – all had levels of institutional capability that were below the predicted values for their level of income in 1982, clearly showing the impact of the oil boom. Similarly, such other oil producers as Iran and Algeria exhibited levels of the IQ index below their predicted values. Other MENA economies conformed more closely to the cross-country pattern, although in general they tended to have levels of institutional capability that were lower than would be predicted on the basis of their level of income in 1982.

By 1992 several MENA economies had moved into closer conformity with the international income-institutional capability pattern. This was due to two distinct phenomena: (i) reductions in the real per capita GNP of a number of GCC countries, Syria and Iran without significant reductions in the index of institutional quality; and (ii) improvements in institutional quality in a number of economies, including the UAE, Saudi Arabia and Morocco (Figure 6).

To test the relationship between income growth and institutional capability we have regressed per capita income growth from 1980 to 1995 directly on the institutional quality index and have also used the index as an argument in a Barro-type growth regression that includes the conventional explanatory variables of relative income, population growth, and the primary school enrolment rate in 1980.[17] We thus treat institutional capability as predetermined at the beginning of the period and test for its impact on future growth. Table 2 presents the regression results. We find that in both the direct regression and in the cross-country growth regression institutional capability is significantly (at the one per cent level) and positively correlated with growth of per capita income. All other variables in the cross-country growth regression conform to the sign and significance patterns observed in the literature, and the explanatory power of both regressions is consistent with results observed elsewhere.[18]

Figure 7 pictures the relationship between the IQ index and the rate of growth of per capita income between 1980 and 1995 together with the plot of the direct regression. Countries with higher levels of institutional capability in the early 1980s grew faster from 1980 to 1995 than those with lower levels. The pattern of residuals formed by the Middle East and North African economies is of some interest. Of the MENA observations, only three – Egypt, Morocco, and Oman – have growth rates which exceed their predicted values on the basis of institutional capability by more than one standard deviation. Iraq, Saudi Arabia and Qatar, on the other hand, grew more slowly than we would have predicted on the basis of their level of institutional capability in 1982 by more than one standard deviation. The majority of MENA economies conformed fairly closely to the international pattern.

TABLE 2: Regression Results

Dependent Variable	Constant	IQ 82	Initial GDP per capita	Population Growth Rate	Gross Primary Enrolment Rate	Average years of school 1980–90	Openness	adj. R^2	N
GDP per capita 1980–95	−2.3820**	0.1567**						.1787	79
GDP per capita 1980–95	2.8837	0.1246**	−0.0002**	−0.7495**	−0.0234			.2961	75
GDP per capita 1980–87	−3.4166**	0.1886**						.2104	79
GDP per capita 1988–95	−1.5819	0.1338**						.0708	79
Total Investment/GDP 1980–95	18.9859**	0.1522*						.0503	79
sub-sample developing countries									
Total Investment/GDP 1980–95	14.5634**	0.4534**						.1641	32
Private Investment/GDP 1980–95	3.3796	0.6003**						.3816	32
TFP Growth 1980–90	−2.0578**	0.0902**	−0.0001					.2256	56
TFP Growth 1980–90	−2.5778**	0.1556**	−0.0001			−0.0397		.2908	56
TFP Growth 1980–90	−2.6730**	0.1493**				−0.0410	0.3132	.2397	55

* Statistically significant at the 5% level
** Statistically significant at the 1% level

FIGURE 7: Institutional Quality and Growth in Per Capita Income (1980–95)

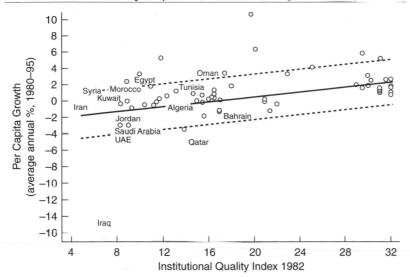

Because the boom to bust cycle of oil prices and growth rates was so strong in the MENA region between 1980 and 1987, we split the sample into two periods 1980–87 and 1988–95 (Figure 8; for an assessment of the long run process of growth in MENA, see Page 1998). The variance of residuals and the pattern of outliers is quite distinct between the two periods. For the sample as a whole, the fit of the regression in the second period is substantially less good. There is a more compact pattern of residuals for the MENA economies in the second period, with all residuals except Kuwait lying within our standard deviation of the regression. The oil states of the GCC conform much more closely to the international pattern in 1988–95 than in the preceding period, and Egypt and Morocco cease to be extreme position outliers. In sum, MENA looks much more like the rest of the world in 1985–95 than in the earlier period.

Introducing other sources of growth does not alter the fundamental conclusion that institutions matter for income growth. Figure 9 presents the partial (orthogonal) relationship between per capita income growth between 1980 and 1995 and the institutional quality index, controlling for relative income, population growth and education. Using this specification, the MENA economies are generally not extreme outliers. Kuwait, Syria, Egypt and Oman

FIGURE 8: **Institutional Quality and Growth in Per Capita Income (1980–87)**

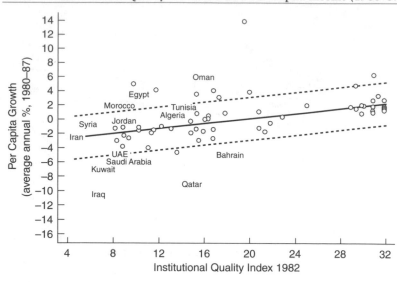

Institutional Quality and Growth in Per Capita Income (1988–95)

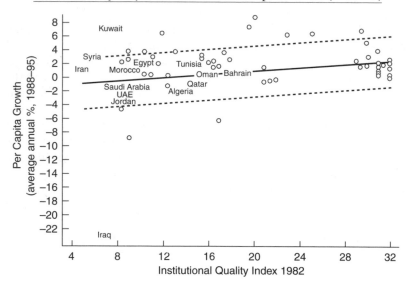

FIGURE 9: **Partial Relationship Per Capita Income Growth (1980–95) and Institutional Quality**

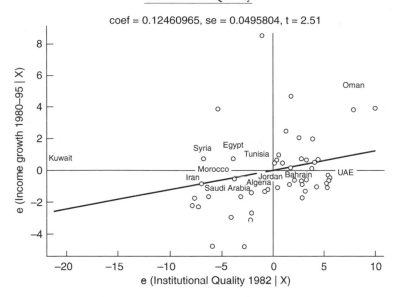

coef = 0.12460965, se = 0.0495804, t = 2.51

continue to exhibit rates of growth that are above their predicted values on the basis of institutional capability, controlling for other sources of growth. Morocco and Tunisia are also positive outliers but are closer to their predicted values.

We find that institutional capability has a significant positive impact (at the one per cent level) on total investment between 1980 and 1995 (Figure 10). Here, in comparison with growth, the pattern of residuals is reversed. We underpredict the level of total investment for the level of institutional capability, except in Lebanon, Oman and Qatar. Jordan, Iran, Algeria, Tunisia and Bahrain all had levels of total investment that exceeded their predicted values by more than one standard deviation.

We have argued that, because private investors consistently rank the institutional environment as a significant determinant of their investment decisions, institutional capability should be closely correlated with private investment. When we regress the ratio of private investment to GDP directly on the IQ index we find that for the whole sample the explanatory power of the regression increases substantially, as does the estimated impact of the institutional

FIGURE 10: Investment and Institutional Quality

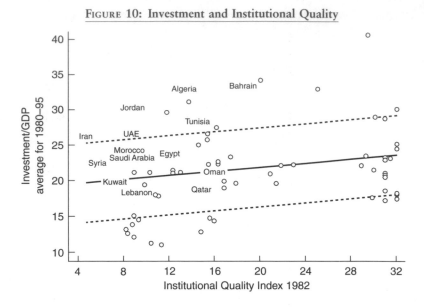

capability variable on investment. The number of MENA economies for which we have consistent private investment data is small, and all of the observations lie within one standard deviation of the regression (Figure 11). Morocco and Tunisia have shares of private investment in GDP which exceed their predicted values, while Egypt's share of private investment is below its fitted value.

It is, of course, possible that the index of institutional capability is closely associated with other determinants of investment behavior. If that is the case, omitting them from our analysis may give an erroneous view of the impact of institutions on investment. Fortunately, the cross-country literature on economic growth has reached a reasonable consensus on other factors influencing the rate of investment. Even controlling for these variables, institutional capability is significantly associated with higher investment.

Figure 12 plots the rate of TFP growth against the institutional capability index. The direct relationship is positive and statistically significant (at the one per cent level).[19] Better institutions result in higher total factor productivity growth. A one standard deviation increase in the IQ adds about 0.8 per cent to the rate of TFP growth. That in itself is higher than the recorded TFP growth for three-quarters of the developing countries in the sample. When we control

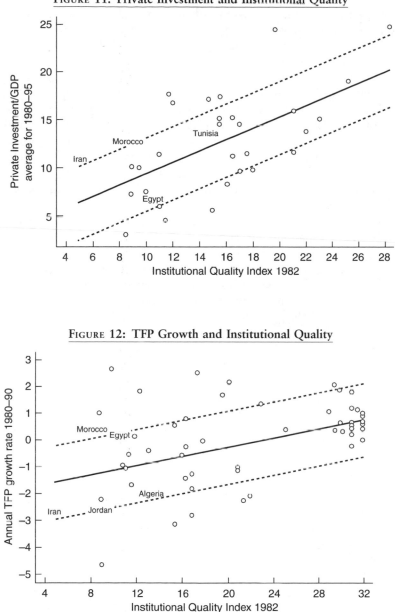

FIGURE 11: **Private Investment and Institutional Quality**

FIGURE 12: **TFP Growth and Institutional Quality**

for other possible factors which would lead to intercountry variations in the rate of TFP growth, the relationship is remarkably robust. Even controlling for relative distance from international best practice, educational attainment, and openness of the economy to trade – three factors strongly correlated with variations in TFP growth rates in cross-country studies (Page 1994) – the index of institutional capability remains strongly (at the one per cent level), positively associated with higher TFP growth.[20]

The pattern of residuals for the MENA economies reveals that in the direct relationship Iran, Iraq, Algeria and Jordan show significantly lower than predicted rates of TFP growth. Egypt and Morocco are the only MENA economies that substantially exceed predicted values. Controlling for income and educational attainment preserves Morocco and Egypt as positive outliers but leaves only Algeria as a significant negative outlier.

Taken together, our results strongly support the conclusion that institutional capability matters for economic growth, both internationally and for the Middle East and North Africa. In general, there is little that is distinct about MENA in this relationship. The economies of the GCC began the 1980s with levels of income and rates of economic growth that were very high relative to their levels of institutional capability, but by the 1990s they were much closer to the international pattern due to declining oil prices and growth rates combined with improved institutional capability. Total investment in the region was high relative to institutional capability. Our results suggest that this was due primarily to higher than predicted levels of public investment. Total factor productivity growth in MENA was similar to what we would have predicted for other countries in the sample on the basis of institutional capability.

INSTITUTIONS AND POLICY REFORM IN MENA

A recent cross-country study (Commander *et al.* 1997) found that for the period 1964–93 good policies, combined with more capable state institutions to implement those policies, produced faster per capita income growth than good policies alone. This section looks briefly at evidence in the MENA region on the interplay of good policies and good institutions on growth.

While a good policy framework covers a host of items, we construct a simple Policy Index as the sum of three indices that measure education policy (rapid accumulation of human capital), trade openness (integration into the world economy) and inflation (macroeconomic stability). This is broadly consistent with key elements of the Washington consensus. Each index is constructed to range from 0 to 10 with higher values representing more reformist policies.[21]

Some observations are warranted about the relationship among our indices in the MENA region. First, the positive correlation among the component indices (IB, IL, IE, and IG) is less pronounced in MENA than for the sample as a whole. While the aggregate IQ index is still highly correlated with IL, IG, and IE (ranging from 0.92 to 0.95), the strength of this relationship is less pronounced with IB (0.63). This reflects the low dispersion of the bureaucratic quality measure in the MENA region (11 countries received a rating of one and the maximum score was only three).

In terms of the component indices of the Policy Index, the positive correlation among the sub-indices is weaker than for the IQ index. This makes sense since it is quite possible to have 'good' policy in one area (such as macroeconomic stability) while neglecting policy reforms in other areas (such as education). The correlation between the Openness Indicator and Macrostability (inflation) Indicator is positive (0.54). The Education Policy Indictor is less strongly correlated with the other two. Given that policy decisions related to macroeconomic stabilization and trade openness are in the domain of similar set of decision makers, this is not unexpected.

The aggregate IQ index and Policy Index are positively correlated (0.69). The IQ index has a stronger relationship with the Education Policy Indicator (0.64) than with either the Macrostability (0.34) or Openness Indicators (0.48). This is consistent with our assertion that the quality of institutions matters more when tackling complex reforms in the social sectors compared to reforms that can be enacted by a small, compact group of actors.

We divide our sample of MENA countries around the mean values of the Institutional Quality Index and the Policy Index. As shown in a scatterplot, countries are thus clustered into a two-by-two matrix (Figure 13). Those above the respective means are judged to have stronger institutional capacity and lower policy distortions. Looking at average per capita income growth rates for each group of countries, we find evidence to support the hypothesis that the impact on growth of good policies was enhanced by better institutions.

During the time period considered, per capita income in many MENA countries was still contracting. Yet countries that combined

FIGURE 13: Institutional Quality and Policy in MENA

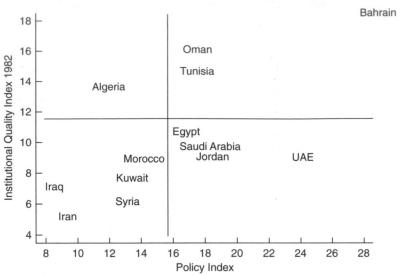

sound policies in a strong institutional setting averaged per capita income growth of about 1 per cent per year. In countries that had similarly good policy environments but weak institutional settings, income per capita fell by about 1.7 per cent a year. Countries that fell below the mean on both the Institutional Quality and Policy Index contracted by an average of 2.5 per cent per year (Figure 14). The evidence suggests that the impact felt from better institutions, perhaps through more efficient implementation of programs and greater certainty in the minds of investors, is substantial. The results also suggest that the benefit from reformist policies on growth is more pronounced than the effect of stronger institutional capacity.

Two notes of caution are warranted in the interpretation made of these results. First, the lack of an adequate number of observations in the MENA region does not permit a statistical testing of the relationships cited, nor the control for factors such as education, income, or other variables. Second, the classification of countries is based against MENA benchmarks. Against international benchmarks, more of the sample would fall into the weak institutional capacity, non-reformist policy category, because institutional capacity and reformist policy are measured against MENA benchmarks rather than international ones.

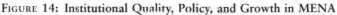

FIGURE 14: Institutional Quality, Policy, and Growth in MENA

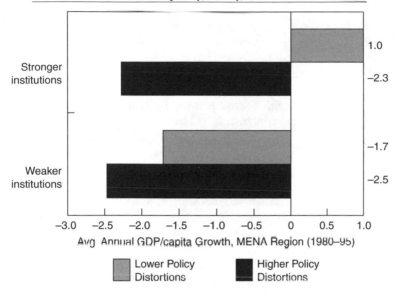

Avg Annual GDP/capita Growth, MENA Region (1980–95)

Lower Policy Distortions | Higher Policy Distortions

INSTITUTIONS AND MARKET INTERVENTIONS – THE CASE OF EXPORT PROMOTION

Support for exporters is one of the most pervasive public policy interventions by governments. Participation in international markets facilitates learning and productivity change, both because it brings firms into contact with international best practice and because it is a form of competitive pressure. Learning through exports is not limited to the exporting firms alone; it spills over into the domestic economy, leading to a generalized improvement in productivity. For example, one recent empirical study of total factor productivity (TFP) growth in a broad cross-section of countries (Pack and Page 1994) finds a significant positive relationship between the economy wide rate of TFP growth and the share of manufactured exports in total exports. A simple interpretation of this result is that the higher the probability that an incremental export will be a manufactured good, the higher the economy-wide rate of productivity growth.

Because exporting firms cannot charge others for the learning they facilitate, economies will tend to underinvest in exports. Indeed, because there are potentially high costs to creating country reputation in export markets, there is a classic coordination failure, and a strong rationale for government action. The policy regimes which individual governments have used to encourage exports range from creation of a 'free trade regime for exporters', to simple uniform subsidies on the value of exports, to highly elaborate schemes involving access to credit, foreign exchange, and publicly provided services.

A recent review of the effectiveness of export promotion efforts in six countries – Korea, Brazil, Kenya, Bolivia, Turkey and India – comes to a surprising conclusion.[22] The two most successful programs of export promotion – those in Korea and Brazil – were highly complex and selective, gave bureaucrats substantial discretionary powers, changed rules frequently, and depended on close interaction between bureaucrats and firms. The two least successful, those in Kenya and Bolivia, consisted of simple, uniform, and non-discretionary subsidies. Elsewhere (Page 1996) we have interpreted these results in terms of an economic contest to facilitate coordination among exporters.

Chart 3 summarizes the essential elements of the export promotion contents in each country, together with an evaluation of their success. The first notable difference between the programs is in the level of commitment of the political leadership to the program goals. Credible, public commitment was important because it communicated to firms and to the bureaucracy that *both* would be judged by the success of the program. Where export promotion programs lacked public commitment from the top leadership, the implementing agencies in each country correspondingly lacked conviction that they would be judged by their success in building exports. Firms often waited lengthy periods to receive benefits; applications were rejected for trivial reasons; and delay and unpredictability undermined any incentive effect of the program.

In the Korean, Brazilian, and Turkish programs, firms and the government entered into enforceable contracts regarding export performance. In the Brazilian and Korean cases, in addition to the rewards for compliance under both schemes, there were also sanctions for non-performance. Competition was thus encouraged by the forward-looking nature of the contracts and by the government's lack of willingness to renegotiate them in response to changing firm-specific circumstances. The success of the Turkish scheme was blunted in part because the performance contracts between the government and firms were not enforced. In the Bolivian, Kenyan and Indian schemes contracts with individual firms were not used. Rather, the

CHART 3: An Evaluation of Export Promotion Programs

Country	Effectiveness	Commitment	Complexity	Discretionality	Corruption	Contracts
Korea 1960–1980	High	High	High	High	Low	Enforced
Brazil 1960–1985	High	High	High	High	Low	Enforced
Turkey 1980–1986	Moderate	High	Moderate	High	Moderate	Not Enforced
Kenya 1975–1990	Low	Low	Low	Low	High	Not Required
Bolivia 1987–1992	Low	Low	Low	Low	Moderate	Not Required
India 1960–1970	Moderate	Moderate to Low	Moderate	Moderate	Moderate	Not Required

Source: Page (1996)

rewards were proportional to past performance, and there were no sanctions for failing to achieve program goals.

Finally, the successful programs depended on the governments' ability to resist pressure from organized private interests. The autonomy of the export promotion authorities was sufficient to ensure broad compliance with the program rules, despite substantial incentives for cheating. Cheating, on the other hand, was one of the hallmarks of the unsuccessful experiences with export promotion. Historical and structural factors undoubtedly played a role in insulating the export bureaucracy in the successful cases, but the scrutiny of the political leadership and its commitment to the export objective must also have heightened accountability and perhaps the perception by bureaucrats of the risks of favoritism.

Chart 4 summarizes our assessment of export promotion programs in Egypt, Jordan, and Lebanon using the same framework (the assessment is based on Roy 1998 and World Bank 1997a). The results emphasize the rudimentary nature of export promotion efforts in all three economies, even in comparison with the least successful international comparators. Our first striking finding is that the level of political commitment to export promotion ranges from only moderate in Jordan to low in Lebanon. Egypt is the only country to have established a public-private council for export promotion under the leadership of the President, but it meets infrequently and has not yet been effective in creating a pro-export culture in either the public administration or in private industry. Ministries involved in export promotion (and export administration) have multiple and overlapping functions and do not cohere around export policy at the cabinet level. In Jordan, there is no high level body charged with export promotion under the chairmanship of the head of government (or state), but the accountabilities among ministries are clearer and there is greater cohesiveness in the cabinet regarding appropriate export policies. In Lebanon, ministerial responsibilities are ill defined, and the political leadership has not committed itself to high level support of export promotion. Basic rule changes, including reform of the customs laws, changes in philo-sanitary and quality inspection procedures, and regulatory reforms affecting air and road transport and port services have not been issued by the executive or successfully passed through parliament in any of the three countries.

Organizational change to improve some aspects of the export regime is underway in Jordan, and to a lesser degree in Egypt. In Jordan, a 'green channel' customs system was introduced to facilitate

CHART 4: Export Regimes in MENA Countries

	Jordan	Lebanon	Egypt
Government Commitment	Moderate Implemented at Ministerial Level No higher export council	Low No clear Ministerial responsibilities	Low-Moderate Export Council Chaired by President meets infrequently Cabinet-level coherence limited
Key Organizational Changes	Green channel for exporters Proposed Aqaba Free Zone		Temporary admission/duty drawback Free trade zones
Needs	Lacks effective Export Promotion Agency Lacks clear strategy for trade-related infrastructure (accelerated progress in telecommunications and transport)	Fragmentation and duplication of controls Lacks strategy for trade-related infrastructure	Lacks effective export promotion agency Lacks strategy for trade-related infrastructure (some reform in transportation and telecommunications)
Efforts to Reduce Corruption	Reform of customs inspection procedures and practices	Planned shift to red and green customs channels	Initiated reform customs
Needs	Customs law drafted but still in Parliament Reform of inspection incomplete	Reform of bonus system of payment Highly complex customs procedures	Multiple steps in Customs Lack of transparency
Complexity of Rules	Moderate	High	Moderate
Rewards	Low	Low	Low
Contracts	Not Used	Not Used	Not Used

duty free access by exporters to intermediate and capital goods. In Egypt, in contrast the temporary admissions and duty drawback systems are still subject to multiple bureaucratic steps, domestic content regulation, and discretionary application of rules (World Bank 1997a identifies eight separate administrative steps to obtain a duty drawback). These hurdles have been described as 'insurmountable' for small and medium enterprises (World Bank 1997a). Lebanon offers no effective duty free access system and, despite low customs duties, imposes substantial transactions costs on importers by the complexity and discretionality of its customs procedures. Both Jordan and Egypt have developed free trade zones, but the existing zones in both countries have failed to attract a wide range of export manufacturing firms due to organizational difficulties, lack of promotion and poor housekeeping. All three economies lack coherent strategies for the development of trade related infrastructure (Page 1998).

Efforts to control corruption have largely focused on customs reform. Jordan's has been the most far-reaching, involving changes in the incentives system for individual customs inspectors. Contrary to the cases of Egypt and Lebanon, individual customs inspectors no longer receive bonuses based on the volume of fines levied. In all three countries some efforts have been made to streamline customs procedures (they are most advanced in Jordan and still in the planning stage in Lebanon), but these have not been fully implemented, in part due to resistance from interest groups.

Performance-based contracts between exporting firms and the export promotion authorities are absent in all three cases. As the three export promotion programs are now structured, there are minimal 'rewards' for superior export performance. In the successful programs sketched out above these rewards ranged from public recognition of exporters by giving awards and prizes, to explicit subsidies. The export promotion regimes in Egypt, Jordan and Lebanon attempt only to correct for anti-export bias arising from the tariff structure, and do not – with the exception of Jordan – even succeed at that. There is no system of recognition of, or awards to, exporters in any of the three economies and none employs subsidies, even to compensate for indirect taxes paid.[23] This could be the consequence of a deliberate decision by government to avoid sanctions for unfair trade practices, but in fact, even such 'WTO friendly' contractual arrangements as guaranteed access to credit for exporters or export promotion services are absent in all three economies. Thus, we conclude that the absence of contractual arrangements reflects lack of a coherent strategy to employ them, rather than an explicit policy decision.[24]

In summary, none of the export promotion regimes reviewed can be classified as even moderately successful. The institutional failures underlying this outcome begin with the 'rule making function', embodied in the level of political commitment of governments to the export promotion strategy, and extend through the provision of public services – for example customs and trade related infrastructure, ending in the absence of an effective economic contest to coordinate behavior among exporters.

The failure to achieve successful export promotion regimes provides another example of the link between institutional capability and effective policy reform. In both Egypt and Jordan, trade reforms – consisting of the elimination of quantitative barriers to imports and reductions in tariffs – have been undertaken to reduce the anti-export bias.[25] In both economies there has been disappointment at the absence of an 'export supply response' accompanied by calls from producers of import substitutes for restoration of protection. The absence of an effective export lobby hinders further momentum in trade reform. But the absence of effective institutional support for exporters hinders rapid expansion of exports. Thus, trade reforms are viewed by the manufacturing sector – and the public at large – as entailing substantial adjustment costs for incumbent producers but offering few tangible benefits.

CONCLUSIONS

We began this chapter by asking the rhetorical question, 'why have many countries failed to heed the advice of the "Washington consensus" and why have those who have taken this policy advice frequently failed to achieve sustained economic success?' For the economies of the Middle East and North Africa, we believe that our results strongly suggest at least a partial answer to the question. There is a missing link in the chain running from policy reform to accelerated growth, and that link is institutional capability.

We have shown that institutional capability – measured by international indices of the state's ability to perform critical institutional functions – is strongly, statistically correlated with economic growth and its sources, investment and total factor productivity growth. We have also shown that institutional capability affects the capacity of governments in MENA to implement change, whether in

51

the reform of economic 'rules' governing such areas as macroeconomic management or trade policy, in the provision of public goods and services such as education and infrastructure, or in the ability of governments to improve the working of markets through coordination of economic activity, as in export promotion. In all of these areas, weak institutional capability and weak organizations impede policy reforms.

When reformist policies are combined with improvements in institutional capability the potential rewards are substantial. Despite MENA's unprecedented economic contraction between 1985 and 1995, those economies with reformist policies and better than average institutions avoided negative growth. Those economies that lagged in policy reform and had worse than average institutions experienced the greatest economic declines. These results parallel the story world-wide: strong institutions combined with reformist policies yield higher growth.

Finally, we have argued that, because the quality of the state's performance in delivering institutional functions increases with income per capita, there is scope for a virtuous circle between institutional reform, policy reform, and growth. Better institutions will facilitate more sustained and successful policy reform, and together they will result in higher incomes per capita, providing the basis for further gains in institutional capability.

Growth-oriented governments in the Middle East and North Africa, therefore, cannot afford to ignore institutional and organizational reform. Institutional capability has increased in MENA, but more remains to be done. While a substantial number of MENA economies have embarked on changes in economic 'rules', ranging from customs laws to investment codes, reform of the organizations which *administer* the rules is still in the early stages. Similarly, codification of the rules governing private provision of public goods and services, and reform of the organizations of the state providing these goods and services will need to be accelerated.

Ultimately, the public administration will need to change itself if Middle Eastern and North African states are to forge the missing link between policy reform and sustained growth.

NOTES

1 The term 'Washington consensus' is due to Williamson (1993). It is also at times referred to as the 'Latin American consensus' (Edwards 1995). There is much less consensus among economists, however, on whether the

industrial and financial policy interventions characteristic of the rapidly growing northeast Asian economies were central to their success. The literature on industrial policy in Asia is enormous and contentious. See for example Amsden (1989), Wade (1990), World Bank (1993), and the symposium in *World Development*, 1994. On the contrast between some elements of the East Asian experience and the Latin American consensus, see Page (1997).

2 In this we largely follow Graham and Naim (1997); however, they do not classify interventions in markets as a separate institutional function in their typology, presumably viewing it as a subset of setting rules and provision of public goods. As we shall argue below, in cases of coordination failures in markets this is too narrow a view.

3 See references in footnote 11 below.

4 See references in footnote 12 below.

5 Many studies have attempted to measure the impact of political variables – such as changes in government, coups, riots, etc. – on growth. These are surveyed in Levine and Renelt (1992). Mauro (1995), Campos and Root (1996), Knack and Keefer (1995) and World Bank (1997a) report on attempts to explain variations in growth rates using measures of bureaucratic efficiency.

6 See, for example, the Private Sector Assessments conducted by the World Bank for more than 30 developing countries.

7 They may be indirectly reflected to the extent that they lower the marginal product of capital and reduce investment demand.

8 We do not mean to suggest, however, that there is unanimity on the scope, pace or sequencing of economic reforms.

9 Indeed, one credible explanation for the recent financial crisis in Indonesia and Thailand is that the institutional mechanisms which had insulated the technocratic managers of the macroeconomy and the central banks in both countries broke down in the second half of the 1990s.

10 On the Korean and Singaporean cases see Campos and Root (1996); on the Latin American cases see Graham and Naim (1997).

11 Based on discussions of investor perceptions in, for example, IFC (1998), Brunetti (1997), FIAS (1997), and World Bank private sector assessments for Tunisia (1994a) and Jordan (1994b) and Lebanon (1995b).

12 For example, country risk is measured by Business Environment Risk Intelligence (BERI), Country Risk Information Service (CRIS), Euromoney, Institutional Investor, Standard and Poor's Rating Group, Political Risk Services (Inter-Country Risk Guide, ICRG, and Coplin O-Leay Rating System), and Moody's Investor Services. The World Economic Forum publishes a Competitiveness Index (openness, government, finance, infrastructure, technology, management, labor and institutions); Freedom House computes an Economic Freedom index (freedom to hold property, earn a living, operate a business, invest one's earnings, trade internationally and participate in a market economy). Transparency International publishes a Corruption Perception index.

13 IB is defined as autonomy from political pressure and strength and expertise to govern without drastic changes in policy or interruption of services. IL is defined as degree to which citizens of a country are willing

to accept the established institutions to make and implement law and adjudicate disputes. IE is defined as freedom from risk of outright confiscation or forced nationalization. IG is defined as freedom for risk of modification of a contract taking the form of repudiation, postponement or scaling down.

14 Thirteen are in Sub-Saharan Africa; 8 in East Asia; 4 in South Asia; 21 in Latin America; 15 in MENA; and 20 in OECD. A list of countries is found in Appendix A.

15 The relatively high measures of institutional quality in Sub-Sahara Africa are somewhat surprising in this and following regional comparisons. This may be due to a significant sample selection bias. With required data series available for only 13 of 27 Sub-Saharan African countries, those countries producing and reporting long series of economic indicators may also be more likely to have higher levels of institutional capacity on average than countries that do not.

16 This provides a 'pattern of development' in the tradition of Chenery (1979). We do not assert any causal relationship between the variables.

17 For a fuller exposition of the model specification, see Keller and Page (1998). That paper also contains the results of causality tests which indicate that institutional variables strongly predict future growth.

18 For a comprehensive early survey, see Levine and Renelt (1992). For a recent well known application see Sachs and Warner (1995). Consistent with recent cross-country econometric work (Pritchett 1997), we find that the education variable is not statistically significantly different from zero.

19 This result differs fundamentally from that of Mauro (1995) who, using a cross-country growth regression framework, is unable to find a significant association between his bureaucratic efficiency index and growth, independent of investment.

20 The IQ index is positive and significant in all specifications even when an index of openness is included as an explanatory variable.

21 Arguing that variations in education policy are more pronounced at the secondary level than at primary level, the education policy index is constructed based on secondary level gross enrolment rates (GE). The index, constructed to vary from 0 to 10, is equal to $\beta^1 * [(GE1990 - GE1980) / (100 - GE1980) * 10] + \beta^2 * (GE1990/10)$, if GE1980 and GE1990 ≤ 100, else = 10. The first component reflects improvements in gross enrolment rates weighted by the initial gap from international best practice. The second component reflects the gross enrolment rate at the end of the period. The weights, $\beta^1 = (100\text{-}GE1980)/10$ and $\beta^2 = (GE1980)/100$, assign higher value to the first component (closing the gap) the further away a country starts from international best practice. The trade openness variable is constructed as the sum of exports and imports as a percentage of gross domestic product, scaled by a factor of 100, with a maximum score of 10. The macroeconomic stability indicator is a composite index (also constructed to range from 0–10) that weights equally the average inflation rate in the period and level of variance.

22 Rodrik (1993). Rodrik is careful to point out that he is reviewing the effectiveness, not the efficiency of the programs. Efficiency could only be

determined by careful comparisons of the costs of the export promotion scheme with its benefits in terms of increases in social welfare.

23 While it is important to recall that the international trading system is less accepting today of export subsidies than during the period when the international comparator schemes were functioning, a range of export incentives is still allowed and used by major trading countries. These are absent in the MENA cases.

24 This conclusion is reinforced by the lack of government commitment to the programs discussed above.

25 Jordan has signed, and Egypt is in the final stages of negotiating, a free trade agreement with the European Union which will 'lock in' these reforms by ensuring duty free access of European goods to domestic markets by 2010.

REFERENCES

Amsden, Alice H. (1989) *Asia's Next Giant: South Korea and Late Industrialization*, New York: Oxford University Press.

Aslund, Anders, Peter Boon and Simon Johnson (1996) 'How to Stabilize. Lesson from Post Communist Countries', *Brookings Papers on Economic Activity*, no. 1.

Barro, Robert J. (1997) *Macroeconomics*, 5th ed., Cambridge, Mass.: MIT Press.

Bosworth, Barry, Susan Collins and Yu-Chin Chen (1995) 'Accounting for Differences in Economic Growth', *The Brookings Institution*, processed.

Brunetti, Ayno (1997) 'Institutional Obstacles to Doing Business', *Policy Research Working Paper*, no. WPS-1759, Washington D.C.: The World Bank.

Bruno, Michael and Willaim Easterly (1996) 'Inflation And Growth: In Search of a Stable Relationship', *Review/Federal Reserve Bank of St. Louis*, vol. 78, no. 3 (May/June).

Campos, Jose Edgardo and Hilton Root (1996) *The Key to the Asian Miracle: Making Shared Growth Credible*, Washington, D.C.: The Brookings Institution.

Chenery, Hollis (1979) *Structural Change and Development Policy*, New York: Oxford University Press.

Chong, Alberto and Cesar Calderon (1997) 'On the Causality and Feedback between Institutional Measures and Economic Growth,' processed. Washington D.C.: The World Bank.

Commander, Simon, Hamid Davoodi and Une J. Lee (1997) 'The Causes and Consequences of Government for Growth and Well-Being', background paper. Washington D.C.: The World Bank.

Cukierman, Alex, Steve Webb and Silin Neyapti (1992) 'Measuring the Independence of Central Bank and its Effect on Policy', *World Bank Economic Review*, vol. 6, no. 3, (September).

Easterly, William (1997) 'Life During Growth', processed Washington D.C.: The World Bank.

Edwards, Sebastian (1995) *Crisis and Reform in Latin America: From Despair to Hope*, New York: Oxford University Press.

Fischer, Stanley (1993) 'Macroeconomic Factors in Growth', paper presented at the conference, 'How Do National Policies Affect Long-Run Growth?' Washington, D.C.: The World Bank (February).

Foreign Investment Advisory Service (1997) 'Strategies of Multinationals and Competition for Foreign Direct Investment: The Opening of Central and Eastern Europe', *Foreign Investment Advisory Service Occasional Paper*, no. 10, International Finance Corporation and The World Bank.

Graham, Carol and Moises Naim (1997) 'The Political Economy of Institutional Reform in Latin America', in Nancy Birdsall (1997) *Beyond Trade-offs: Market Reforms and Equitable Growth in Latin America*, Washington D.C.: IADB.

IFC (1995) 'Trends in Private Investment in Developing Countries – Statistics for 1970–94', *International Finance Corporation Discussion Paper*, no. 28.

—— (1998) 'How Businesses See Government: Responses from Private Sector Surveys in 69 Countries', *International Finance Corporation Discussion Paper*, no. 33, Washington D.C.

IMEDE (1989) *World Competitiveness Report*, World Economic Forum, vol. 3, no. 3, Geneva: World Economic Forum.

Keller, Jennifer and John Page (1998) 'Governance and Growth: Some New Evidence and a Surprise', processed Washington D.C.: The World Bank.

Knack, S. and P. Keefer (1995) 'Institutions and Economic Performance: Cross-country Tests Using Alternative Institutional Measures', *Economics and Politics*, 7(3): 207–27.

Krueger, Anne O. (1974) 'The Political Economy of the Rent Seeking Society', *American Economic Review*, vol. 64, no. 3: 291–303.

Levine, Ross and David Renelt (1992) 'A Sensitivity Analysis of Cross-Country Growth Regressions', *American Economic Review*, 82: 942–63.

Mauro, Paolo (1995) 'Corruption and Growth', *Quarterly Journal of Economics*, 109: 681–712.

Naim, Moises (1993) 'Good Economics and Ugly Politics: The Venezuelan Reforms', *International Economic Insights*, vol. 3, no. 4, July/August: 45–8.

Pack, Howard and John Page, Jr. (1994) 'Accumulation, Exports, and Growth in the High-Performing Asian Economies', *Carnegie-Rochester Conference Series On Public Policy* 40: 199–250 (June).

Page, John (1994) 'The East Asia Miracle: Four Lessons for Development Policy', *NEBR Macroeconomics Annual*, Cambridge, MA: MIT Press.

—— (1996) 'Does Governance Matter?', processed Washington D.C.: The World Bank.

—— (1997) 'Getting Ready for Globalization', processed Washington D.C.: The World Bank.

—— (1998) 'From Boom to Bust – and Back? The Crisis of Growth in the Middle East and North Africa' in Shafik (1998b).

Pritchett, Lant (1997) 'Has Education had a Growth Payoff in the MENA Region?', processed The World Bank.

Rodrik, Dani (1993) 'Taking Trade Policy Seriously: Export Subsidization as a Case Study in Policy Effectiveness', *NBER Working Paper*, no. 4567, Cambridge, MA: National Bureau of Economic Research.

Roubini, Nouriel and Jeffrey Sachs (1989) 'Government Spending and Budget Deficits, Industrial Economies', *NBER Working Paper no. 2919*, Cambridge, MA: National Bureau of Economic Research.

Roy, Jayanta (1998) 'Trade Facilitation: The World Bank Experience', a paper presented at the Trade Facilitation Symposium, Geneva: World Trade Organization (WTO).

Sachs, Jeffrey and Andrew M. Warner (1995) *Economic Convergence and Economic Policies*, Cambridge, MA: National Bureau of Economic Research.

Shafik, Nemat (ed., 1998a) *Economic Challenges Facing Middle Eastern and North African Countries: Alternative Futures*, in association with Economic Research Forum for the Arab Countries, Iran and Turkey, London and New York: Macmillan Press.

—— (ed., 1998b) *Prospects for Middle Eastern and North African Economies – From Boom to Bust and Back?*, in association with Economic Research Forum for the Arab Countries, Iran and Turkey, London and New York: Macmillan Press.

Tendler, Judith (1997) *Good Government In The Tropics*, Baltimore: Johns Hopkins Press.

Wade, Robert (1996) 'Comparing Irrigation Authorities in India and Korea', Washington, D.C.: The World Bank.

—— (1990) *Governing the Market: Economic Theory and The Role of the Government in East Asian Industrialization*, Princeton: Princeton University Press.

Williamson, John (1993) 'Democracy and The "Washington Consensus"', *World Development*, vol. 21, no. 8, August: 1329–36.

World Bank (1991, 1994 and 1997a) *World Development Reports*, New York: Oxford University Press.

—— (1993) *The East Asian Miracle: Economic Growth and Public Policy*, New York: Oxford University Press.

—— (1994a) *Tunisia: Private Sector Assessment*, Report no. 12945, Washington D.C.: The World Bank.

—— (1994b) *Jordan: Private Sector Assessment*, Report no. 14405, Washington D.C.: The World Bank.

—— (1995a) *Claiming the Future: Choosing Prosperity in the Middle East and North Africa*, Washington D.C.: The World Bank.

—— (1995b) *Lebanon: Private Sector Assessment*, Report no. 13956, Washington D.C.: The World Bank.

—— (1996) *Global Economic Prospects and the Developing Countries*, Washington D.C.: The World Bank.

—— (1997b) *Country Economic Memorandum. Egypt: Issues in Sustaining Economic Growth*, Report no. 16207, Washington D.C.: The World Bank.

—— (1998) *Assessing Aid: What Works, What Doesn't, and Why*, Washington, D.C.: Oxford University Press.

World Development 1994. vol. 22, no. 4, April.

APPENDIX A
LIST OF COUNTRIES IN THE DATA SET

ALGERIA[2]
ARGENTINA[2, 3]
AUSTRALIA[2]
AUSTRIA[2]
BAHRAIN
BANGLADESH[2, 3]
BELGIUM[2]
BOLIVIA[3]
BRAZIL[2, 3]
CAMEROON[2]
CANADA[2]
CHILE[2, 3]
COLOMBIA[2, 3]
COSTA RICA[3]
DENMARK[2]
DOMINICAN REPUBLIC[2, 3]
ECUADOR[2, 3]
EGYPT[2, 3]
EL SALVADOR[3]
FINLAND[2]
FRANCE[2]
GABON
GHANA[2, 3]
GREECE[2]
GUATEMALA[3]
HAITI[2]
HONDURAS

HONG KONG
INDIA[2, 3]
INDONESIA[2, 3]
IRAN[2, 3]
IRAQ[4]
IRELAND[2]
ITALY[2]
JAMAICA[2]
JAPAN[2]
JORDAN[2]
KENYA[2, 3]
KOREA[2, 3]
KUWAIT
LEBANON[5]
MALAWI[3]
MALAYSIA[2, 3]
MEXICO[2, 3]
MOROCCO[2, 3]
NETHERLANDS[2]
NEW ZEALAND[2]
NICARAGUA[2]
NIGERIA[2, 3]
NORWAY[2]
OMAN
PAKISTAN[2, 3]
PANAMA[2, 3]
PARAGUAY[3]

PERU[2, 3]
PHILIPPINES[2, 3]
PORTUGAL[2]
QATAR[4]
SAUDI ARABIA
SENEGAL
SINGAPORE[2]
SPAIN[2]
SRI LANKA[2, 3]
SWEDEN[2]
SWITZERLAND[2]
SYRIA
TAIWAN[1, 4]
TANZANIA[4]
THAILAND[2]
TOGO
TRINIDAD[2]
TUNISIA[3]
UAE
UGANDA[4]
UK[2]
URUGUAY[2, 3]
USA[2]
VENEZUELA[2, 3]
ZAIRE[2]
ZAMBIA
ZIMBABWE[2]

[1] *Included only in regional summary of IQ Index.*
[2] *Included in TFP estimates.*
[3] *Included in private investment estimates.*
[4] *Missing required data for the Barro-type growth regression.*
[5] *Excluded from most estimates because of data limitations.*

Chapter Three

Structural Obstacles to Economic Adjustment in the MENA Region: The International Trade Aspects

Massoud Karshenas *

INTRODUCTION

Two aspects of the problems of economic adjustment in the MENA region have been highlighted in the recent literature. The first one relates to the slow pace of structural reform in the region compared to other parts of the world, e.g., Latin America, Central and Eastern Europe and even parts of Sub-Saharan Africa. The second pertains to the apparent lack of commensurate supply response in situations where limited economic reform has been introduced. This is reflected, for example, in low rates and slow growth of private investment and low rates of foreign direct investment inflows in the region by international standards (World Bank 1995; Page 1998; Riordan *et al.* 1998; Hoekman 1998; El-Erian and El-Gamal 1997).

The explanations for the first problem, namely, the apparently slow pace of economic reform, have been sought in various political and socio-cultural attributes of the countries in the region (Waterbury 1998). The explanations put forward for the second aspect of adjustment problems, namely the weak responses by domestic private capital and foreign capital to reforms, attribute the lack of credibility of the liberalization measures introduced or announced by the governments in the region to the gradual and slow pace of reform (Shafik 1998; Hoekman 1998). Indeed, various authors have suggested that perhaps joining multilateral pacts like the membership of WTO or the European Union Mediterranean Initiative would

---

* I would like to acknowledge helpful comments by Hassan Hakimian and Robert Mabro, subject to the usual disclaimers.

enhance the credibility of the gradualist approach to reform in the region.

In this chapter, I will argue that the reasons for the slow pace of reform in the MENA region may have more to do with the underlying structures of these economies – arising from their resource endowments and their past experience of development as well as external economic constraints facing them – rather than the idiosyncrasies of their political systems. Since politics is very much country specific, in order to explain general tendencies at the regional level, perhaps it would be more plausible to start from the shared structural features of the economies in question rather than making overgeneralizations about political tendencies at a regional level. It would be absurd to maintain that different countries share the same political predilections merely because they are located in the same region. I also argue that the question of credibility of economic reform is as much the outcome of the conformity of the pronounced reforms with the objective economic conditions which make such reforms effective. A reform programme which is devised without due consideration to the underlying structural constraints of the economy, even if it offers large immediate incentives to the business community and even when it is implemented with speed and by a ruthlessly resolute government, is unlikely to instil the type of confidence which is necessary for the long term commitment of investment by the private sector.

One of the key issues of economic adjustment in the MENA region since the early 1980s, the so-called post-oil boom period, has been the necessity for the countries in the region to develop alternative sources of foreign exchange revenue by improving their competitiveness and diversifying their export base. Trade liberalization is the linchpin of the proposed reforms, which are meant to shift the region's growth strategy from a protectionist, public sector dominated one to an export-led strategy in which the private sector plays a more prominent role. Nevertheless, very little research has been done on the type of activities in which the MENA countries may have a comparative advantage. In most of the literature it is assumed, either explicitly or implicitly, that under a liberalized trade regime, with other appropriate adjustment policies in place, the market will automatically take care of competitiveness issues and an appropriate structure for trade. In this chapter, I argue that under the present conditions in the world economy where important changes are taking place with the implementation of the Uruguay Round agreement, and where the major market for the MENA region exports, i.e., the European Union, has been very selective in import liberalization, it is important to have some idea of comparative advantages in the MENA economies before advocating drastic liberalization attempts. Such an understanding would be also necessary to predict and cope with the dislocations that trade liberalization may create in the short to medium run. It can also contribute to understanding the reasons for the slow pace of reform in the MENA region, and the apparent lack of credibility of reforms referred to above.

The purpose of this chapter is not to conduct a detailed analysis of the disaggregated lines of activity in which various MENA countries may have, or may be able to develop, comparative advantages. It is rather more concerned with broad sectoral patterns of specialization and trade, and the constraints imposed by general levels of resource availability as well as by international trade agreements.

SKILLS, NATURAL RESOURCES, AND COMPETITIVE ADVANTAGES

According to conventional trade theory, under certain assumptions, variations in resource endowments across different countries should explain variations in the composition of exports, at least in the early stages of industrialization, where intra-industry trade is not important. The relative abundance of capital, labour, skills, and natural resources are thus expected to be important determinants of the type of specialization in different countries or regions. This proposition has been subject to a great deal of controversy and has given rise to various empirical tests with mixed results. Nevertheless, here we shall consider it as a useful starting point. It is plausible that in hitherto closed economies possessing rich natural resources relative to the size of their labour force, the wages of simple unskilled labour relative to the international prices of manufactured goods is likely to be higher, as compared with overpopulated countries with a poor natural resource base. The latter group of countries is therefore expected to have a competitive edge over the former in less technologically sophisticated labour-intensive type of manufacturing and processing activities. Of course, the natural resource-rich, high-wage economy can, over time, develop a competitive edge in more skill-intensive manufacturing and services if it can upgrade the skills of its labour force and adopt more sophisticated technologies. In doing so, however, it has to be able to compete with countries at higher levels of industrialization and

61

technological know-how. Again, it is not implausible that countries with relatively higher stock of skilled labour relative to natural resources would have a competitive edge in skill-intensive manufacturing and services, as compared with countries with a large stock of natural resources but meagre skills.

In the above, I have concentrated on factors other than capital, because of the international mobility of capital (Wood 1994). In fact, a main assumption in the literature on adjustment in the MENA region has been that, with the right market incentives, foreign capital will make an important contribution to investment in the region. This is not, however, an entirely satisfactory reason for excluding capital because even with high international capital mobility it takes time to augment physical capital, during which other factors, e.g., the stock of skills, would be also changing. Another reason for excluding capital is that in hitherto closed economies the existing stock of capital is likely to have an inappropriate structure, involving substantial restructuring with high costs following the opening up to international competition. However, to the extent that the existing stock of capital enhances the productivity of particular factors, e.g., irrigation in agriculture enhancing the productivity of land, the exclusion of capital can give rise to misleading conclusions. We shall keep this caveat in mind, while focusing on the three remaining factors of production, namely natural resources, labour and skills.

The MENA region has been known for its abundant hydrocarbon and mineral natural resources. What is less known, but perhaps even more important particularly for the non-oil exporting countries in the region, is the relatively high agricultural land/labour ratios in the region compared to other countries in Asia. A comparison with Asia and Latin America in terms of land/labour ratio and agricultural labour productivity will be instructive. Table 1 shows labour/land ratios, agricultural production and labour productivity in 35 countries in MENA, Asia and Latin America. Output and productivity are measured in wheat equivalent units at 1980 international prices to enable us to conduct comparisons across countries. As can be seen, labour/land ratios in Asia in 1965 were on average five times higher than in the MENA region. There are of course exceptions such as Lebanon and particularly Egypt, where labour/land ratios are much higher than the MENA average. However, once we allow for the quality of land in these countries, a similar gap between these countries and the Asian countries would emerge. This is reflected in the output/labour ratios shown in the last three columns of the Table.

TABLE 1: Agricultural Land, Output and Labour Productivity in Asia, Latin America and the MENA Region, 1965–90

	Output	Labour/Land Ratio	Output Labour Ratio		
	1965	1965	1965	1980	1990
MENA					
Algeria	7	36	4408	7888	8546
Egypt	27	1696	5963	6799	8724
Iran	20	59	5643	8444	11142
Iraq	7	119	6343	8715	11600
Jordan	2	92	17558	25979	38012
Lebanon	2	523	13123	26707	52560
Libya	1	15	8020	23165	30995
Morocco	12	93	5077	5809	8027
Syria	7	39	10153	20345	21202
Tunisia	5	88	8483	10529	13567
Turkey	52	299	4713	7617	8812
MENA (median)	7	92	6343	8715	11600
MENA (mean)	13	278	8135	13818	19381
Asia					
Bangladesh	30.4	1637	1931	2039	2046
China	379.0	866	1231	1449	2190
India	278.6	851	1847	2204	2804
Indonesia	47.6	751	1646	2581	3674
Korea, Rep.	14.3	2343	2682	4737	7425
Malaysia	6.7	427	3571	6138	9092
Pakistan	39.2	426	3800	4627	5771
Philippines	26.2	934	3699	5181	5392
Sri Lanka	6.3	1024	2863	3133	2911
Thailand	28.2	977	2301	3327	3467
Asia (median)	29	900	2492	3230	3570
Asia (mean)	86	1024	2557	3542	4477
Latin America					
Argentina	64.0	9	40231	69462	85594
Bolivia	3.2	24	4564	6486	7571
Brazil	122.2	73	9315	12865	16713
Chile	9.5	51	13378	20924	30698
Colombia	18.5	63	7566	10981	13676
Dominican Rep.	3.8	198	6040	7541	7566
Ecuador	7.4	190	8247	10322	13595
El Salvador	2.6	445	4568	6567	5973
Jamaica	1.4	535	5266	5017	4649
Mexico	44.2	65	6886	8798	9430
Panama	1.6	123	7708	12037	13370
Peru	10.5	58	6079	5255	5490
Uruguay	8.0	14	37220	48067	66352
Venezuela	8.2	40	10431	16117	20764
Latin America (median)	8	64	7637	10651	13482
Latin America (mean)	22	135	11964	17174	21531
t-Test for difference between the Means	(MENA and Asia)		4.41	4.01	3.27
	(MENA and Latin America)		−1.15	−0.60	−0.27

Notes: Output is measured in wheat equivalent units in mn tons in 1980 world relative prices. Labour/Land ratio is in persons per 000 ha of agricultural land, and labour productivity in kg per head in wheat eq. units. Medians and means refer to the countries in the table. Means are simple averages.
Source: FAO Data Bank, FAOSTAT (1998) and Karshenas (1998).

Average labour productivity in agriculture in the MENA region is three to four times higher than a corresponding average in Asia.[1] This applies to both oil and non-oil economies in the region. Even in the case of Egypt, where labour/land ratios were well over the Asian average in 1965, the average product of labour was double the Asian average in that year (Table 1). This reflects the higher quality of agricultural land in Egypt and the fact that Egyptian agricultural land is one hundred per cent irrigated.

Of course, hydrocarbon based and other mineral resources are equally, if not more, important than agricultural land in most MENA countries. However, to the extent that the existence of these other natural resources has given rise to fast rates of expansion of non-agricultural employment in the region, and thus high rates of emigration from rural and agricultural areas, the agricultural land/labour ratios are also likely to reflect the broader picture of natural resource availability in the region. There are, of course, countries in other regions at a much higher stage of economic development, where high land/labour ratios and high levels of agricultural labour productivity reflect the engagement of the larger part of the labour force in manufacturing and services and the use of highly capital and technology intensive methods in agriculture. What distinguishes economies of this type from natural resource-based economies such as the MENA countries, is the much higher skill/land ratios in the former.

Assuming that agricultural labour productivity across countries at early stages of development would be highly correlated with reservation wages of simple unskilled labour, these figures indicate that the wheat equivalent wages of unskilled labour in the MENA region are likely to be much higher than in Asia. Clearly, the MENA economies cannot be competitive in low skilled labour intensive manufacturing in relation to populous countries in Asia such as India, China, Indonesia and Bangladesh. Considering that in these countries close to 70 per cent of the labour force is still engaged in agriculture, they seem to be in possession of 'unlimited' supplies of cheap labour for a long time to come. This leaves MENA countries the possibility of becoming specialized in more skill-intensive manufacturing, or in processing of bulky minerals where transport costs are high.

As shown in Table 1, the MENA region's labour/land ratio seems to be comparable to Latin America's. However, agricultural labour productivity rates are higher on average in Latin America than in

MENA (although productivity differences between the two regions are not statistically significant). A significant difference between the two regions, however, is the much higher stock of skills or human capital per labourer in Latin America compared to the MENA region. This can be seen in Table 2, where a comparison of adult illiteracy rates and mean years of schooling is given for the different regions. In fact, if we exclude the South Asian economies such as India, Bangladesh and Pakistan from the Asian sample, the human capital situation in East Asia also becomes considerably more favourable compared to the MENA region. Adult illiteracy amongst the female population is particularly high, by any standards, in the MENA region.

Formal education plays an important enabling role in the process of learning and skill formation in the economy, but a part of the necessary skills in the economy are also generated within the production process through learning by doing or through on the job training by firms. Since a large part of the non-agricultural labour in the MENA region is likely to be first generation rural migrants during the rapid urbanization of the oil-boom years, and considering the young age structure of the labour force, the existing stock of industrial skills in these economies is likely to be even lower in relative terms than that suggested by the education data shown in Table 2. In terms of skill/natural resource (or land) ratio, the MENA region therefore seems to be lagging behind Latin America and is well below Asia – particularly the Far East.

The above points can be looked at from a different angle by comparing wage differentials across the countries. Ideally, one would compare wages of labour with similar skill levels and hours of work. However, since such data is not readily available, we shall compare manufacturing wage differentials across the countries, which gives only a rough idea of the relation between wage differentials and relative factor availabilities. Table 3 shows wage rates in the manufacturing sector for the three regions for the 1963–95 period, in dollar terms at market exchange rates. Wages are measured as total compensation of labour divided by the number of manufacturing employees. As can be seen, the wage differentials between the regions are in line with the agricultural productivity differentials in Table 1. This is particularly the case for the 1960s, when skill differentials between the regions were not as acute as in later years. On average, wages seem to be three to four times higher in the MENA region than in Asia, but not significantly different from Latin America averages.

TABLE 2: Adult Illiteracy and Mean Years of Schooling in the MENA Region, Asia and Latin America, 1994

	% Adult illiteracy (15⁺ age group)			Mean years of Schooling (Adults aged 25⁺)	
	Total	Female	Male	Female	Male
MENA					
Algeria	51	65	37	0.8	4.4
Egypt	55	71	40	1.9	3.9
Iran	52	64	41	3.1	4.6
Iraq	48	59	36	3.9	5.7
Jordan	26	38	14	4.0	6.0
Lebanon	23	31	14	3.5	5.3
Libya	44	60	30	1.3	5.5
Morocco	58	71	46	1.5	4.1
Syria	41	57	26	3.1	5.2
Tunisia	42	53	32	1.2	3.0
Turkey	24	36	12	1.8	3.8
MENA (median)	44	59	32	1.9	4.6
MENA (mean)	42	55	30	2.4	4.7
Asia					
Bangladesh	68	81	56	0.9	3.1
China	32	45	20	3.6	6.0
India	56	71	42	1.2	3.5
Indonesia	28	37	20	2.9	5.0
Korea, Rep.	5	9	2	6.1	8.0
Malaysia	26	35	17	5.0	5.6
Pakistan	69	82	57	0.7	3.0
Philippines	12	13	12	7.0	7.8
Sri Lanka	13	19	8	6.1	7.7
Thailand	9	13	5	3.3	4.3
Asia (median)	27	36	18	3.5	5.3
Asia (mean)	32	40	24	3.7	5.4
East Asia (median)	13	19	12	5.0	6.0
East Asia (mean)	18	24	12	4.9	6.3
Latin America					
Argentina	5	6	5	8.9	8.5
Bolivia	28	36	19	3.0	5.5
Brazil	22	23	20	3.8	4.0
Chile	8	8	7	7.2	7.8
Colombia	15	16	14	7.3	6.9
Dominican Rep.	20	22	18	4.0	4.6
Ecuador	17	20	15	5.3	5.8
El Salvador	31	35	27	4.1	4.1
Jamaica	2	2	2	5.2	5.3
Mexico	15	18	13	4.6	4.8
Panama	14	14	14	6.9	6.6
Peru	18	26	11	5.7	7.1
Uruguay	5	5	4	8.2	7.4
Venezuela	14	12	16	6.2	6.4
Latin America (median)	15	17	14	5.5	6.1
Latin America (mean)	15	17	13	5.7	6.1
t-Test for difference (MENA and Asia)	1.21	1.44	0.85	−1.61	−1.06
between the Means (MENA and East Asia)	4.41	4.49	4.06	−3.54	−2.63
(MENA and Latin America)	6.47	7.91	4.46	−5.9	−3.0

Source: World Bank (1998) and UNDP, Women's Indicators Database (1997).

TABLE 3: Manufacturing Wages in Asia, Latin America and the MENA Region, 1963–95

	Average Dollar Wage Rates		
	1963–70	1975–85	1985–95
MENA			
Algeria	2096	5569	5946
Egypt	571	1894	2628
Iran	568	6986	4805
Iraq	819	3588	–
Jordan	532	3531	3561
Libya	1668	6166	
Morocco	1367	3209	3123
Syria	454	2856	5834
Tunisia	940	2808	5126
Turkey	1085	3727	5432
MENA (median)	880	3559	4966
MENA (mean)	1010	4033	4557
Asia			
Bangladesh	322	477	627
China	–	436	380
India	397	892	1213
Indonesia	139	745	895
Korea, Rep.	342	2558	9313
Malaysia	688	2082	3425
Pakistan	382	1035	1639
Philippines	627	1081	1816
Sri Lanka	442	460	641
Thailand	495	1495	2262
Asia (median)	397	963	1426
Asia (mean)	426	1126	2221
Latin America			
Argentina	–	5223	6519
Bolivia	830	3037	2143
Brazil		2407	6193
Chile	1404	4360	5379
Colombia	950	2400	2811
Dominican Rep.	838	1826	998
Ecuador	874	3802	3384
El Salvador	769	2984	3637
Jamaica	1753	4828	3949
Mexico	–	3865	5286
Panama	1880	4224	5823
Peru	–	–	–
Uruguay	963	3205	4248
Venezuela	2366	8615	5788
Latin America (median)	957	3802	4248
Latin America (mean)	1263	3906	4320
t-Test for difference (MENA & Asia)	3.22	5.12	2.51
between the Means (MENA & Latin America)	–1.10	0.18	0.39

Notes: Wages refer to total compensation of labour in US $ terms at market exchange rate, divided by total number of employees in the manufacturing sector.
Source: UNIDO, INDSTAT (1996).

This wage gap between MENA and Asia is likely to be more the result of the relative resource availabilities in the two regions, than of institutional factors such as minimum wage legislation, union power, etc. The fact that, for example, industrial wages in 1963–70 in Turkey were more than three times higher than in Korea is a reflection of the fact that labour/land ratio in Korea during this period was several times higher than in Turkey (see Tables 1 and 3). In fact, in the MENA region manufacturing real wages have shown a remarkable degree of downward flexibility during the adjustment period since the early 1980s, when oil and other mineral and agricultural commodity prices were falling in real terms. This can be seen from Table 4, which shows the trend growth rates in real wages, employment, and productivity in the manufacturing sector for the MENA region and Latin American countries during major adjustment periods over the 1980s. An

TABLE 4: Growth of Real Wages, Output, Employment and Labour Productivity in the Manufacturing Sector

	Average Annual Rate of Change of:			
	Real Wages[1]	Output	Employment	Productivity
MENA				
Egypt (85–92)	−9.5	−0.1	1.9	−2.0
Iran (77–92)	−2.2	1.4	3.9	−2.5
Morocco (78–92)	−5.7	2.2	5.5	−3.3
Tunisia (80–92)	−1.4	2.5	1.4	1.1
Turkey (79–88)	−3.5	8.3	2.0	6.3
Median	−3.5	2.2	2.0	−2.0
Latin America				
Argentina (75–92)	2.0	−0.3	−3.9	3.6
Brazil (80–92)	1.7	1.9	0.0	1.9
Colombia (80–92)	0.0	3.0	0.0	3.0
Mexico (80–92)	−2.9	0.5	−1.5	2.0
Chile (73–82)	6.4	1.0	−4.7	5.7
Median	1.7	1.0	−1.5	3.0
Asia				
India (80–92)	4.9	6.8	−0.1	6.9
Korea (80–92)	7.3	9.8	4.3	5.5
Malaysia (80–92)	3.1	9.7	5.6	4.1
Pakistan (80–92)	1.4	4.0	0.6	3.4
Thailand (80–92)	7.0	5.5	2.1	3.4
Median	4.9	6.8	2.1	4.1

Notes: 1. Real product wages.
Sources: Based on UNIDO, INDSTAT (1996).

interesting difference between the two regions is that, while in the MENA region the main burden of adjustment seems to be borne by real wages, in Latin America real wages seem to be stickier, and the main brunt is borne by employment. The conventional models of union power and wage bargaining seem to be more relevant to the experience of Latin America than that of the MENA region.

The above suggests that in the early 1980s, when most MENA economies were required to embark on adjustment policies in order to deal with serious internal and external imbalances in the face of large negative external shocks, the nature of their resource availabilities posed serious limits to competitiveness and export diversification in areas other than primary commodities. In order to follow an export oriented industrialization strategy, the MENA region had to compete, on the one hand, with countries such as the highly populated Asian economies with much lower wage levels and higher skills, and, on the other, with Latin American countries or some of the more industrialized Asian countries with comparable wage levels but much higher human capital. In theory, of course, it is expected that upon trade liberalization in hitherto closed economies, wage levels would find their equilibrium value in accordance with the comparative advantages of the countries in question. However, in economies that have been subject to substantial negative external shocks, as was the case of the MENA economies during the 1980s, and where the structure of skills and capital stocks have evolved in a relatively closed economic environment, the required adjustment in wages following a sudden liberalization of foreign trade can be overwhelming. To develop this point further, we first need to examine MENA's emerging pattern of export diversification in the context of its relative resource endowments.

PATTERNS OF EXPORT SPECIALIZATION

The patterns of export specialization in the MENA region by the early 1980s were broadly in line with the relative resource availability in the region, as examined in the last section. In the region's oil exporting economies, primary products formed between 90 and 100 per cent of total exports in 1980; even in non-oil economies, the share of primary exports in total exports was in general over 65 per cent.[2] Manufacturing exports, however, grew rapidly in some MENA economies during the 1980s. In order to examine the relationship between the patterns of resource availability and export speicialization in the MENA region, I have used the data in the international comparative study of patterns of export specialization by Wood and Berge (1997). On the basis of a simple two-factor trade model, these authors have conducted a cross-country regression analysis of the relationship between manufacturing/primary commodity export specialization and skill/natural resource availability across different countries.[3] Using a sample of 114 countries, they find a robust positive relationship between manufacturing/primary export ratio and skill/natural resource availability in different countries.[4] I have reproduced their regression line in Figure 1, together with average observations for MENA and a few other regions for the year 1989. As can be seen, the regions can be ranked according to their relative skill ratios ranging from Sub-Saharan Africa at the bottom to MENA, Latin America, South Asia, East Asia and high-performing East Asia (consisting of Hong Kong, Indonesia, Korea, Malaysia, Singapore, Taiwan and Thailand). The manufacturing export share increases with the value of relative skill ratio.

The MENA region seems to have an above normal share of manufacturing exports relative to its average skill ratio. For instance, while the average skill/land ratio in MENA countries is lower than in Latin America, their average manufacturing export ratio is higher than in Latin America. However, this is mainly the result of the manufacturing export performance in a few non-oil-exporting

FIGURE 1: Manufacturing Exports and Resource Endowments, 1989

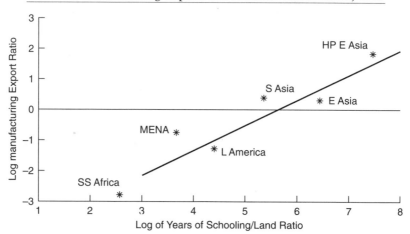

Source: Based on Wood and Berge (1997).

countries, as shown in Figure 2. In particular, countries such as Morocco, Tunisia and Turkey seem to have well above normal rates of manufacturing trade specialization. The relatively high share of manufactured exports in these countries is a very recent phenomenon. In fact, in all the MENA countries depicted in Figure 2, the share of manufacturing exports shows a steep climb since the early 1980s. For example, the share of manufacturing exports in Turkey increased from about 27 per cent in 1980 to almost 69 per cent in 1990. In the case of Tunisia, it increased from 35 per cent to 69 per cent, in Morocco from 26 per cent to 53 per cent, in Syria from 6 per cent to 40 per cent, in Egypt from 11 per cent to 66 per cent, and in Jordan from 34 per cent to 51 per cent (World Bank data). Such impressive increases in the share of manufactures, however, should be considered in the context of the overall growth of exports. With slow rates of growth of overall exports, reductions in primary commodity export revenues would lead to an automatic increase in the share of manufacturing exports. As can be seen from Figure 3, amongst the major non-oil-exporting countries in the region only Turkey and Tunisia exhibited noticeable increases in the ratio of merchandise exports to GDP. Even in these two countries, the export/GDP ratio stabilized somewhat during the 1990s, after impressive increases in the 1980s. Trends in per capita real merchandise exports, shown in

FIGURE 2: **Manufacturing Exports and Resource Endowments, 1989**

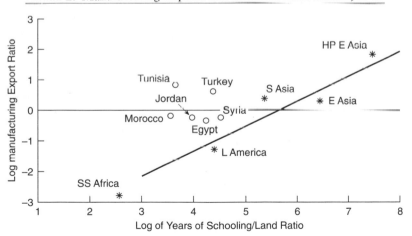

Source: Based on Wood and Berge (1997).

FIGURE 3: Merchandise Exports GDP Ratios, 1963–96

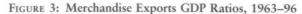

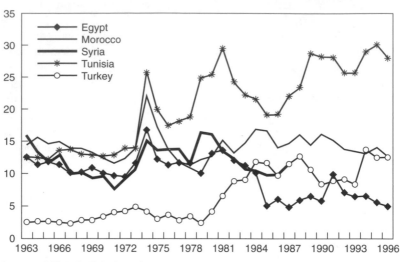

Source: World Bank, STARS Database (1996).

Figure 4, also indicate that only Turkey and Tunisia, and to a much lesser extent Morocco, witnessed spectacular increases in their export growth during the 1980s. These are, of course, the three countries that started their adjustment policies earliest and which have gone further than other MENA economies in pursuit of liberalization policies. It is therefore important to form an overview of the characteristics of manufacturing exports and the forces driving export expansion in these countries.

One of the main characteristics of manufacturing exports from the MENA economies – as highlighted by various authors – is the predominance of low technology, labour intensive commodities (mostly textiles and clothing). Using an index of intra-industry trade as a measure of the complexity and sophistication of manufacturing exports, various researchers have found that the intra-industry trade orientation index for MENA countries is well below countries with similar levels of per capita income and wages in Central and Eastern Europe and Latin America (Havrylyshyn and Kunzel 1997; Hoekman 1998). This is consistent with the evidence on low levels of skill/ natural resource ratios in the MENA region discussed above. The manufacturing export drive in the MENA countries since the 1980s

FIGURE 4: Per Capita Real Merchandise Exports, 1963-96

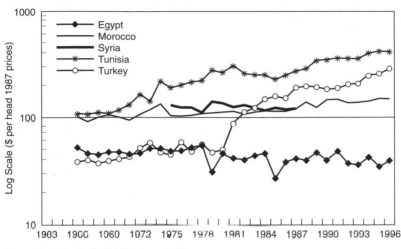

Source: World Bank, STARS Database (1996).

has thus been based on enhancing price/cost competitiveness in traditional exports rather than on product innovation and developing niches in high quality products.

An important contributing to the growth of this type of manufacturing export has been preferential treatment in the European Union and other industrialized country markets. A large part of the manufacturing exports from the MENA countries has been in textiles and clothing, which are effectively protected from Asian competition through Multifibre Agreement (MFA) quotas. The MENA countries have also actively promoted their manufacturing exports since the early 1980s through the provision of a considerable amount of direct subsidies. During the 1980s, for example, Turkey provided substantial direct subsidies for manufacturing exports in the form of tax rebates, subsidized credits, and duty-free imports. According to estimates by Senses (1990) and Uygur (1996), such direct subsidies were equivalent to over 20 per cent of the value of manufacturing exports during the 1980s and the early 1990s. Estimates by Togan (1993) indicate that the effective rate of protection for export-oriented industries such as weaving was about 100 to 300 per cent during the 1983–91 period, while for clothing it increased from about 200 per cent in the early 1980s to over 6000 per cent in 1991. The cost of such large subsidies, which are, in a way, necessary to enable the MENA countries to attain cost competitiveness vis-à-vis the low wage Asian countries in low skilled labour intensive manufactures, is partly born by other sectors of the economy. To the extent that foreign loans are available, such subsidies can be also financed by increased foreign borrowing. It is not surprising that during the period of adjustment the total stock of foreign debt in countries such as Turkey, Tunisia and Morocco increased dramatically.[5]

A further important element behind cost reduction in export oriented industries during the 1980s was the substantial real wage compression that took place during this period. As shown in Table 4, in some countries like Turkey and Tunisia this took place despite a positive rate of labour productivity growth in the manufacturing sector. Of course, as noted above, according to conventional trade theory, this downward movement of wages is an important mechanism of adjustment in economies that have been subject to negative external shocks. However, in order to attain cost competitiveness in conventional labour-intensive manufacturing activities, the necessary wage adjustment in the MENA region (as discussed in the previous section) would be dramatic. As I have argued elsewhere (Karshenas 1997), the historically evolved family structures and other social institutions in the MENA region would have made further downward adjustment to wages beyond what has already taken place since the early 1980s, extremely difficult. Changes in family structures and other social customs and habits, for example, attitudes to female labour force participation, involve much longer adjustment periods than other economic variables. Any drastic trade liberalization attempts under these circumstances, rather than enhancing the credibility of the reform programme, could easily prove counter-productive.

FUTURE CHALLENGES

In the near future, the MENA economies are unlikely to be able to compete with the Asian economies in low skill manufacturing exports, once they lose their preferential advantages in the European Union's markets with the phasing in of the Uruguay Round agreement. With the build-up of foreign debt, continued subsidization of this type of manufacturing exports also becomes increasingly problematic. Furthermore, new competition from the Central and East European countries with roughly similar per capita incomes

74

and wages as the MENA region, but with much higher levels of education and industrial skills, is going to increase market pressures on the MENA countries. Under these conditions, it is difficult for the MENA region to be able to attract foreign direct investment in industry either. Recent trends in processed manufacturing exports to the European Union, surveyed by European firms in MENA and Central and Eastern Europe, confirm these points. Between 1989 and 1994, this export category increased from 10.4 to 17.1 per cent of total exports to EU from Central and Eastern Europe. However, the corresponding shares for the MENA region were 1.6 and 1.7 per cent in the same period (Hoekman 1998: 112). It should also be noted that the main concentration of this export category from the MENA region, i.e., clothing, still benefits from the current MFA restrictions.

With current levels of education and skills relative to their natural resources, one area in which some MENA countries may have comparative advantage under a free trade regime is in agricultural and other primary exports.[6] For the countries in the region with relatively higher than average skill levels, the processing of primary commodities and agricultural products could be another source of comparative advantage. However, this potential source of relatively profitable exports is also blocked by the EU's protective policies. A major part of exports from MENA region to Europe until the mid-20th Century consisted of agricultural exports. The introduction of the Common Agricultural Policy at the early stages of the formation of the European Common Market appears to have contributed to undermining this source of export activity in the MENA region. It is not unlikely that the adoption of increasingly inward oriented development strategies in the MENA economies in the post-war period was connected to the erosion of this source of outward orientation following the introduction of the Common Agricultural Policy in Europe.[7] The much-publicized European Union Mediterranean Initiative, by excluding agricultural trade issues from its agenda for the time being, has not resolved this problem either. It seems that in the short to medium term, the EU's protection policies are likely to be a stumbling block for liberalization and export diversification in the MENA region. In the long run, it is essential for the region to build up its human capital and skill levels in order to be able to benefit from the opportunities provided by the global economy by developing potential sources of dynamic comparative advantages.

CONCLUSION

The starting point of this chapter was the recognition of the urgent need for the MENA economies to diversify their export base so as to take advantage of the new opportunities provided by the global economy. This has become a vital prerequisite for sustained growth in the region in the post-oil era since the early 1980s and is likely to remain so with present projections for the price of and demand for oil and other primary commodities in the international economy. The slow pace of economic reform and lack of response of domestic and foreign investment to economic reform over the past two decades has thus been a serious cause of concern for the MENA countries. In this chapter, I have concentrated on some of the fundamental structural features of the MENA economies as the possible causes for the sluggishness of economic reform and adjustment. The basic premise of the arguments developed above has been that economic development is essentially a path dependent process, in the sense that the past experience of development limits the set of choices available to societies at any point in time.

A prominent feature of the MENA economies, inherited from the past experience of development, is the low stock of skills and human capital compared to other countries with similar levels of per capita income. This may have come about as a result of the substitution of other types of capital for human skills, encouraged by the relative abundance of financial capital and made possible by the rich natural resource endowments in the region. This feature of the MENA economies, which is reflected in relatively low human skill/natural resource ratios by international standards, has proved particularly inimical to export diversification at a time when the new automated technologies demand high levels of general skills and education. As noted above, high rates of manufacturing export growth in a select few MENA countries since the early 1980s have been attained on the basis of traditional, low skill intensive exports. This has been made possible by relatively high rates of subsidization and by lowering wages. It has also been aided by preferential treatment in European markets. Given the wide wage gap between the MENA economies and the low wage Asian economies, this strategy is unlikely to lead to sustained rates growth of manufacturing exports in the MENA region. The prevailing social institutions, for example, patriarchal family structures and attitudes to female labour force participation in the non-agricultural sectors, would set a limit to the degree to which real wage reduction can be relied on as the main equilibrating mechanism for dealing with foreign exchange shortages.

The past experience of development seems to have 'locked' the MENA economies into social institutions and skill patterns that are inappropriate in the context of new technological realities and the prevailing trends for primary commodity prices in the global economy. The slow pace of economic reform and adjustment in the region, as compared to regions such as Latin America or Central and Eastern Europe, may not be unrelated to this configuration of skill/wage ratios in the MENA economies, as it takes time to bring about the necessary adjustments in the stock of skills or change social institutions that limit the downward flexibility of wages. This, of course, does not mean that the lack of serious reform attempts by the governments in the region have not played a part in the slow pace of adjustment in the MENA countries. Inadequate policy responses are, however, likely to be reflected in the differential reform records in different MENA countries rather than a general phenomenon that can explain the slow pace of adjustment in the region as a whole. For example, country specific policy responses, as determined by domestic political factors, set reforming countries such as Turkey and Tunisia apart from late adjusters such as Syria, Egypt or Iran. The success of the early reforming countries in cumulatively building up competitive niches in the international market can, in time, introduce a qualitative gap between these countries and the laggards. However, a major obstacle to competitiveness in manufacturing and processing activities which seems to be general to all the countries in the MENA region still seems to be the low levels of skill and human capital. Therefore, in addition to the usual liberaliztion policies which are aimed at improving the efficiency of resource use, it is also imperative for MENA countries to develop specific strategies to address the serious educational and human skill gap in the region.

NOTES

1 The lower labour productivity levels in Asia should not, of course, be interpreted as indicating a technologically more backward agriculture in Asia than in the MENA region. On the contrary, the wide application of the green revolution technologies and the much higher intensity of cultivation in Asia has meant that they have achieved some of the highest levels of land productivity in the world. The reason for Asia's lower labour productivity levels is the region's much higher population pressure on land compared to the MENA region.

2 In 1980, the share of primary exports in total exports in Egypt, Jordan, Morocco, Syria, Tunisia and Turkey were respectively, 89%, 66.2%, 74%, 94%, 65%, and 73% (World Bank, STAR5 databank 1996).

3 Wood and Berge (1997) assume primary commodity production and labour intensive manufacturing have similar degrees of skilled labour/ simple labour ratios, and hence confine their analysis to the effect of the skill/natural resource ratio on export specialization. They also show that this restriction is not rejected by the data. Such a restriction is also convenient for the analysis of trade specialization in the case of MENA economies, because, as noted above, these economies are unlikely to be able to compete with Asia in low-skilled labour-intensive manufacturing.

4 They use mean years of schooling as a proxy for skills and total area of land as a proxy for natural resources. Their reasoning for the use of total area of land, rather than agricultural land, as a proxy for natural resources, is that the former may be a better indicator of all natural resources including minerals.

5 In Turkey the stock of foreign debt increased from 15.9 bn dollars in 1980 to 79.8 bn dollars in 1996. In Tunisia it increased from 3.5 bn dollars in 1980 to 9.9 bn dollars in 1996, and in Morocco it increased from 9.2 bn dollars to 21.8 bn dollars (World Bank data).

6 This may appear counter-intuitive, as most MENA economies have a large agricultural trade deficit, and the binding constraints on agricultural output seems to be shortage of water rather than availability of cultivable land. This, however, does not preclude the possibility of restructuring agricultural output and trade towards more export oriented products. The efficiency gains resulting from such restructuring may even give rise to a lower agricultural trade deficit while maintaining the current per capita food consumption levels.

7 Economists have often treated the adoption of development strategies as exogenous decisions by governments, or in recent literature increasingly as a function of the interests of a bureaucratic clique. In my opinion, however, there is a large element of endogeneity in government policies. If potential sources of profitable exports exist, it is unlikely that, under normal circumstances, governments would find it possible or desirable to shun these.

REFERENCES

Aricanli T. and D. Rodrik (eds, 1990) *The Political Economy of Turkey: Debt, Adjustment and Sustainability*, London: Macmillan.

El-Erian, M. and H. El-Gamal (1997) 'Attracting Foreign Investment to Arab Countries: Getting the Basics Right', *Working Paper 9718*, Cairo: Economic Research Forum for the Arab Countries, Iran and Turkey (ERF).

Food and Agricultural Organization of the United Nations (FAO) (1998) *Agricultural Database*, Rome: FAOSTAT.

Havrylyshyn O. and P. Kunzel (1997) 'Intra-Industry Trade of Arab Countries: An Indicator of Potential Competitiveness', *IMF Working Paper*, Washington DC: International Monetary Fund.

Hockman, B. (1998) 'The World Trade Organization, the European Union, and the Arab World: Trade Policy Priorities and Pitfalls', in Shafik (1998), ch. 4: 96–131.

Karshenas, M. (1998) 'Purchasing Power Parities and the Interntional Comparison of Real Agricultural Output and Productivity', *mimeo*, London: School of Oriental and African Studies, Economics Deaprtment.

—— (1997) 'Economic Liberalization, Competitiveness and Women's Employment in the Middle East and North Africa', *Working Paper 9705*, Cairo: Economic Research Forum for the Arab Countries, Iran and Turkey (ERF).

Page, J. (1998) 'From Boom to Bust – and Back? The Crisis of Growth in the Middle East and North Africa', in Shafik (1998), ch. 5: 133–158.

Riordan, E.M., U. Dadush, J. Jalali, S. Streifel, M. Brahmbhatt, and K. Takagaki (1998) 'The World Economy and its Implications for the Middle East and North Africa, 1995–2010', in Shafik (1998), ch. 2: 15–46.

Senses, F. (1990) 'An Assessment of the Pattern of Turkish Manufactured Export Growth in the 1980s and its Prospects', in Aricanli and Rodrik (1990), ch. 3: 60–77

Shafik, N. (ed., 1998) *Prospects for Middle Eastern and North African Economies: From Boom to Bust and Back?*, London: Macmillan.

Togan, S. (1993) *1980'li Yillarda Turk Dis Ticaret Rejimi ve Dis Ticaretin Liberizasyonu*, Ankara: Eximbank Publishers.

UNDP (1997) *Women's Indicators Database*, New York: United Nations.

UNIDO (1996) *Industrial Statistics Database*, Vienna: United Nations Industrial Development Organization.

Uygur, E. (1996) 'Export Policies and Export Performance: The Case of Turkey', *Working Paper 9707*, Cairo: Economic Research Forum for the Arab Countries, Iran and Turkey (ERF).

Waterbury, J. (1998) 'The State and Economic Transition in the Middle East and North Africa', in Shafik (1998), ch. 6: 159–177.

Wood, A. (1994) *North-South Trade, Employment and Inequality: Changing Fortunes in a Skill-Driven World*, Oxford: Clarendon Press.

Wood, A. and K. Berge (1997) 'Exporting Manufactures: Human Resources, Natural Resources, and Trade Policy', *Journal of Development Studies*, vol. 34, no. 1 (October): 35–59.

World Bank (1995) *Claiming the Future: Choosing Prosperity in the Middle East and North Africa*, Washington, D.C.: The World Bank.

World Bank (1996) *Socio-economic Time Series Access and Retrieval System* (STARS), Wahshington, D.C.: The World Bank.

World Bank (1998) *World Development Indicators* (WDI) Database, Washington D.C.: The World Bank.

Chapter Four

From MENA to East Asia and Back: Lessons of Globalization, Crisis and Economic Reform

Hassan Hakimian

INTRODUCTION

Until the onset of the Asian crisis, East Asia's economic successes were much admired, and spoke favourably of the experience of globalization in the developing regions. The Asian 'model' inspired and informed key debates on development policy and was a common point of reference for liberalization and outward-oriented economic policies, which the development orthodoxy has strongly advocated since the early 1980s.[1]

In the MENA context, the wider application and general attractions of this model have been influenced by two sets of considerations: the region's faltering growth trend in recent decades on one hand; and its apparent failure to take advantage of increasing global opportunities on the other. Much of the recent literature on economic reform in the MENA region has thus emphasized an urgent need for sound macroeconomic policies including domestic economic liberalization and a more open approach to the international economy (see, for instance, World Bank 1995; Shafik 1998b; Handoussa 1997).

Until recently, some of this literature was somewhat optimistic about the potential outcome of globalization. Upbeat accounts of external opportunities abounded in which success was largely a function of the choice of appropriate economic policies alone.[2] We were reminded that MENA states faced an historic opportunity for catching up with new and real hopes of convergence 'in the twenty-first century' (Handoussa 1997: 4).[3]

The dramatic reversal of Asia's financial and economic fortunes since the second half of 1997 has, however, cast a new, critical light on

80

this perspective. As controversies have arisen over the causes and consequences of this crisis, the remarkable consensus that once united mainstream development economists over the perceived benefits of globalization has been weakened. This has led to new questions about the underlying tenets, character and sustainability of the Asian 'miracle' as well as its implications for other regions and 'emerging' economies.

This chapter examines the recent Asian crisis and evaluates its lessons and implications for policy debates and development prospects in the MENA region. The experiences of East Asian and MENA economies are, in many ways, antithetical. East Asian economies have been characterized widely as models of openness and beacons of economic orthodoxy and macroeconomic stability. In contrast, the MENA states have been viewed as inward-looking, interventionist, over-reliant on natural riches and hence vulnerable to large external shocks. Moreover, MENA's tardiness in introducing economic reforms and adjustment has been widely interpreted as contributing to its deteriorating position in the world economy.

Given the differences between the two regions and especially the limited extent of reforms in the MENA countries, it may be argued that any comparisons between them may be premature and unlikely to produce useful insights. While it is undoubtedly true that any crisis has its own specific (regional) characteristics, drawing lessons from Asia's recent woes may prove useful for at least two reasons.

First, several countries in the MENA region (notably, Morocco, Jordan, Tunisia, Turkey and Egypt) have embarked on economic reforms in recent years and more countries are likely to follow in the near future. Whether already committed to reforms or still pondering over the costs and benefits of full participation in the global economy, MENA countries can usefully learn from Asia's experiences of both prolonged boom in the past and bust in more recent years.

A second point relates to the significance of the crisis itself. Largely unforeseen, this calamitous event which swept Asia in the second half of 1997 has helped bring 'to the fore some of the structural and institutional challenges posed by globalization' (World Bank 1998b). Its lessons and implications are of interest beyond the region itself and will be the subject of wide ranging debate in the years to come.

The structure of this chapter is as follows. The next section provides an overview of arguments in favour of restructuring MENA's position in the world economy. First, we review MENA's recent 'crisis

81

of growth', arguing that a poor growth record in MENA cannot be merely ascribed to lack of economic reforms, as it is also related to factors such as rapid demographic growth and lack of diversification. This is followed by an examination of MENA's position in the wider international economy. The following two sections then take up the theme of globalization and its opportunities and risks for developing regions in light of the Asian crisis. After discussing the features of this crisis, we draw lessons from it for other developing countries and regions. We then confront the Asian lessons with MENA's realities, focusing on challenges and prospects for economic reform in the latter in the light of lessons from the former.

PROSPECTS AND PROMISES OF GLOBALIZATION IN MENA

A Crisis of Growth?

MENA's comparatively poor economic performance in recent years has been a common focal point in the literature dealing with economic reform and liberalization. Various analysts and researchers have highlighted the region's weak growth record since the early 1980s and its inflexible production structures as providing a strong rationale for extensive economic reforms in the area (Page 1998; World Bank 1995; Shafik 1998a and 1998b; Handoussa 1997).

It is widely recognized that economic performance in the MENA region faltered after the oil-boom prosperity of the 1970s. Real GNP per capita in the region contracted throughout the 1980s, falling on average by about 2.4 per cent per annum. This contrasted sharply with East Asia's growth rate of 6 per cent and South Asia's 3.5 per cent in the same period (World Bank 1998a).

Figure 1 depicts the comparative growth performance for different regions in five-yearly intervals since 1975. It can be seen that MENA's strong growth performance of the late 1970s remains an exception to date and largely attributable to the strength of OPEC and the oil-boom in that period. The 1980s debacle was followed by a moderate recovery in the first half of the 1990s, raising the region's average growth in income per head to marginally above zero (0.5 per cent). However, this is still well below MENA's potential and considerably inferior to the performance of other areas (with the exception of Africa). For instance, East Asia continued with an impressive annual real growth rate of 8 per cent until recently and South Asia's growth rate has topped 2.5 per cent per annum in the 1990s.

FIGURE 1: Comparative Growth Performance – World Regions, 1975–95
(Average annual % change in real GNP per capita)

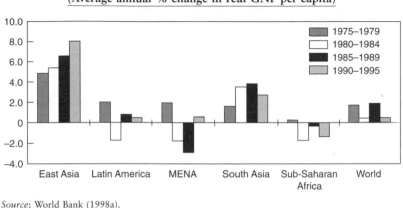

Source: World Bank (1998a).

Table 1 provides a more disaggregated perspective on growth by contrasting the performance of a selected group of East Asian and MENA countries in the past two and a half decades. It can be seen that almost all countries in the former group (with the exception of the Philippines) experienced impressive growth rates until the mid-1990s. The individual country growth experience of the MENA region is, however, far more varied and disappointing. As stated before, this applies specially to the 1980s, but is also true of more recent years. Several MENA countries have continued to experience falling real per capita incomes (for instance, Qatar, Saudi Arabia, Algeria and UAE), while others have been only moderately making up for the 1980s' reversals (Iran, Syria, Tunisia; in the case of Turkey the catching up was over the 1970s' decline).

As stated before, this inferior growth record, and its deteriorating trend especially in the 1980s, has been a cause of serious concern in numerous studies in recent years. Alarmed by the scale and extent of what has been referred to as the region's 'crisis of growth' or 'the crash' of the 1980s (Page 1998), various studies have legitimately sought an explanation and proposed remedies. A broad consensus has emerged which has attributed MENA's disappointing track record to the pursuit of old-fashioned statist and inward-looking policies, and stressed the need for a radical policy overhaul in favour of outward orientation and more market-friendly approaches to development. Among policies specified for the

83

TABLE 1: Comparative Growth Rates – MENA and Selected East Asian
Economies, 1970–95
(Average annual % change in real GNP per apita)

	1970–79	1980–89	1990–95
East Asia:			
Hong Kong	6.7	5.9	3.7
Singapore	7.0	5.5	6.4
Korea	8.0	12.7	6.8
Malaysia	5.0	2.9	6.3
Indonesia	4.4	4.4	6.2
Thailand	4.3	5.2	7.8
Philippines	3.1	−0.6	0.9
MENA:			
Algeria	3.4	0.0	−2.5
Egypt	4.9	3.9	−0.2
Iran	−2.9[a]	−3.2	2.5
Iraq	6.9	−9.6	n/a
Jordan	n/a	−6.6[b]	1.7
Kuwait	−1.1	−5.0	8.4
Libya	−0.5	−8.4	n/a
Morocco	2.5	1.9	−0.1
Oman	4.3	4.6	0.5
Qatar	−3.9[c]	−4.9	−6.0
Saudi Arabia	3.1[d]	−5.3	−1.9
Syria	5.4	−1.5	4.5
Tunisia	5.2	1.0	2.4
Turkey	−18.3	1.8	2.5
UAE	−0.9	−5.0	−2.4

Notes: [a] For 1975–79   [c] For 1971–79
 [b] For 1984–89   [d] For 1974–79
Source: World Bank, (1998a).

MENA region are: reducing the role of the state; empowering the private sector; and promoting exports (Page 1998: 154–56; Riordan *et al.* 1998).

In the rest of this section, we will argue that while there is a strong case for reforms in the region, there is a stronger case which concerns MENA countries' need to *diversify* their economic structures rather than merely improve their growth record.

First, trends in *per capita* income are likely to over-state MENA's inferior growth record due to the erosive effect of population growth in the region. Table 2 shows demographic trends in a comparative context suggesting that variations in living standards in MENA may

TABLE 2: Population Growth Rates: World Regions, 1975 – 95
(Average annual %)

	1975–79	1980–84	1985–89	1980–89	1990–95
East Asia	1.69	1.56	1.69	1.62	1.36
Latin America	2.32	2.15	1.99	2.07	1.77
MENA Region	2.98	3.18	3.16	3.17	2.76
South Asia	2.40	2.32	2.26	2.29	1.97
Sub-Saharan Africa	2.88	3.13	2.78	2.95	2.81
Low & Middle income countries	2.02	1.99	2.02	2.00	1.71
World	1.79	1.75	1.79	1.77	1.54

Source: World Bank (1998a).

have as much to do with demographic forces as with sluggish economic growth.

It can be seen that the MENA region has consistently recorded the highest population growth rate in the world since 1975, at a pace well above that for the low and middle income countries. Only Sub-Saharan Africa has in recent times (the 1990s) surpassed the record of demographic growth in MENA. Moreover, both MENA and Africa have, until recently, been immune from a general trend of demographic transitions, which has checked population growth in various regions. In both these regions, the population growth rate has hovered around 3 per cent per annum in the past two and a half decades. This contrasts, for instance, with the experience of both East and South Asia, where annual population growth rates have declined sharply after the 1970s and were below 2 per cent by the 1990s.

The case of the small Gulf states as well as Saudi Arabia and Libya, which have experienced some of the highest population growth rates in the world in the past two decades (often exceeding 4 per cent per annum) illustrates perhaps best the pervasive effect of demographic growth in the region. These economies have small population bases and high per capita incomes. Moreover, whether through natural increases or incoming migrant populations, excessive population growth rates in their case is more likely a sign of relative prosperity than of relative decline.

A second caveat regarding MENA's growth record, and particularly the individual country variations within it, is that the observed growth pattern does not seem to lend itself to ready-made explanations or policy prescriptions. There is no clear dividing line between the economic performance of countries pursuing statist and those pursuing market-oriented policies. For instance, Syria, with perhaps one of the most statist regimes in the region, exhibits one of the highest growth records in the 1970s and 1990s. Egypt and, to a lesser extent, Algeria seem to reflect a similar anomaly.[4] Although some of the literature has emphasized that reforming countries (such as Tunisia, Morocco and Jordan) have out-performed non-reformers in recent years (Shafik 1998a: 2), the evidence is perhaps too recent and short, and the sample of countries affected by reforms too small to warrant generalizations of this type as yet.

A third and final observation relates to structural characteristics of the MENA economies, namely, the predominance of the oil sector and its direct and indirect influence over growth prospects in the region. Both the 1970s boom and the 1980s bust were closely driven by large swings in international oil prices. The growth crisis of the 1980s, in fact, deepened after the mid-1980s, reflecting the international oil price crash of 1986. A re-examination of Figure 1 shows that in the first half of the decade, GNP per capita in the region contracted by 1.8 per cent per annum. This widened to just under 3 per cent during 1985–89. It was largely against the backdrop of this major oil price crash that the MENA region recorded both its worst recent growth record over time and compared to other regions.[5]

The oil sector's pervasive influence in the region is seen in the fact that in the Gulf countries, oil accounted for just over a third of domestic output and as much as 95 per cent of the total exports in 1993. For other oil exporters, these shares were 10 per cent and 85 per cent, respectively (World Bank 1995: 17). This makes the oil economies not only vulnerable to declining terms of trade for their major export item, but also highly susceptible to erratic and volatile price trends.[6] As a result, their growth prospects have been dampened by the declining real price of oil since the late 1970s, but also by a much greater instability in their merchandise exports earnings.[7] Moreover, non-oil exporters are affected indirectly as their principal foreign export earnings (migrant workers' remittances and the volume of OPEC aid) are strongly associated with oil price movements and the fortunes of the oil economies.

Nevertheless, despite the proviso about the supposed link between MENA's recent growth record and its policy orientations, it remains true that the region's record is less than a success story. The comparative perspective helps demonstrate that MENA has not been able to sustain the prosperity of the 1970s or achieve its full economic potential. It also means that continuing along these lines could mean deeper relative stagnation in the future and possibly more painful adjustments in the years to come.

Missing Out on External Opportunities

MENA's 'crisis of growth', as described above, has also focused attention on its relatively unfavourable position in the international economy in recent decades. This has featured prominently in much of the recent literature, which has argued for a new role for MENA in the global economy to identify new sources of long term growth.

Riordan *et al.* (1998), for instance, urge an active strategy for promoting manufactured exports as the 'new engine of growth' for the region. Similarly, Hoekman (1998) considers membership of the WTO and regional enlargement schemes like the European Union's Mediterranean Initiative to be beneficial and capable of improving the slow supply response to reforms, emanating from their low credibility and slow pace in MENA.[8] The rationale for these arguments is partly rooted in the changing character of the global economy and partly in the opportunities the MENA countries have been missing out on until now, due to their inward-looking orientation.

Like other developing nations, MENA countries find themselves in a world characterized by a massive rise in the 'cross-border flows of goods, services, investment and factors of production' (Safadi 1997: 19). Reflecting the underlying process of globalization, international trade has grown faster than national incomes throughout the post-war period. Between 1970 and 1994, the developing countries managed to increase their share of global trade from 15 per cent to 23 per cent and their share of global manufactured exports from 6 per cent to almost 25 per cent (ESCAP 1997). Capital flows have also expanded phenomenally: net foreign direct investment and portfolio investment in developing countries grew at a rate of 23.2 per cent per annum between 1989 and 1997 alone (rising from $18.3 billion to an estimated figure of $120 billion; IMF 1997: 65). In this context of ever increasing global trends, more and more economies have jettisoned import substitution industrialization strategies in favour of outward-oriented policies, thus hoping to be able to create competitive industries, facilitate technology transfer and exploit economies of scale (Safadi 1997: 22; Nugent 1997).

Cushioned by their mineral riches, however, the MENA countries have generally managed to buck these trends. This is seen from an examination of both their foreign trade and investment experiences.

Table 3 shows MENA countries' poor record in attracting Foreign Direct Investment (FDI) compared to other regions. It can be seen that for LDCs as a whole there has been a significant expansion in foreign investment inflows since the mid-1980s. Between 1985–90 and

TABLE 3: Foreign Direct Investment Inflows: Selected Regions and Host Countring, 1985–96
(Annual averages in US$ million)

	1985–90	1991–93	1994–96
All countries	141,930	183,597	313,745
Developed countries	116,744	124,415	188,624
(% of all countries)	(82.2)	(67.8)	(60.1)
Developing countries	24,736	54,789	114,254
(% of all countries)	(17.4)	(29.8)	(36.4)
MENA	2,420	3,774	2,387
(% of all countries)	(1.7)	(2.0)	(0.8)
(% of LDCs)	(9.9)	(6.9)	(2.1)
– Egypt	1,086	402	830
– Turkey	340	763	738
– Saudi Arabia	586	483	−885
– Morocco	83	410	412
– Tunisia	80	404	322
South, East and Southeast Asia	12,357	32,058	69,283
(% of all countries)	(8.7)	(17.5)	(22.1)
– China	2,654	14,346	36,605
– Singapore	2,952	3,926	7,880
– Malaysia	1,054	4,729	4,533
– Hong Kong	1,597	1,419	4,310
– Thailand	1,017	1,953	1,923
– Taiwan	879	1,022	1,599
– Korea	705	832	1,637
– Philippines	413	670	1,529
Latin America and the Caribbean	8,145	16,544	36,845
(% of all countries)	(5.7)	(9.0)	(11.7)
– Mexico	2,618	4,515	10,358
– Brazil	1,315	1,485	6,187
– Argentina	914	2,825	5,075
– Chile	700	677	3,428
– Bermuda	1,143	2,929	1,510

Source: UNCTAD (1997 & 1999: Annex Table B1).

1994–96, their share of total world FDI doubled from 17.4 per cent to 36.4 per cent. However, as is commonly known, this trend has been highly concentrated in a few countries led by the fast growing Asian economies (notably China, Singapore, Hong Kong and Malaysia) and a handful of Latin American economies (Mexico, Brazil, Chile and Argentina).

By contrast, average annual inflows of FDI in the MENA region almost stagnated in the same period at around $2.5 billion per annum. This was about one-quarter of the annual inflows for Mexico alone (1994–96) and well below the total for any one of the other major host nations in Latin America.[9] MENA's share of world FDI, indeed, declined from 1.7 per cent in 1985–90 to less than 1 per cent in 1994–96. Its share of total FDI in LDCs also shrank from about 10 per cent to 2.1 per cent in the same period. Within MENA, only Egypt and Turkey have played hosts to sizeable sums of FDI recently (each with under a billion dollars per annum and even so only about half of that for the Philippines).

An examination of global equity capital flows depicts an even more dismal picture for the region. International equity flows to emerging markets rose eighteen-fold between 1986 and 1993 (rising to $61.2 billion from $3.4 billion). Asia apportioned almost 64 per cent of the total by the end of the period, followed by Latin America (33 per cent). 'Other' countries, including MENA, by contrast, accounted for the remaining 3 per cent – or a total of just $2.2 billion (El-Erian and Kumar 1995: 318).[10]

A similar picture emerges from an examination of MENA's integration in global trade. Figure 2 shows the evolution of MENA and selected regions' degree of openness (defined as imports plus exports taken as a proportion of GDP) over time. Again East Asia stands out by virtue of its consistently increasing openness since the early 1970s (it trebled its integration index from 19 per cent in 1970 to almost 58 per cent in 1995). Similarly, South Asia saw a rise in its trade integration index from 12 per cent to 30 per cent. However, for the MENA region the index declined by almost one-third between the 1970s and 1990s (falling from 73.3 per cent in 1974–79 to 53 per cent in 1990–95). Even these generally high ratios reflect the continued, although declining, importance of oil exports in the MENA region. On the assumption that these made up some 80 per cent of all exports, MENA's non-fuel trade integration index too has been declining – albeit less dramatically (from about 40 per cent to 33 per cent in the same period).

FIGURE 2: Trade Integration: Selected Regions, 1970–96

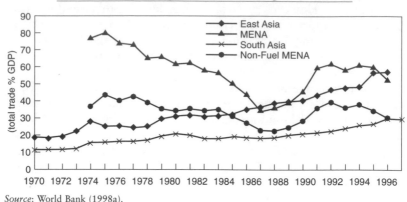

Source: World Bank (1998a).

These trends show that MENA's integration tempo has been largely dictated by oil exports (notice, for instance, the influence of the 1970s oil-boom and the 1980s oil price crash, as discussed in the last section, on the region's integration trend). Secondly, even in terms of non-fuel trade, the region's degree of integration, which was about three times higher than South Asia's to start with, has just about levelled off with the latter.

To sum up, this section has demonstrated that a growing body of thought in recent years has stressed the need for MENA countries to adopt market-led policies to stimulate their economies. Alongside domestic reforms, adopting outward-oriented policies has been seen as crucial to MENA's ability to meet the present and future challenges of globalization. The region has failed to maintain its own past standards, has fallen behind other regions and faces uncertain prospects if it continues to rely on its oil riches into the future. In this context, therefore, turning to the global economy can understandably be elevated to a position of holding the key to much of the region's weaknesses.

But as we shall see from the experience of East Asia, the global economy can pose as much risk as it can offer opportunities. Other regions like MENA need to weigh both of those against each other before drawing firm conclusions about the promises of globalization.

This is now what we turn to, by first looking at the Asian crisis and then drawing lessons from it both generally and for the MENA region particularly.

THE FEATURES AND SIGNIFICANCE OF THE ASIAN CRISIS

The Asian crisis first surfaced in Thailand with the abandonment of the Thai currency's peg against the US dollar on 2 July 1997. After that, market volatility and turmoil accelerated sharply, spreading first to other neighbouring ASEAN countries (Indonesia, Philippines, Malaysia) and later beyond (including other so-called emerging economies of Latin America and Eastern Europe). By early 1998, economic slowdown and business failures were widespread in Asia; many projects had been put on hold or were cancelled; the burden of foreign debt had mounted with companies squeezed through falling currencies and high interest rates; the cost of living and unemployment were both climbing steeply; and property prices had collapsed widely. Food riots in Indonesia and forced expatriation of migrants from Malaysia and Thailand were other grim realities facing what had, until recently, been one of the world's most vibrant areas.

Perhaps one of the most prominent features of the Asian crisis was that it happened rather quietly and its early stages went almost undetected.[11] This feature is all the more surprising for an event that was subsequently dubbed 'the world's most important development in 1997' and was likened in significance to the collapse of the Soviet Union in 1991 (*The Economist*, 20 December 1997).

Although some alarms had been raised earlier about the Asian economies, these warnings went largely unnoticed (see, for instance, Krugman 1994; UNCTAD 1996). They were few and far between and tended to be subsumed in the euphoria which surrounded Asia's hitherto impressive successes. They were also mainly concerned with the possibilities of a *cyclical* slowdown in growth (rather than a full-blown international financial crisis) and mistook the timing of the crisis.[12] Even when the crisis had got under way, the tendency to underestimate its extent and full ramifications was not absent.[13]

This widespread inability to predict the crisis derived partly from the unfamiliar characteristics of the crisis itself (see below for more on this). It also indicated difficulties of a *conceptual* nature for the conventional wisdom in its handling of the crisis from its early stages. With its perception of macroeconomic fragility mainly rooted in public sector weaknesses, the orthodox approach proved ill suited to detect a crisis that, by most accounts, originated in the decisions and behaviour of *private* sector agents. In particular, the signalling instruments or variables used in the past to predict and monitor crises proved poor indicators in this instance, leading some to argue that the Asian crisis was in fact *unpredictable* judged by conventional macroeconomic criteria (Salvatore 1998; Furman and Stiglitz 1998).[14]

The second distinguishing aspect of the Asian crisis, as suggested above, was its 'unorthodox' characteristics. The Thai crisis stood against a background of exceptional economic performance since 1990 with an overall track-record that was the envy of most LDCs.[15] By 1996, certain stress signs had surfaced, namely, a modest slowdown in growth; a persistent current account deficit, a rise in short-term debt and a sharp slow-down in export receipts. None of these, however, seemed unduly alarming.[16]

There were also sharp contrasts between the Thai macroeconomic setting and other crises in the past (e.g., Mexico in 1994): public sector accounts were sound; sovereign debt was negligible; currency over-valuation was moderate; and international reserves were healthy and had been gradually built up throughout the 1990s.[17] Further-more, Asian economies were characterized by high investment ratios, in sharp contrast with Mexico's where large foreign savings financing the current account deficit were channelled to consumption (see IMF 1997).[18]

A third feature of the crisis stems from, and reflects, the above two points: its unpredictability and unorthodox nature. It seems that the controversy around this crisis has brought to an end the broad development consensus which had been achieved since the early 1980s (the so-called Washington consensus). This consensus had been built around the twin goals of macroeconomic stability and outward-oriented development and was set against a background of the receding powers of the state. But as the beacons of this strategy in Asia were engulfed in financial turmoil by mid-1997, the consensus behind that strategy itself started to come under a new wave of scrutiny.

Tension was evident at different levels of discussion and debate about the crisis: from conflicting analyses of its causes[19] to differing crisis management strategies and remedial measures prescribed. This is best seen in the divergent analyses and policy prescriptions that emerged from the IMF and the World Bank.

The crisis seemed to reinforce the IMF's faith in conventional policy measures such as macro stability and deregulation to restore investors' confidence in the region. But it also led to controversies over the Fund's short-term shock therapy measures. In particular, critics viewed its standard financial package – a combination of tight fiscal and monetary policies meant to curb inflation and to support ailing currencies – as too deflationary and ill-suited to the conditions of the Asian economies affected by the crisis (Chang 1997: B7).[20]

By contrast, the World Bank's position – articulated in the works of its then Senior Vice President, Joseph Stiglitz – brought into question some of the underlying tenets of the 'Washington consensus', and called for a new ('Post-Washington') consensus.

In Stiglitz' view, the 'Washington consensus' addressed the development problems of debt-ridden, high inflation countries of Latin America in the 1980s. These concerns had little applicability to Asia, where a vibrant, but *under*-regulated corporate sector was the spearhead of the miracle that transformed the region. The state provided essential partnership and back-up, but it did not go far enough in providing the regulatory and supervisory framework necessary either to prevent or contain the crisis. For the state to perform this type of strategic role, in fact, would require redrawing the lines of power and responsibility between private and public sectors well beyond that allowed or envisaged by conventional development thinking.

In contrast to the Washington consensus, which has primarily focused on downsizing the state and public sectors in LDCs, the 'Post-Washington' consensus advocates capacity-building and improving the quality of the state machinery to make it more effective in performing its expected functions. The approach also seeks a shift of emphasis from *macro*- to *micro*-fundamentals; and from deregulation to regulation of the private sector (Stiglitz 1998a).

Although prospects for achieving an eventual consensus are not yet clear, the shift of perspective implied by the 'Post-Washington consensus' is significant. Discussions of the Asian crisis may not have a final and determining role in achieving a new consensus (if and when it materializes). Nevertheless, it is clear that they have been instrumental in initiating this wider process of debate with a potential for a real paradigm shift in conventional thinking on development.

LESSONS OF THE CRISIS

From the dazzling heights of success and prosperity to the depth of crisis and volatility, the Asian economies witnessed a spectacular turnaround in their fortunes after late 1997. Below, we draw a few pertinent observations on the crisis and its likely ramifications for the future of development thinking and policy. The next section will relate these lessons to the Middle Eastern economies.

The first point to make is that the Asian crisis both emanated from, and brought to the fore, some of the structural and institutional challenges posed by the *globalization* model itself. This was manifest both in the national and international dimensions of the crisis.

At the domestic level, it is remarkable that a burst property bubble in one relatively small country such as Thailand could have blown up into a major international crisis with a calamitous effect on the region and beyond. This was at least partly facilitated by the unprecedented degree of integration achieved in the Thai economy between various sectors and markets during its rapid growth phase in the 1990s – or during its heyday of deregulation. While the close linkages forged between the assets, equity and currency markets positively contributed to accelerated growth on the upswing of the economic cycle, the crisis was later to manifest that they also carried the seeds of a more precipitous future downswing. This tendency was no doubt magnified significantly by the large inflows of short-term international capital that oiled Thailand's economic expansion.

As the discussion in the last section demonstrated, the Thai crisis was not a classic currency or debt crisis, although each had a part to play in it. In terms of foreign reserves, for instance, Thailand's situation was healthy by regional and international standards throughout the 1990s.[21] The over-valuation of the bhat in the period leading to the crisis, too, is considered to have been modest.[22]

Thailand had experienced a rapid expansion of its foreign debt with an annual average growth rate of 18 per cent after 1994 and reaching a total of US\$ 90.5 billion by the end of 1996. By conventional debt criteria, however, the situation was far from alarming.[23] More significant was the structure of debt and its uses. For instance, over four-fifths of it was concentrated in the private sector in 1996 and just over half consisted of short-term loans with less than one year maturity (Bank of Thailand figures). Moreover, commercial banks had the lion's share of foreign debt within the private sector. With increased access to international financial markets, the banks' foreign liabilities grew sharply in the mid-1990s: from 6–7 per cent of their total liabilities in 1990–93 to about a quarter by 1995–96. Growth was particularly fast during the property boom of 1993 and 1994, when the foreign liabilities of the banking sector rose by a staggering 110 per cent and 121 per cent, respectively (Bank of Thailand).

This was probably the Achilles' heel of the Thai economy. It manifested also the link between the international capital markets (of which Thailand had become a beneficiary in the 1990) and the bubbling property market at home. Channelling vast amounts of mainly short-term foreign funds into the domestic property market contributed to its over-heating and was potentially destabilizing. This was because rising property prices inflated the balance sheets of the banks with exposure in the construction sector, exaggerating their financial 'health' and raising their credit standing among international investors who were too eager to lend to emerging markets. When the property bubble finally burst and the peg system was abandoned, banks with foreign currency debt exposure and those financing construction sector projects were, not surprisingly, amongst the worst affected. The sudden reversal of the flow of short-term international capital further accentuated the crisis in two ways: it contributed to the collapse of property prices and precipitated currency depreciation. In both cases, the solvency of the banks was imperilled as they were subjected to the double crunch of collapsing asset prices and a rising debt burden.[24]

All this indicated key features of the globalization experience in Thailand, namely, an unprecedented degree of integration and linkage between the international and the domestic economy on the one hand, and between different domestic sectors, on the other.

A second lesson relates to the perceived roots of the crisis. Ever since debate about the Asian crisis began, opinion has been sharply divided between those maintaining that the crisis resulted from international market failures and those attributing it to the institutional and structural weaknesses of the Asian economies themselves (see, for instance, Chang *et al.* 1998). On the whole, the latter viewpoint has been dominant, with most proponents of the 'Washington consensus' laying the blame for the crisis squarely at the door of domestic factors such as non-transparent corporate governance or misguided government policies in Asia.[25] An extreme version of this viewpoint has gone so far as to suggest that the peculiarities of Asian capitalism (dubbed 'crony capitalism') are to be blamed for triggering the crisis (see Wade 1998, and Johnson 1998, for a critique of this thesis; Chang *et al.* 1998 query its 'orientalist' overtones).

Exclusive emphasis on the domestic roots of the crisis is not only simplistic but also ironic, in the light of the importance attached to globalization and external opportunities in the first instance as explanatory factors behind Asia's past miracles.

As cogently described by Stiglitz, 'In their haste to place exclusive blame on the governments in the region, many critics have also forgotten that every loan requires not just a borrower, but also a lender' (1998b). This raises the thorny question of the international regulation of capitalism – a rather difficult area with few ready-made solutions to date. The international economy is still the only market that is not regulated by an overarching institution or authority, yet it continues to grow in size and complexity. In this context, the Asian crisis has reminded us again about the need for safeguards against misallocation of resources on an *international* scale and for mechanisms to thwart international instability.

A third lesson of the crisis relates to the speed of 'contamination' and the regional character of the crisis itself. Despite local variations in the severity of the crisis, the speed of the contagion reflected the close degree of regional integration forged between Asian economies over the years. The success of these economies, arguably, owed more to the fact that, like Europe, they 'shared a region, and close economic links ... rather than a common "Asian model"' (*The Economist* 20 December 1997: 15). It is perhaps no surprise that this common characteristic (regionalism) was proved as strong a characteristic of the 'Asian model' in a time of crisis as during the growth and prosperity phase.[26]

Yet, despite strong regional links, these economies lacked sufficient common mechanisms against, and were ill-prepared to cope with, crises affecting the whole region. Such mechanisms could have assisted them with both crisis prevention and management. In the early stages of the crisis, for instance, there was increased local enthusiasm for setting up an 'Asian Monetary Fund'. Potentially deriving strength from Japan's reserves, this type of regional monetary authority could have played a positive role in stabilizing currency volatility in the region. Being unenthusiastic about a regional rival to the IMF, however, the American opposition seemed to have sunk the project at an early stage, making it, in the words of Amnuay Virawan, Thailand's former Deputy Prime Minister and Finance Minister, 'dead on arrival' (1998).

A fourth lesson relates to the nature of the tension between globalization and its social impact. Discussions of the risks associated with globalization have hitherto focused on social exclusion and the impact of trade on particular segments, regions and social strata.[27] The Asian crisis has broadened this concern by focusing on the risks of globalization for vulnerable groups even in relatively prosperous and well-to-do countries.

On account of both its severity and constituency, the crisis has underlined the importance of the need for effective safety nets and social insurance mechanisms, no matter how successful a country's experience of globalization may be.

Indonesia, Thailand, Korea and, to a lesser extent, Malaysia were hard hit by financial melt-down and the ensuing severe economic slowdown, and witnessed rising unemployment, escalating food costs, widespread business closures, and extensive social hardship.

Given the Asian governments' slender social security and welfare systems,[28] decisive, internationally-coordinated action was required to soften the adverse welfare effects of the crisis and to help avert unnecessary austerity and social disintegration in the countries most affected.

Lastly, the experience of boom and bust in Asia has led to a rethink about the balance of benefits and risks associated with globalization. A more sober account of such costs and benefits is the most likely outcome of this kind of re-evaluation.

As far as other regions and parts of the world (including the MENA region) are concerned, perhaps the principal message of the crisis is that the costs of globalization may have been *under*estimated so far, resulting in an unduly upbeat view of its *net* benefits. But if East Asia's successes were instrumental in driving such optimism in the past, its recent financial woes can help provide a more balanced perspective on the net potential benefits of globalization.

It appears that no matter what the outcome of the Asian debacle, perceptions of globalization may have changed already. Developing countries will be more cautious in their approach to outward-oriented reforms, particularly the liberalization of their capital accounts. They will want to examine the liberalization package carefully by its contents rather than by its promises alone. For their part, the developed world institutions – public and private sectors alike – will be more prudent in designating where the next 'miracle' lies. More realism about globalization and its promises, then, may well be the general outcome of this crisis.

To sum up this section, we have highlighted five main lessons from the Asian crisis. These are:

- It reflects inherent characteristics and contradictions of the globalization experience.

- It cannot be reduced to 'internal' or 'domestic' weaknesses and problems in the Asian countries – rather, the international architecture too needs to be put under the spotlight.
- It has very strong regional characteristics, suggesting the need for region-wide crisis prevention and management strategies.
- Just as the role of the state was critical in Asia's success phase, its importance cannot be discounted during crisis, especially in softening its social impact and in taking a lead role in getting the economy moving again.
- Overall, this experience should lead to a more realistic view of the costs and benefits of globalization as a future strategy for developing countries.

It is now time to take these and other lessons and perspectives from Asia back to the MENA region.

THE MENA REGION AFTER THE ASIAN CRISIS

The immediate impact of the Asian upheaval on the MENA region was limited. The trade impact consisted principally of reduced demand for oil imports (Asia, including Japan, accounted for 57 per cent of the Middle East's mineral exports in 1996; UNCTAD 1998: 29) and took several months to materialize.[29]

An immediate or short-term financial impact on the region was also noticeably absent. At the peak of market volatility in late October 1997, only Turkey's stock market appeared to be mildly affected, indicating a substantial degree of general insulation for the MENA region from the global markets.[30]

Although insulation at the height of financial turmoil may have appeared as a blessing for the region's economies, and despite an apparent lack of immediate relevance, this section argues that Asia's lessons are, nevertheless, pertinent for the future direction of MENA's development. Three points, in particular, are discussed below: capability to draw on and utilize effectively foreign resources under globalization, regional dynamics and integration, and the transformed role of state.

A first lesson for MENA countries after the Asian debacle is that globalization is not a panacea and its outcome is predicated upon individual economies' ability to tread a fine balance between the opportunities it offers and the risks it entails. For instance, the sudden expansion in external resources following liberalization can be as much a source of crisis and instability as an opportunity for expansion and growth. This was, for instance, the experience of Thailand, as discussed in the last section. Similarly, Mexico's crisis in 1994 erupted against the background of a big private consumption boom fuelled by massive foreign capital inflows. The result was a severe foreign debt crisis and the spectre of default on sovereign debt. A similar event happened in Iran after the end of the war with Iraq. The drive for post-war reconstruction and the ensuing liberalization of imports led to a massive foreign shopping spree and a serious foreign debt with a large short-term component.[31] In these cases, opening up to the outside world was associated with heightened risks of further macroeconomic shocks and disequilibria. Yet, absent in all these cases were adequate monitoring mechanisms for overseeing capital inflows and the use of external funds thus generated.

It may well be that by lowering import prices, liberalization encourages consumption and mitigates domestic savings (Gavin *et al.* 1997: 173). However, what the Asian experience has also shown is that even when additional external resources are channelled to *investment*, the type and *quality* of such investment is important for determining the ultimate sustainability of capital flows (see the discussion of the real estate boom and bust fuelled by foreign capital flows in Thailand in the last section).

A second lesson is that to make the most of the globalization experience, MENA countries will have to promote increased economic relations within the region. Currently, MENA's inter-regional integration is limited and largely confined to the pervasive influence of the oil price cycle. There are a number of reasons why growing intra MENA cooperation and closer economic union between MENA countries will be complementary to their experience of globalization.

First, limited regional integration can actually distort the results of globalization in the MENA region. This is best seen in the case of the EU-Mediterranean Initiative. In the absence of due integration between the MENA partners, this free trade initiative risks 'verticalizing' MENA trade with the EU and creating a 'hub and spokes' system in which the EU would be the 'hub' and the individual Mediterranean countries the 'spokes' (ERF 1998: 73). This may have adverse consequences on the region's ability to draw in FDI and may, ironically, draw investment towards the European Union.[32]

A second reason for regional integration has to do with the risks of globalization and derives from the Asian experience of boom and bust, as discussed above. As we saw, East Asian successes – and later crisis – were magnified by the *regional* features and linkages of these economies. The crisis, in particular, brought to the fore potential vulnerability and exposure to regional disturbances and hence the need for adequate safeguards against such shocks. In a world increasingly carved up between different trade and currency blocs, economic unions and investment zones, the MENA countries too will have to seriously consider the benefits of initiating similar cooperation mechanisms among themselves as a way of reducing risks associated with globalization. For instance, with the liberalization of capital accounts and the increased risks of currency and stock market volatility, a regional monetary authority or currency stabilization fund may be necessary to coordinate monetary and exchange policies in a more integrated Middle East in the future.[33]

The final rationale for regional cooperation and co-ordination has to do with the growing tendency for global capital mobility between nation states and its challenges for individual countries concerned. In a regional context with geographical proximity of the markets, there may be a tendency among those businesses which are increasingly mobile to engage in 'competitive bidding between countries' (Rodrik 1997: 81–2). Reducing this risk presents a positive externality for all host countries and dealing with it requires cooperation measures such as regional exchanges of information by tax authorities and joint conventions for reducing tax evasion through foreign direct investment.

This brings us to the third and final 'Asian' lesson for the MENA region: emphasis on macro stability and 'sound' economic fundamentals, while necessary, is unlikely to prove sufficient for sustainable long term growth. This, in turn, raises important new questions for the role of state in the economy – particularly in a global context.

As we saw in the last section, the accent of the Washington consensus has for long been on the *quantitative* diminution of the state in the economy. Yet, the Asian crisis – and with it the Post-Washington 'consensus' – have raised important new questions regarding the *quality* and type of state intervention. This concerns the state's *capability* to engage in critical areas of the economy, such as creating and exploiting dynamic comparative advantages, picking and promoting winners, providing an appropriate regulatory framework, monitoring the use of internal and external resources and ability to avert and manage crises.

The Asian crisis has served to demonstrate the inadequacy of the traditional 'state versus markets' debates in development economics. A narrow emphasis on downsizing the public sector overlooks the importance of the type and quality of state intervention in the economy and its capability to address the opportunities and risks of globalization. Asia reminds us that even where markets are buoyant and successful, the possibility of misallocation of resources is real. The private sector – even when operating in 'market friendly' and stable macroeconomic environments – is prone to making 'bad' decisions and to leading the economy down the path of precipitous economic instability and crisis. In brief, not all economic ills can be put down to inherent weaknesses in the public sector. On the contrary, a capable, high calibre state machinery and institutions may well be the key to ensuring that the pursuit of private interest today does not carry with it the seeds of public destruction tomorrow.

This in turn may require investing in and upgrading the *quality* of states in the MENA region – rather than aiming to erode them. This is a different story to that accepted in conventional wisdom until recently and we owe it to the Asian crisis.

CONCLUSION

This chapter has argued that East Asia's past successes have led to an optimistic paradigm in development that has emphasized the link between 'sound' development policies and performance. While Asia's achievements have been considerable, hopes that other countries can now 'choose to remain poor or become prosperous' by virtue of their choice of policies alone may well be inflated in the light of lessons learnt from the Asian crisis.

Even accepting the expected benefits of globalization (and this chapter has not debated these), its potential costs may have been underestimated until recently. The Asian crisis has raised some novel issues and focused our attention on new risks associated with outward-oriented policies. The full extent of some of these risks is probably not fully understood yet (e.g., risks due to capital account liberalization, or an unprecedented integration between the local, regional and international assets, equity and currency markets).

As far as MENA is concerned, we drew three principal lessons from the Asian crisis. First, the risks stemming from globalization need to be carefully balanced against its promises. Second, the risks are probably accentuated for individual countries trying 'to go it alone'; instead measures such as regional cooperation and integration may help better prepare them to reap the benefits offered by the global markets. Third and last, whether for exploiting opportunities or for facing up to the likely risks of globalization, the states concerned need to acquire new capabilities and an upgrading – not weakening – of their existing abilities in managing the economy.

In closing, a healthy outcome of the Asian crisis is perhaps its contribution to the end of an era of consensus dominated by unwavering faith in open-door policies. While the experience of the Asian crisis has not negated the case for outward orientation, it has, nevertheless, highlighted hitherto discounted risks and challenges *en route* to the glory associated with globalization. It can thus help restore some balance to claims and counterclaims about what can or cannot be achieved through such policies in practice. Hopefully, the MENA countries can draw on some of these lessons.

NOTES

1 The World Bank's seminal work in 1993 epitomizes the copious literature on the East Asian model of development in recent years (World Bank 1993). Krueger (1995) argues that East Asia's superior economic performance is attributable to its outward-oriented macro-economic policies. Birdsall *et al.* (1997) and Page (1997) draw lessons from, and examine the implications of, Asian success stories for Latin America. For similar literature on the MENA region, see Gangnes and Naya (1997).

2 For instance, 'no country' was thought 'destined to be poor because of a bad endowment of natural resources, an isolated location, or a concentration on certain products.' On the contrary, countries could now 'choose, *through their policies*, to be rich – or to be poor' (World Bank 1995: 1; emphasis added).

3 The reasons why prospects have improved radically is that now 'any country with advanced human resources' can acquire an 'edge in international markets' by 'competing in process technology, by adopting better organization methods, and by taking advantage of their lower wage rates' (Handoussa 1997: 4).

4 In fact, both Syria and Egypt were among the twenty fastest growing countries classified by the World Bank during the period 1960–85 (World Bank 1995: 3). The list was topped by Botswana, followed by Asia's High Performance Economies (Taiwan, Indonesia, Hong Kong, Singapore, Korea and Japan).

5 This comparison includes Latin America and even Sub-Saharan Africa, both of which sustained serious recessions in the 1980s. As a result of the 1986 oil price crash, almost all oil exporters suffered negative growth rates in 1987 ranging from − 5 per cent (Libya, Oman and Iran) to

between −6 per cent and −10 per cent (Bahrain, Saudi Arabia and Kuwait; World Bank data).

6 Even ignoring the recent oil price crash in 1997–98, the real purchasing power of a barrel of oil (measured against MENA's imports of manufactured goods from industrial nations) has been lower in the 1990s compared to the 1970s.

7 Riordan *et al.* find that the real international purchasing power of exports for MENA was twice as volatile as for other developing nations and nearly four times that of industrial countries. Moreover, instability for the oil-exporters exceeded that of the non-oil exporters by a factor of three (1998: 19–21).

8 Likewise, Diwan *et al.* (1998) consider the impact of the implementation of the Uruguay round and the enlargement of the EU to the East. They find that these are likely to result in a welfare loss for MENA, but argue that reforms will be needed to make them more flexible and to help them make up, in overseas markets, for lost markets at home.

9 MENA's FDI was only 58 per cent higher than total FDI for the small island of Bermuda, with a population of just over 60,000!

10 Stock markets in the Middle East are generally either non-existent or small by international standards. In terms of market capitalization, the largest regional markets are in Turkey, Jordan, Egypt, Morocco, Iran and Tunisia. The first four are, however, the most active (El Erian and Kumar 1995: 322–25).

11 According to *The Guardian*, 'for a crisis that has caused shock waves throughout the world financial system, it had a quiet start' (30 March 1998). This characteristic was widespread and spanned both private sector institutions dealing with Asia and multilateral agencies such as the World Bank and the IMF. A 1996 investment research report by Morgan Stanley predicted: 'Many of the problems besetting the Thai market today will dissipate over the coming months, leading to a potentially stronger performance next year' (*Bangkok Post* 6 January 1997). The IMF, too, was candid enough, in retrospect, to admit that its staff had failed to forecast the crisis, resulting in excessive optimism in its baseline projections for 1997 (IMF 1997: 40).

12 Krugman is widely credited with having articulated strong scepticism about the sustainability of the Asian miracle a few years before the crisis (1994). But as he admits, 'even pessimists ... expected a modest downturn, and we expected the longer-term slowdown in growth to emerge only gradually' (Krugman 1998a: 1). Similarly, UNCTAD's 1996 *Trade and Development Report* focused on the difficulties, mainly for second-tier Newly Industrializing Economies of Southeast Asia, of maintaining competitiveness in labour-intensive manufactures because of the entry into the market of low-cost producers (UNCTAD 1996). In this sense, it focused on the need for a change of gear with respect to *industrial* policy rather than the possibility of a financial crisis.

13 In September 1997, a few months after the Thai currency flotation and the spread of the crisis to other neighbouring ASEAN countries (Indonesia, the Philippines and Malaysia), the World Bank President, James Wolfensohn, described the Thai crisis as a 'hiccup' since it was not

going 'to stop the future development of Asia' (reported in *Bangkok Post* 20 September 1997).

14 These were largely a set of macroeconomic indicators or 'fundamentals' rooted in the concerns of the 'Washington consensus' with macroeconomic management and stability: public sector and current account deficits, inflation, debt and debt service ratios, foreign reserves, etc. (see Salvatore 1998, for an extensive discussion of these variables).

15 Thailand's economic performance in the years preceding the crisis was robust by most accounts. There was an annual average real growth rate of 8.6 per cent between 1990–96, a healthy fiscal surplus of just under 3 per cent and an average inflation figure of about 5 per cent for the same period. Domestic savings also stood at a healthy proportion to GDP of over one-third and a similar external debt service ratio of 4.5 per cent seemed to give little cause for concern.

16 Although a growth rate of 6.4 per cent in 1996 was Thailand's lowest growth rate in the 1990s and the first ever to fall below 8 per cent in recent times, it was still a healthy figure by international standards and exceeded the growth rates for Japan, Hong Kong and Taiwan. Similarly, Thailand's current account deficit in 1995 was proportionately lower than that for Malaysia (8 per cent of GDP against the latter's 10 per cent; IMF 1997: 50) and was hardly a new phenomenon. It had, in fact, peaked in 1990 at 8.3 per cent of GDP and, after falling to 5 per cent in 1993, it was back up at 8 per cent and 7.9 per cent in 1995 and 1996, respectively (Bank of Thailand figures).

17 Only about one-fifth of the total foreign debt was government-owned with a negligible fraction made up of short-term public debt. Currency over-valuation was at about 15 per cent (compared with double that for Mexico) and foreign reserves amounted to an annual average sum of $26.5 billion for the period 1990–96 (Bank of Thailand figures).

18 It is worth remembering that the high level and superior *quality* of investment in East Asia were earlier considered as a cornerstone of the Asian Miracle (World Bank 1993).

19 Views on the causes of the crisis are wide ranging. Jeff Sachs, for instance, blames the sudden deterioration in investor sentiments and the ensuing 'panic' for Asia's problems (Sachs 1997; Radelet and Sachs 1998). Krugman (1998b) offers an alternative explanation based on the 'moral hazard' affecting the banks' investment allocation decisions in the region. Dornbusch (1998) focuses on 'vulnerability' as the main factor explaining the big Asian melt-down, stipulating the main roots of vulnerability in 'a shaky banking system, made more shaky by the dollar debts of its clients, a very large and short-dated [private] foreign debt ... and a total lack of transparency and a pervasive overlay of corruption.' See Chang *et al.* (1998) for a critical perspective and a general discussion of contending viewpoints on Asia.

20 According to *The Economist*, Asian governments too (in particular, Indonesia, Korea and Thailand) have feared that the Fund's hidden agenda is to open doors for US business as pressures have mounted on the Thai and Korean governments to allow foreigners to buy up local banks and finance companies (13 December 1997).

21 At the end of 1996, Thailand's total reserves ($37.7 billion) were only
marginally below those of the UK and Switzerland and came second after
Singapore with one of the highest reserve ratios in the world: 240.2 per
cent for M0 and 207.5 per cent for M1 (Tatom 1998: 6). Less reassuring
was, of course, a high short-term debt to reserves ratio, which indicated a
far less favourable foreign liquidity position.

22 The real effective exchange rate rose about 16 per cent over the two year
period between April 1995 and June 1997 (Tatom 1998: 4).

23 As a percentage of the GDP, debt service was still in line with the 1990s'
norms (an average of 4.5 per cent for 1990–96), although the debt
service ratio (out of exports) was continuing to rise (it had reached
12.3 per cent by 1996, partly accentuated by sluggish export earnings
during 1996).

24 This process was, of course, complicated by corruption and political
influences over the channelling of funds and the selection of construction
projects.

25 The IMF's account of the crisis has been in terms of the domestic
economic and institutional weaknesses of the economies affected. These
vulnerabilities were, in the IMF's judgement, accentuated by lack of
'decisive government action' in the area to avert a full-scale deterioration
of 'investor sentiments' (IMF 1997). Among these delayed policies were:
macro measures to address the problem of overheating and unsustainable
external imbalances, as well as the deregulation of the banking sector to
allow for increased foreign competition.

26 Asian economies are highly integrated through trade: in 1996, about
52 per cent of Asia's total merchandise exports and 54 per cent of total
imports were interregional. These ratios were even higher for some
categories: 63 per cent for agricultural products, 85 per cent for mining
products and 80 per cent for tourism (UNCTAD 1998: 27).

27 Rodrik, for instance, has argued that the asymmetry in the international
mobility of capital and labour is not only likely to shift the demand curve
for labour inward but it will also make it more elastic. The result is a
disproportionate impact on wages in the event of cyclical variations in
demand (1997: 4–7).

28 Comparative data on social security expenditures are not readily available
for the Asian economies. The following, however, should give an idea of
the limited scale of their welfare states. Public health expenditure
averaged 1–1.9 per cent of GDP only for Hong Kong, Singapore, Korea,
Thailand, Indonesia and Malaysia during 1992–94 compared to 5.5–7 per
cent for the UK, US, Germany and Japan in 1994. Similarly, social
security taxes were virtually non-existent in the Asian countries
mentioned. Korea was an exception with 7.7 per cent of government
revenue coming from these taxes in 1994 (compared to 34.2 per cent in
the US and 46.2 per cent in Germany in 1993; World Bank 1997). It is
obvious that, in meeting the social consequences of the crisis, the social
security systems of these countries need to be overhauled.

29 A severe and serious slump in the international price of oil began in the
last quarter of 1997 – approximately three months after the start of the
Thai crisis. The crisis in Asia, however, was but one factor in the oil price

crash. Other contributing factors were: international stock-piling of oil; prolonged mild winters in the Northern Hemisphere; and a 10 per cent rise in OPEC member countries' production quota in November 1997. The international price of crude petroleum fell by 6 per cent in 1997 and by 21.4 per cent in 1998 (see UNCTAD 1998: 6–7).

30 It has been observed that the Egyptian equity market was more adversely affected by the massacre of tourists in Luxor in November 1997 than by world market volatility a few months earlier (Khayat 1997/8: 11).

31 Three-quarters of Iran's estimated $23 billion total debt in 1993 were short-term mostly related to trade finance; see Hakimian and Karshenas 2000).

32 This is because, in the absence of sufficient integration among Mediterranean countries, an EU-based enterprise would benefit from preferential access not only to Mediterranean countries but also at the same time to the East European markets. But an enterprise based in one individual country of the MENA region would only enjoy preferential access to EU markets (ERF 1998).

33 Although less than perfect, the experience of regional cooperation in the Middle Eastern energy markets may be relevant in this context. However, both internal difficulties encountered by OPEC as a producers' association and a largely hostile reception to it elsewhere are reminders of the likely substantial political and institutional obstacles to this type of body both within and beyond the region.

REFERENCES

Alizadeh, P. (ed., 2000) *Iran's Economy – Dilemmas of an Islamic State*, London: I.B. Tauris, forthcoming.

Bangkok Post, Bangkok, Thailand.

Bank of Thailand, Monthly Bulletin of Statistics, online service, Bangkok, Thailand.

Birdsall N. and Federick Jaspersen (eds, 1997) *Pathways to Growth, Comparing East Asia and Latin America*, Washington, D.C.: The Johns Hopkins University Press for the Inter-American Development Bank.

Chang, H-J (1997) 'A Crisis From Underregulation', *Los Angeles Times*, (31 December).

Chang, H-J, Gabriel Palma and D. Hugh Whittaker (1998) 'The Asian Crisis: Introduction,' *Cambridge Journal of Economics*, vol. 22, no. 6: 649–52.

Diwan, Ishac, Chang-Po Yang and Zhi Wang (1998) 'The Arab Economies, The Uruguay Round Predicament, and the European Union Wildcard', ch. 3 in Shafik (1998b).

Dornbusch R. (1998) 'Asian Crisis Themes', unpublished paper, Massachusetts Institute of Technology, (February).

The Economist, various issues, London.

El-Erian, M. A. and M. S. Kumar (1995) 'Emerging Equity Markets in the Middle Eastern Countries,' *IMF Staff Papers*, vol. 42, no. 2, (June).

ERF (1998) *Economic Trends in the MENA Region*, Cairo: The Economic Research Forum for the Arab Countries, Iran and Turkey.

ESCAP (1997) 'Economic and Social Survey of Asia and the Pacific,' New York: United Nations, Economic and Social Commission for Asia and the Pacific.

Furman, J. and J.E. Stiglitz (1998) 'Economic Crises: Evidence and Insights from East Asia,' *Brookings Papers on Economic Activity*, no. 2: 1–135.

Gangnes B. and Seiji Naya (1997) 'Why East Asian Economies Have Been Successful: Some Lessons for Other Developing Countries,' in Handoussa (1997).

Gavin, M., Ricardo Hausmann, and Ernesto Talvi (1997) 'Saving, Growth and Macroeconomic Vulnerability,' in Birdsall *et al.* (1997).

The Guardian, daily newspaper, London.

Hakimian H. and M. Karshenas (2000) 'Dilemmas and Prospects for Economic Reform and Reconstruction in Iran,' in Alizadeh (2000).

Handoussa H. (ed., 1997) *Economic Transition in the Middle East – Global Challenges and Adjustment Strategies*, Cairo: The American University in Cairo Press.

Hoekman, B. (1998) 'The World Trade Organization, the European Union, and the Arab World: Trade Policy Priorities and Pitfalls,' ch. 4 in Shafik (1998b).

IMF (1997) 'World Economic Outlook – Interim Assessment,' Washington D.C.: International Monetary Fund, (December).

Ito, T. and Anne O. Krueger (eds, 1995) *Growth Theories in Light of East Asian Experience*, Chicago and London: The University of Chicago Press.

Johnson, C. (1998) 'Economic Crisis in East Asia: the Clash of Capitalisms,' *Cambridge Journal of Economics*, vol. 22, no. 6: 653–61.

Khayat, D. (1997/8) 'Asia's Turbulence and the Egyptian Finance Market,' *Forum*, Economic Research Forum for the Arab Countries, Iran and Turkey, vol. 4, no. 3, (December 1997–January 1998).

Krueger Anne O. (1995) 'East Asian Experience and Endogenous Growth Theory,' in Ito and Krueger (1995).

Krugman, P. (1994) 'The Myth of Asia's Miracle,' *Foreign Affairs*, (November/December).

Krugman, P. (1998a) 'What Happened to Asia?', unpublished paper, January.

Krugman, P. (1998b) 'Will Asia Bounce Back?', unpublished speech for Credit Suisse First Boston, Hong Kong, (March).

Nugent, G. (1997) 'From Import Substitution to Outward Orientation: Some Institutional and Political Economy Conditions for Reform,' ch. 5 in Handoussa (1997).

Page, J. (1997) 'The East Asian Miracle and the Latin American Consensus: Can the Twain Ever Meet?,' in Birdsall *et al.* (1997).

—— (1998) 'From Boom to Bust – and Back? The Crisis of Growth in the Middle East and North Africa,' in Shafik (1998b).

Radelet, S. and Jeffrey D. Sachs (1998) 'The East Asian Financial Crisis: Diagnosis, Remedies, Prospects,' *Brookings Papers on Economic Activity*, vol. 1: 1–90.

Riordan, E. M., U. Dadush, J. Jalali, S. Streifel, M. Brahmbhatt, and K. Takagaki (1998) 'The World Economy and Implications for the Middle East and North Africa, 1995–2010', ch. 2 in Shafik (1998b).

Rodrik, D. (1997) *Has Globalization Gone Too Far?*, Washington D.C.: Institute for International Economics.

Sachs, J. (1997) 'Personal View,' *The Financial Times*, (July 30).

Safadi, R. (1997) 'Global Challenges and Opportunities Facing MENA Countries at the Dawn of the Twenty-First Century', ch. 2 in Handoussa (1997).

Salvatore, D. (1998) 'Capital Flows, Current Account Deficits, and Financial Crises in Emerging Market Economies,' *International Trade Journal*, (Spring): 5–22.

Shafik, N. (ed., 1998a) *Economic Challenges Facing Middle Eastern and North African Countries – Alternative Futures*, Basingstoke and London: Macmillan Press.

Shafik, N. (ed., 1998b) *Prospects for Middle Eastern and North African Economies – From Boom to Bust and Back?*, Basingstoke and London: Macmillan Press.

Stiglitz J.E. (1998a) 'More Instruments and Broader Goals: Moving toward the Post-Washington Consensus,' WIDER Annual Lectures 2, UNU World Institute for Development Economics Research (UNU/WIDER), Helsinki, Finland, January.

Stiglitz, J.E. (1998b) 'Bad Private-Sector Decisions', *Wall Street Journal*, (February 4).

Tatom, John A. (1998) 'Float or Fail? Lessons from the 1997 Thai Currency Crisis,' *Economic Focus*, Zurich: UBS Economic Research, Union Bank of Switzerland, (March).

UNCTAD (1997 and 1999) *World Investment Report*, New York and Geneva: United Nations Conference on Trade and Development.

—— (1996 and 1998) *Trade and Development Report*, New York and Geneva: United Nations Conference on Trade and Development.

Virawan, A. (1998) 'East Asia After the Bubble Burst,' text of speech at the Institute of Developing Economies, Tokyo, in *Bangkok Post*, (6 February 1998).

The World Bank (1993) *The East Asian Miracle – Economic Growth and Public Policy*, Oxford and New York: Oxford University Press.

The World Bank (1995) *Claiming the Future – Choosing Prosperity in the Middle East and North Africa'*, Washington, D.C.

The World Bank (1998a) *World Development Indicators*, CD ROM, Washington, D.C.

The World Bank (1998b) 'The East Asia Crisis and the Role of the World Bank,' World Bank Information Kiosk Announcement, Mr. Sandstrom's Statement – East Asia, 2/13; updated on: Wednesday, 18 February 1998.

Part II
Processes and Outcomes

Chapter Five

The Politics of Economic Liberalization: Comparing Egypt and Syria

Raymond Hinnebusch

APPROACHES TO THE POLITICS OF ECONOMIC REFORM

The dominant, mainstream approach to economic liberalization in the Middle East tends to view it as the inevitable response to economic crisis. The neo-liberal Washington consensus assumes that there is one rational objective formula for economic success: failure to pursue it in the Middle East is viewed as a function of political irrationality – patrimonial/rentier states harness the economy to their power requisites, using it as a source of patronage and control at the expense of economic rationality.

The assumption that indigenous political culture is at odds with the supposedly universal and objective requisites of economic development reflects Orientalist cultural exceptionalism and fails to grasp the extent to which neoliberal economics is, at least partly, an ideology reflective of the interests of global capital and neglectful of those of LDCs and, in particular, their subordinate classes (Ayubi 1993: 28; 1995: 332). This approach also comes close to either an economic or cultural determinism which ignores the role of interests and the political process in shaping policy.

The assumptions of this chapter are different in several ways: 1) It accepts that economic crisis precipitates policy changes and that economic policy decisions are indeed taken chiefly on political grounds; but it views the political rationality of state-building – maximizing legitimacy and stability – as just as valid as economic rationality. 2) As such, it assumes that policy-makers must design packages involving trade-offs and compromises between politics and economics while seeking, in the long run, to reconcile the two; 3)

Economic policy is viewed as neither fully determined by economics or culture, nor the product of rational optimization insulated from social forces; rather, it results from a political process in which elite strategies will take account of the balance of domestic social forces as well as international pressures and opportunities.

Comparing case studies can provide insights into the complex pattern of variables at work. This chapter will compare the experiences of two once populist-etatist authoritarian republics which have subsequently taken somewhat different post-populist paths to economic liberalization: Egypt, a pioneer of liberalization and Syria, one of the states most resistant to it. This analysis applies chiefly to such initially authoritarian-populist regimes and will be of lesser relevance to other types of state.

FRAMEWORK OF ANALYSIS

The Starting Point: Authoritarian Populism

Economic liberalization in the Middle East has been governed by the post-populist evolution of the authoritarian-populist regimes which have dominated the region starting in the 1950s. These regimes, launched by military coups led by radical officers, initially aimed to consolidate power against the traditional upper class by co-opting middle and lower strata. Their strategy of economic development aimed to break economic dependency and launch state-led import substitute industrialization (ISI). Nationalizations and land reform served both political consolidation and the economic logic of statist development by breaking oligarchic control of the economy and vesting it in the hands of the state (Ayubi 1992: 89–105). Statist economic strategies have, however, been universally exhausted and further economic development seemingly requires economic liberalization. However, it cannot proceed far unless it is made compatible with a political logic allowing these regimes to adapt to their "post-populist" environment without compromising their stability and security.

Domestic Economy: Crisis and Response

In examining the evolution of the domestic economy, two separate but inevitably intertwined factors are being assessed. On the one hand, the economic ills of the statist system which produce pressures for liberalization are analysed; on the other hand, the economy registers the impact of the state's policy responses to economic ills which re-shape the economy over time – reducing or increasing pressures for further economic reform.

Economic liberalization normally has its origins in a crisis of the statist economy. Its pace and degree will be shaped firstly by the severity of the crisis of capital accumulation and other economic imbalances (balance of payments, budget deficits, debt, unemployment). But crises have not exerted consistent pressure on policy-makers; instead pressures have fluctuated, with peaks, interspersed with periods of liberalization and recovery, relieving pressures for further liberalization.

Moreover, responses to crises depend on opportunities, above all the likely availability of sources of private investment needed to replace the role of the state. There is, for example, frequently a hope that much hidden or expatriate capital could be mobilized by liberalization. The latter cannot, however, be taken for granted given the speculative and commercial tradition of local capitalism, the high incidence of capital flight and the historic reluctance of investors to fund strategic industries – all the problems which precipitated the statist model in the first place. Significant foreign capital, 'shy' of this unstable region, can only be expected in later stages of liberalization.

Policy-makers will therefore likely attempt to liberalize in ways which preserve the accomplishments of the ISI period, notably the most 'strategic' parts of the public sector. They will also search for substitutes for private investment, notably geopolitical or petroleum rent, which will allow them to tailor the extent and pace of liberalization. Specifically, they will attempt to calibrate liberalization so that statist dismantling does not exceed private sector and market ability to fill the vacuum from the decline of state investment, and will start with the 'easiest' measures, such as trade liberalization and leave those which challenge vested interests – notably privatization, until last.

In fact, policy makers have aimed at, and to an extent attained, a certain ideal-typical sequence in their liberalization strategies. The first response to the statist exhaustions of the sixties and early seventies was typically selective trade liberalization and laws encouraging private/foreign investment (*infitah*). Further integration into the world market (through exchange rate and price liberalization) and structural adjustment are logical next steps needed to encourage the growth of the private sector. Once the market appears to be functioning (and creating new employment), reform and later privatization of the public sector becomes less risky (second *infitah*). In practice, of course, policy makers have not always been able to exercise such rational control over the process. This is partly because the first *infitah* has tended to generate debt and deficits which, owing to rent influxes, have gone unaddressed, leading to a later, deeper crisis, more painful austerity and greater vulnerability to international pressures for further liberalization. Despite such zigzags, the long term tendency has been an incremental deepening of liberalization.

Forces Shaping Economic Liberalization Policy

It is a fallacy to think that decision-makers respond purely to economic troubles and pressures. Rather, their response is filtered, so to speak, by international conditions, domestic social forces and political calculations. These three factors are discussed briefly below.

The International System

The international system shapes the security imperatives to which all policy, including economic policy, is likely to be subordinated, as well as determining the options available to regimes when responding to economic pressures.

State security is the most immediate preoccupation of regimes in the Middle East, especially those involved in intense conflicts with neighbouring powers. The 1967 defeat of Egypt and Syria defined their main security imperatives: the Israeli threat and the drive for recovery of the occupied territories. This decisively shaped their alignments in the bi-polar arena: state elites had to decide whether Soviet arms or American diplomacy, or some combination thereof, would best serve their goals. The consequences of such choices inevitably found their way into every other policy decision, including economic strategy. Switching to American patronage required some economic liberalization; reliance on the Soviets delayed it.

The intersection of security preoccupations with developments in the regional petroleum economy also had a profound effect in shaping subsequent economic policy options and responses. The 1967 war forced the nationalist states, Egypt and Syria, to end the ideological cold war with the conservative Arab oil-producing states in return for financial help to rebuild their armies. The 1970s oil boom increased the prestige and resources of these oil producers – boosting, in Heikel's words, *tharwa* (resources) over *thawra* (revolution) (1978: 261–62).

114

The resulting dependence of the nationalist states on transfers from and labour markets in the oil states made them vulnerable to the pressures of these Arab donors to moderate their strategies and open their economies (Dessouki 1982: 319–347). The opportunity to acquire petroleum-related rent thus initially acted as an incentive to liberalization. Once access to rent was acquired during the oil boom, it relieved pressures for further liberalization. However, the mid-1980s oil price bust and the resulting economic imbalances renewed liberalization pressures on these states.

Finally, the transformation in the global arena after the end of the Cold War has reshaped the environment in which decision-makers operate. Just as bipolarity opened the door to nationalist models of development in which statist import substitute industrialization aimed to break dependency on the West, so its end undermined such models. Under bipolarity, the Soviet bloc provided an alternative source of aid, technology and markets which allowed nationalist states to flout the IMF and Western aid donors. Soviet arms and political protection made nationalist policies possible and superpower competition allowed Egypt, in particular, to get economic aid from both East and West.

Once the declining ability of Soviet aid to meet states needs forced the beginning of economic liberalization and integration into the international market, formerly statist states became vulnerable to IMF and Western lender pressures for further economic liberalization (Ayubi 1993; Owen 1992: 139–165). The 1990s end to bipolarity and the Gulf War underlined the need to placate the American world hegemon, while the globalization of capitalism destroyed the remaining credibility of national development models and opened up potential new opportunities for foreign investment and export markets. The Gulf war – often taken as the defining transition event to the post-bi-polar world – generally accelerated economic liberalization.

State formation and the balance of social forces

The State: The authoritarian-populist state has a natural resistance to liberalization: the product of a populist movement against the bourgeoisie, its initial constituents – unionized workers, public employees, and small peasants – are threatened by liberalization while its historic bourgeois rivals are most likely to benefit from and be strengthened by liberalization.

To minimize the risks of, and the resistance to, liberalization and to gain the necessary backing for it, the state must literally alter its social base – away from its initial middle-lower class coalition and toward a new alliance with the bourgeoisie. The pace and degree of this realignment is conditioned by the specific pattern of state formation in a country, notably, the relative power of an intra-regime 'state bourgeoisie' prepared for liberalization as opposed to the counter-vailing power of populist interests incorporated into the state and resistant to liberalization.

Reconstruction and incorporation of the bourgeoisie: Liberal-ization cannot go very far without an entrepreneurial bourgeoisie which, being willing to invest, can provide a viable alternative to the public sector; which is prepared to reach a *modus vivendi* with the state; and which acquires an interest in, and the power to push for, economic liberalization. A key variable determining liberalization will, therefore, be the extent of survival of a bourgeoisie from the pre-etatist era and/or the reconstruction and political incorporation of a new one.

In the Arab Middle East, however, the bourgeoisie is neither united nor an unabashed promoter of economic liberalization. Typically, a state-dependent wing, especially rent-seeking elements, wants only selective liberalization. Trade liberalization is often supported by the commercial bourgeoisie which is content with speculative, commer-cial and middle man ventures, while the industrial bourgeoisie may favour joint ventures with foreign capital but needs protection from foreign competition. The attitude of the bourgeoisie toward economic liberalization will be decisive for its pace and extent.

Elite strategies

Ruling elites must mediate between the external and internal arenas and among internal social forces. Internally, they enjoy a good measure of autonomy of both the statist vested interests embedded in state structures and of the bourgeoisie since these – more or less – check each other. Elites can therefore, to a considerable extent, determine the pace and scope of reform according to their own goals and interests while adapting it to economic and external exigencies.

The state elite's priority is to maximize its autonomy and regime security. Generally, this requires keeping the political and economic logics as compatible as possible since, if one or the other is excessively neglected, the regime will be threatened. Given the great uncertainties involved in economic liberalization, this dictates a selective, incremental opening to the market rather than precipitous, extensive withdrawal of the state from economic management. It is the responsibility of the top leader to balance economic and political logic (Ayubi 1993: 29–31; Ayubi 1995: 338; Heydemann 1992: 11–39).

Economic logic cannot, of course, be neglected. In a sense, it deals the hand which leaders have to play. Whether they can achieve the aim of the game – to keep state retrenchment from exceeding the ability of the private sector to fill the gap – is partly determined by the severity of economic troubles and by opportunities to elicit private investment. There is not necessarily a conflict between economic and political logic. Economic liberalization allows elites to diversify their coalitions by co-opting the bourgeoisie (Ehteshami and Murphy 1996: 753–72). In the longer term, elites realize that capitalist development is inescapable if the economic base of the state is to be protected. Nor does liberalization necessarily generate threats by the bourgeoisie to the power of the state elite since the bourgeoisie is weak in the early stages of liberalization, and liberalization may give the capitalist class a stake in regime survival – even if, in the long term, it potentially increases bourgeois power to curb the autonomy of state elites.

Nevertheless, it is political logic which determines how elites play the economic hand they are dealt. Their policies will typically be shaped firstly, by calculations as to the impact of liberalization on the regime coalition; and secondly, by whether they seek to transform this initially populist social base or merely widen and consolidate it. If they seek coalition transformation, the trick will be to co-opt the bourgeoisie through substantial liberalization while marginalizing populist and statist elements at least cost. If the elites seek to defend, consolidate or maximize their inherited coalition, they will allow enough liberalization to co-opt the bourgeoisie while still appeasing the statist/populist interests, thus avoiding excessive dependency on either wing of their coalition.

Leadership and factional politics determine such choices. The extent of coalition alteration sought by a regime is often most immediately dictated by whether the power needs of the top leader are best served by balancing or transforming the regime coalition. This will play a major role in determining the extent of economic liberalization he pursues. Within the broad limits of the leader's strategy, shorter term conflicts between political and economic logic and the consequent extent and pace of liberalization may in part be resolved by intraregime bureaucratic politics – a struggle between liberalizing *technos* who put their faith in market revival and *politicos* sceptical as to whether the private sector will invest in strategic industries and concerned about the political dangers of attacking populism. In this process, the top leader either leads or arbitrates.

The actual pace of liberalization will vary according to the leader's goals and the scenarios he faces. In general terms, the record suggests that the following conditions govern speedup and slowdown in the pace of liberalization. On the one hand, economic liberalization accelerates when the leader seeks to transform his coalition and when mounting economic difficulties are matched with opportunities for investment, thereby giving the *technos* the upper hand in bureaucratic politics. On the other hand, liberalization slows when the leader seeks to consolidate his coalition through balancing etatist/populist and private sector constituencies, when political resistance to liberalization mounts, and when rent is available as a substitute, thereby giving *politicos* the upper hand.

In the long term, elite strategies also vary according to the *stage* of liberalization. Early in the transition period, when the regime remains dependent on a mixed public-private sector economy, elites are more likely to follow a balancing strategy in which the bourgeoisie is included but etatist/populist interests are still appeased. In later stages of liberalization when, presumably, private and foreign investment increasingly replace public investment, the weight of bourgeois and foreign investor demands and expectations increasingly overshadow statist/populist resistance to liberalization in the policy process.

This analysis reflects the lack of evidence that regime elites act as members of a wider economic 'ruling class' (Waterbury 1992). To be sure, state elites may be 'embourgeoized' but if vital state interests are threatened and seem to conflict with the wider class interests of the bourgeoisie, they normally give priority to state interests. However, if state interests are not threatened, the elites' class interests do make them increasingly responsive to the bourgeoisie, less responsive to their initial popular constituency and hence more receptive to economic liberalization. And, the more economic liberalization widens state dependence on the market economy, the more state interests – in stability – may be seen to coincide with bourgeois class interests.

Figure 1 identifies the main forces determining economic liberalization, as in the foregoing argument. It suggests that policy responses to economic variables are 'filtered' by international conditions, the balance of social forces in the state and elite interests and strategies.

FIGURE 1: Forces Determining Extent of Economic Liberalization

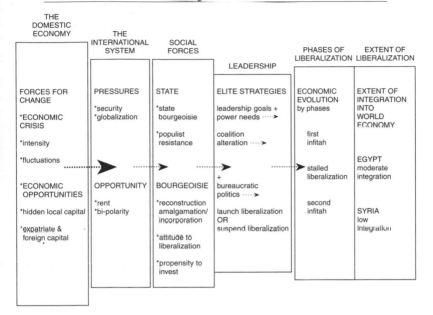

These factors determine the phases and extent of liberalization policies and outcomes which, in turn, 'feed back' on the economic situation, reducing or intensifying pressures for further reform.

CASE STUDIES: EGYPT AND SYRIA

The Comparative Evolution of Political Economy

In, both Syria and Egypt, the first stage of economic liberalization – appropriately called *infitah* (opening) – took the form of selective trade liberalization and new laws encouraging private investment. In Egypt, the immediate aim was to attract the external aid needed to rescue the crumbling war economy. In the longer term, the expectation was that it would generate new foreign, Arab and private investment to complement and eventually overshadow the stagnant public sector as the main engine of development. This strategy, combined with the inflow of aid and oil-related earnings, stimulated considerable private sector revival in the 1970s. However, it chiefly fostered tertiary activities, notably commerce and tourism, and the export of labour to the oil producing Gulf countries, while investment in productive or export industries lagged. This produced an import and consumption boom, fuelling trade and payments imbalances, budget deficits and debt. However, the inflow of aid and oil-related earnings, such as worker's remittances, relieved pressures to address these imbalances and to pursue economic liberalization more thoroughly (Hinnebusch 1985; Waterbury 1983).

By the late eighties, the decline in oil prices and accumulated debt sparked a foreign exchange and debt service crisis. Debt had climbed from $2 billion in 1970 to $50 billion (Richards and Waterbury 1996: 226). This, together with Gulf war opportunities for debt reduction and IMF pressures, opened the door to a second round of liberalization in the early nineties with three major prongs: 1) the correction of macro-economic imbalances through reductions in subsidies, budget deficits and balance of payments deficits enjoyed some success, specifically in cutting budget deficits; 2) deepened integration into the international market through further trade liberalization, banking reforms and the unification of exchange rates resulted in a major influx of expatriate or domestic capital held abroad. That liberalization was also generating, to an extent, its own internal momentum was evident from the way further adjustments to deal with the perverse outcomes of earlier half-way liberalization measures in banking and exchange rate reforms were self-initiated by the government. For example, the private and joint venture banking system set up under *infitah* had merely resulted in Egyptian capital being exported, in part because interest rates were set too low. To reverse this and capture Egyptian worker's remittances, the banking system had to be further liberalized, allowing the market a greater role in setting interest rates and advancing the convertibility of the pound. 3) Finally, only after the Gulf war did private investment stimulation through public sector privatization and reductions in labour protections seriously begin; privatization and private investment in industry has, however, advanced slowly (Richards and Waterbury, 1996: 224–29; Hinnebusch 1993b).

In **Syria**, disinvestment and market scarcities in the early 1970s were met by limited trade liberalization and encouragement of private sector merchants. In the later 1970s, a rent inflow fuelled a two-track policy: a new state-led round of ISI which in turn fostered a class of private contractors and middlemen.

However, the Islamic uprising which started in the late seventies soured government-business relations and stunted private sector takeoff. Then, growing military burdens, and rent depletion in the eighties following contractions of external aid (due to the collapse of oil prices), resulted in a second statist exhaustion. The deteriorating trade imbalance, fiscal and foreign exchange crises and mounting debt forced austerity – cutbacks in public spending and investment – which further depressed the economy. By the late 1980s, the government began to look to the private sector to fill the gap.

This, plus post-Gulf war rents and opportunities, led to a second wave of liberalization including the end to certain state foreign trade monopolies, relaxation of price controls and new concessionary investment and tax laws. The result was a spurt of private investment and exports which began to overshadow public sector ISI. But Syria has preserved a mixed public/private sector strategy. Privatization of the public sector is not on the agenda though joint private-public ventures are emerging as a substitute for it (Hinnebusch 1995; Perthes 1992a and 1992b). Moreover, by the late nineties, long-expected further liberalization measures had not materialized.

Explanatory variables

The pace and extent of economic liberalization is appreciably different in Egypt and Syria. Compared to Egypt, in Syria the weight of the public sector is greater and the level of integration into the world market is lower. What explains such variations in the liberalization mix? Policy makers respond to economic pressures differently in part because responses are filtered through different international and social contexts which shape different options, costs, benefits and leadership calculations. The contextual differences between Egypt and Syria will be suggested below.

The International System

The international system has presented Egypt and Syria with very different incentive structures which have profoundly shaped economic options. Egypt perceived an opportunity from the 1973 war to re-align Westward (exploiting bipolar competition), in order to get American diplomatic help in the recovery of the Sinai, which Soviet arms had not achieved. Egypt's economy was in deep crisis and Sadat was promised economic aid in return for a settlement with Israel. The 1973 oil boom provided a further incentive to open the economy in order to get aid and investment from the conservative Gulf oil producing states and to export surplus labour. Egypt's march toward peace with Israel was paralleled by an influx of Western aid contingent on moves toward economic liberalization. When Camp David cut Egypt's access to Arab Gulf aid, its economic dependency on the U.S. was radically heightened. While US-provided strategic rent relieved pressures for more liberalization in the eighties, by the nineties this was declining. Egypt's debt crisis and the collapse of bipolarity further increased IMF leverage on the government, while the Gulf war made it possible to reassert access to strategic rent, providing the essential prerequisite – massive debt relief – for the second wave of liberalization. That this debt relief was made conditional on IMF sponsored reforms added teeth to international pressures on Egypt's policy-makers (Amin 1982: 285–315; Hinnebusch 1985: 40–77; Hinnebusch 1993b: 159–63).

For **Syria** there was no comparable opportunity for post-1973 Western realignment, particularly once Egypt embarked on a separate peace which destroyed Syria's diplomatic bargaining hand. On the other hand, the oil boom and the Arab aid flows to Syria as a front line state, particularly after Camp David, provided a substitute for substantial economic liberalization. Syria was able to effect a diversification of rent and dependency between the USSR, the Arab oil producers and Iran which allowed it greater autonomy than Egypt enjoyed and subjected Damascus to no comparable international pressures for liberalization.

The end of bipolarity and the Gulf war did provide the incentive and an opportunity for Syria to begin a Westward re-alignment and to enter the peace process – albeit much later and more tentatively than in Egypt. This created a climate conducive to Syria's own second liberalization. But Syria's Gulf war aid windfall also relieved immediate economic troubles and, being from the Gulf Arab states, was not conditional, unlike Egypt's Western-provided debt relief. The regime's peace diplomacy has proceeded largely unconstrained by economic pressures and the peace process has as yet provided no immediate economic incentives (aid or investment prospects) for further liberalization. On the contrary, by the late nineties, its suspension seemed to put all further moves toward economic liberalization in abeyance.

State and Social Forces

State Formation: In **Egypt**, state building centred on Nasser who used his charisma and popular support to make the presidency an interventionist force for re-distribution at the expense of the bourgeoisie. On the other hand, an established bureaucracy readily controlled a deferent society while recruiting its senior ranks from bourgeois families – who, commanding the public sector, were transformed into a state bourgeoisie through high salaries, corruption and business on the side.

Because Nasser's power consolidation did not depend on. a strong ideological party, there were no mechanisms through which the political elite could be replenished with plebeian elements having a stake in his populist policies and through which the lower strata of society could be organized to balance the state bourgeoisie's growing interest in liberalization. As such, once Nasser was gone, there was little obstacle to transformation of the state's social base through purges of the left and new bourgeois recruitment under Sadat. A new social contract between the state and the bourgeoisie, in which Sadat retained authoritarian power but curbed redistributionist intervention, replaced the previous populist one between state and masses whereby the latter were promised a minimum level of welfare. Sadat's lopsided political liberalization turned parliament, press, judiciary and interest groups into vehicles for the bourgeoisie to advance its interests inside the regime. Controlled party pluralization provided some safety values for opposition to economic liberalization but no institutional mechanisms to protect the interests of the lower strata (Hinnebusch 1985).

The state had not, however, lost its autonomy of the private bourgeoisie and economic policy remained, to some extent, constrained, though to a declining degree, by etatist interests and fear of popular backlash. Senior bureaucrats and public sector managers remained a key constituency and were able to ward off privatization until the 1990s; by then their view was ambivalent as some calculated they could survive privatization and/or benefit from the higher salaries and opportunities offered by private business. Since the late seventies, reform had also been deterred by government fear of popular rebellion such as the 1977 food riots. Then, in the early Mubarak years, reform was blocked by a reaction against the abuses of the *infitah* bourgeoisie and the resulting debt and inequality. Trade unions were assertive in their defence of the public sector, striking alliances with opposition parties and public sector managers. By 1990, however, the opposition was so badly split along pro- and anti-reform lines and by the secular opposition's fear of the Islamic movement, that the regime regained its autonomy of society. The

Islamists, the most credible opposition force, were largely silent on economic reform; much of the mainstream Islamic leadership, consisting of the bourgeoisie which made fortunes in the Gulf, probably supported it. As the threat that the public could be mobilized against reform declined, the regime felt freer to launch its second wave of liberalization (Hinnebusch 1995: 305–20; Springborg 1989).

In **Syria**'s more intractable society, the 1960s Ba'th regime, facing powerful opposition from the urban upper class and Islamists, had to mobilize a popular base to survive. It relied on a dual strategy. Before 1970 a strong ideological party rooted in plebeian strata institutionalized populism. Secondly, especially under Asad, recruitment of the core military elite from property-less minorities, especially Alawites, who used the state as a ladder of advancement, gave the regime's dominant social forces a greater stake in defending etatist and populist policies than was the case in Egypt. The party *apparatchiki* and bureaucrats who staff the very structures of the state have ideological and material stakes in the public sector and the state's role in the economy. The public sector remains a critical source of revenue which cannot readily be replaced by taxation of the private sector as long as the latter is able to evade taxation. Elites who have been enriched through smuggling or payoffs from business to evade regulations profit from state regulation of trade. The demands of the huge army for priority claims on economic resources enjoys legitimacy as long as the conflict with Israel persists. The regime's precarious legitimacy rests in part on providing welfare and economic opportunity for the popular strata in its original constituency. As such, political logic requires that it protect its peasant base from the encroachment of a revived landed bourgeoisie. The potentially dangerous urban mass, susceptible to bourgeois-backed Islamicism, must be placated with cheap food and jobs.

Thus, the Syrian state is more at odds with the bourgeoisie than the Egyptian state, and no state-bourgeoisie social contract has displaced the populist one. This has delayed and narrowed the scope of liberalization compared to Egypt. To be sure, this is changing. On the one hand, as state patronage resources declined under economic austerity in the eighties, those dependent on it had to diversify their interests by going into business. On the other hand, Asad sought to increase his autonomy of the party and army by fostering and incorporating a private, albeit state-dependent bourgeoisie. But the state bourgeoisie is weaker than in Egypt. Asad accorded the private sector new access to policy-makers but, compared to Egypt, it has not colonized the army and party, while populist constituencies have been less excluded from access to state elites. Hence, the state strives for a balance between the bourgeoisie and its plebeian constituencies, a strategy which necessarily limits the extent of economic liberalization (Hinnebusch 1990, 1995: 305–20, 1997: 249–65).

Reconstruction and incorporation of the bourgeoisie: In **Egypt**, the bourgeoisie as an economic force capable of driving capitalist development, is far more reconstructed than in Syria. Never as damaged or as pushed from power as in Syria, it had a head start on reconstruction. The amalgamation of the originally middle class ruling military elite and families of old and new wealth is complete and the alienation of the bourgeoisie, which now sees the regime as a full partner, has been largely overcome. The *infitah* commercial/rent-seeking bourgeoisie generated more debt and dependency than productive investment, but Egypt's industrialists have revived and, compared to Syria, the bourgeoisie is larger, more diversified and enjoys more extensive transnational connections: it is reaching the point where the regime can start expecting it to provide the bulk of new investment. Indeed, Egypt is now regarded as an emerging market capable of attracting mobile international capital.

The bourgeoisie is not powerful enough to force the state into liberalization measures it does not want, but there is more of a power balance between the two forces in Egypt than in Syria. The ministerial elite remains dominated by former statists and can still unilaterally alter business conditions, insists on intrusive regulation and, in its attack on Islamic investment companies in the 1980s, showed hostility to independent capitalist forces. However, the bourgeoisie can also sometimes derail economic initiatives taken against its wishes. Its influence has been on a steady rise. It has won a proliferation of tax exemptions, has vetoed government banking policies, and is literally richer than the state. Through its associations, parliament, and the ruling NDP, it actively seeks to shape the emerging capitalist legal framework. The Egyptian Businessman's Association (EBA) has semi-institutionalized access to parliamentary committees considering economic legislation and is even consulted over cabinet level implementation. When the bourgeoisie is united and the state not threatened by its demands, it is unstoppable in contests with other social forces.

While the growing political power of business is an essential ingredient in economic reform, it does not translate uniformly into economic reform since the bourgeoisie is split or ambivalent on the issue. Reform is therefore being shaped in part by an intra-bourgeois political struggle. Those most strongly in favour of reform are the some 5,000 agents of foreign firms, and the 7,500 import agents who dominate the *infitah* bourgeoisie. The American Chamber of Commerce in Egypt, a powerful grouping of ministers, Egyptian business leaders and American investors, has openly lobbied for privatization, supported by USAID. However, private industrialists whose linkages to the public sector have provided benefits, such as low priced inputs and state contracts, are ambivalent about privatization, and lobby for continued protection from foreign competition. Because they are willing to invest in Egypt, their demands cannot be ignored if economic liberalization is to succeed. In addition, the private sector has an Islamic wing which favours some economic liberalization but not Westernization. These splits and ambivalence in the bourgeoisie give the government greater autonomy to follow its own – or the IMF's – preferences (Hinnebusch 1993b: 165–67).

In **Syria**, the bourgeoisie is much less reconstructed. The private bourgeoisie was more damaged and alienated from the state and only recently and partially reconciled to the regime. It remains largely commercial and rent-seeking, its industrial wing is quite weak and foreign partners are absent. Etatist development also fostered a new bourgeoisie of state-dependent middle men and contractors in league with state elites of plebeian origin; at the core of this alliance is a 'military-mercantile complex' of Alawi officers and Damascene Sunni businessmen. Former sharp antagonism between the state and the upper classes has been bridged as the political elite has acquired a stake in new inequalities but amalgamation between the elite and the private bourgeoisie has been delayed by the sectarian barrier – i.e. to Alawi-Sunni intermarriages – and some bourgeois support for the Islamic uprising in the 1980s.

There is now a marriage of convenience between the Alawi-dominated political elite and the Sunni-dominated private bourgeoisie. Business partnerships exist and each needs the other – business needs political patrons and state elites require access to the wider market. However, the state can neither wholly trust nor afford excessive dependence on the bourgeoisie. Officials insist that private investors are only interested in quick high profit ventures and that the economy cannot do without a public sector to invest in strategic sectors. Business lacks confidence in the absence of rule of law, a proper investment climate and facilities, and the foreign partners bringing integration into the world market. The relation of less favoured and smaller business elements to the Alawi barons still resembles the payment of mafia style protection money. Joint public-private ventures, an intermediary stage which deepens alliances between the state and the bourgeoisie, remain in their infancy (Bahout 1994; Perthes 1991: 31–37, 1992a: 207–30; Hinnebusch 1995: 313–15).

Nor is the bourgeoisie necessarily united on economic policy or an unabashed promoter of economic liberalization. In the early nineties, it largely accepted the regime's strategy of incremental liberalization, being happy with the new opportunities to get rich and with political and monetary stability. Politically connected elements wanted the state's role as a source of contracts and monopolies to continue. Finally, however, by the late nineties, the bourgeoisie was increasingly frustrated at the lack of further movement toward liberalization.

Elite Interests and Strategies

Egypt's course cannot be detached from Sadat's political strategy. He inherited Nasser's office but not his popular support and, as such, chose to root his rule in the support of the bourgeoisie – the social force which was both most strategic and most prepared to support a leader promising a reversal of Nasser's populism. As this course inflamed opposition, Sadat encouraged the political re-emergence of the Muslim brotherhood and the liberal Wafd – each representative of different segments of the bourgeoisie alienated from the state under Nasser. The decision to launch *infitah* followed a purge of statists, including Prime Minister Aziz Sidqi, who had defended public sector dominance (Hinnebusch 1985: 40–77).

Once *infitah* was established as Egypt's economic strategy, intra-elite conflicts centred on its proper scope and management. They typically pitted liberalizing economists convinced of the greater efficiency of a fully capitalist economy against more statist minded bureaucrats and state managers allied with politicians fearful of public reaction to the rollback of subsidies and public sector employment. One watershed was Sadat's 1977 responsiveness to pressures from the IMF and Western bankers to cut subsidies: he overruled the objections of his still relatively statist economy and finance ministers. This triggered the 1977 'food riots' which shattered much of the legitimacy Sadat had carefully built up, forced the government to back down, and deterred for over a decade further attempts at radical cuts in the social safety net for the poor (Hinnebusch 1985: 131–57).

The next president, Husni Mubarak, sought to consolidate his base by balancing statist/populist interests against those of the *infitah*. *Infitah*, rather than producing a dynamic capitalist alternative to Nasserite statism, had stimulated a consumption boom that put Egypt in debt; Mubarak insisted that it would be reformed, not reversed, but the government's freedom of action was boxed in by conflicting domestic constraints. The public sector was still the main engine of investment, defended by public sector managers and unionized labour, while Mubarak's reference to the IMF as a 'quack doctor' reflected his scepticism that the market would, if only unchained by the state, work wonders for Egypt. Attacking populist policies seemed likely to fuel Islamic fundamentalism or spark off renewed insurrection. On the other hand, *infitah* had itself created a richer bourgeoisie which vetoed several government efforts to raise taxes or funnel foreign currency into state banks to cope with the financial imbalances. So constrained, the regime opted for incrementalism – e.g. gradually shaving subsidies, and raising taxes on imported luxuries. Unable to undertake radical reform, it chiefly concentrated on negotiations with creditors for a rescheduling of debts – merely postponing the day of reckoning (Springborg 1989; Sullivan 1990: 317–34; Richards 1991).

By the mid-1980s, elites acknowledged the economy was sick, but shared no agreement on the proper medicine. Nevertheless, after the Gulf war, economic liberalism in elite ranks gained the upper hand: the global triumph of capitalism reduced other options while major debt relief provided the resources and opportunity for reform. Mubarak now saw himself less as a cautious consensus man and more as a decisive reformer embracing once scorned IMF prescriptions. Privatization, taboo a few years previously, was seemingly embraced even by the Minister of Industry.

Elites remained determined that reform should not jeopardize the regime's stability, but also now feared that failure to reform would be more dangerous in the long run since the stagnant public sector could no longer absorb job seekers and unemployment was climbing. Moreover, the decline of the opposition parties and the seeming quiescence of the 'street' gave them some confidence that liberalization was possible without rebellion from below (Hinnebusch 1993b).

The Politics of Economic Liberalization

The Syrian regime enjoys greater autonomy from society than does the Egyptian state, and within Syria's authoritarian presidential regime, Asad's views are decisive. In contrast to Sadat, Asad, on coming to power, sought alteration, not transformation of the regime. His main aim was to maximize the autonomy, stability and resources needed to continue the struggle against Israel, albeit in a more realistic way. Such political considerations shaped economic policy. Early economic liberalization was meant to win support from the bourgeoisie to counterbalance the left-wing party; thereafter Asad steered between an emerging bourgeoisie and his initial party-populist base. The Islamic uprising forced him to fall back on his populist alliance, showed the dangers of dependence on the bourgeoisie and retarded liberalization. By the nineties, however, Asad was ready to return to balancing, tilting toward a second *infitah*. The combination of politically dangerous economic stagnation and geopolitically-dictated realignment toward the West required some internal liberalization. It also provided the opportunity to re-diversify the regime's bases and thereby enhance the autonomy needed to pursue the Madrid peace process. This meant more thoroughly including the bourgeoisie, thereby reducing dependence on the army and party.

Yet Asad's pragmatic nature and his disinclination to be too far ahead of the elite consensus in economic (as opposed to strategic) matters, deterred him from imposing policy specifics. These were left to his lieutenants, with the President intervening only when the elite was divided or if an economic failure threatened the regime's political base. There existed an elite consensus that the economic crisis of the eighties showed that some economic liberalization was unavoidable and that a private sector partnership was needed to reduce the state's economic burdens; but also that the public sector remained essential to avoid excessive regime dependence on the bourgeoisie and excessive economic dependence on the market-before much of one was in place.

This has dictated a strategy of selective and sequenced economic liberalization. For example, it was believed that public sector reform could only progress once private sector investment could absorb the resulting unemployment (Sukkar 1994: 26–43). In the meantime, a division of labour was sought in which the public sector continued to meet local needs and served the regime's constituency while the private sector specialized in production for export. This would diversify the country's economic base, minimize risk and enhance the regime's ability to balance between bureaucracy and bourgeoisie.

Within these parameters, the extent and pace of liberalization is determined in good part by bureaucratic politics: an intra-regime competition between liberalizing *'technos'* and statist *'politicos'*. In the early nineties, Asad reshuffled the deck by pushing the party from its monopoly of policy making while giving business semi-institutionalized access to policy makers. In this contest, failures of the statist economy enhanced the political clout of the liberalizers while better economic times increased the ability of politicos to defend the statist status quo (Hinnebusch 1997: 249–65; Perthes 1995: 203–71).

Nevertheless, at least in the absence of major economic crisis, statist interests remained strong enough to block further liberalization measures except those the president could be brought to endorse personally. By the late nineties, however, the increasing frailty of the president and the stalling of the peace process had paralyzed further innovations in economic policy.

CONCLUSION

Explaining Differences in Economic Liberalization

Differences between Egypt and Syria can be explained by the impact of multiple variables – international context, the balance of social forces, and elite strategies.

The international context was far more favourable to liberalization in Egypt. There, the occupation crisis drove a realignment with the US and an Israeli peace which won a rent windfall and required some economic liberalization. Rent disguised domestic economic ills but the resulting high level of dependency on and vulnerability to international pressure eventually forced a second *infitah*. For Syria, in good part because Sadat's separate peace stalled diplomacy on the Syrian front, there was no comparable Western realignment or external incentive for liberalization, while Gulf aid provided an alternative to US re-alignment, enabling a diversification of economic dependency and allowing greater autonomy than that enjoyed by Egypt. Even Egypt's post-Gulf war rent was conditional while Syria's was not. Then, the seeming exhaustion of the peace process between Syria and Israel put further economic liberalization on hold.

The balance of domestic social forces, notably between the state and the bourgeoisie, was tilted more toward liberalization in Egypt than in Syria. In neither case has the bourgeoisie captured state power, but in Egypt, unlike Syria, it could be said to share power with state elites. This is an artefact of different patterns of state formation. In the easier Egyptian environment for state building, charisma and bureaucracy were enough to consolidate the regime, leaving it, post-Nasser, in the hands of the state bourgeoisie and lacking a populist party able to exercise countervailing power and constrain a leadership favouring liberalization. Under Sadat, the amalgamation of the state elite and families of old and new wealth was completed and the alienation of the bourgeoisie largely overcome while Sadat's lopsided political liberalization opened the regime to bourgeois power-sharing. Moreover, the Egyptian bourgeoisie is larger, more diversified and has more extensive transnational connections than Syria's: it and foreign investors may be reaching a point where they can provide the bulk of new investment.

In Syria's more intractable society, reliance on party and sect entrenched more tenacious statist/populist interests resistant to liberalization. The bourgeoisie remains largely commercial and rent-seeking, lacking foreign partners and unable to substitute for the public sector. There is now a marriage of convenience between the Alawi political elite and the Sunni private bourgeoisie; but amalgamation is delayed by the sectarian barrier. The bourgeoisie remains weaker than the state and the elite continues to balance between bourgeois and populist interests rather than sharing power with the former.

Finally elite strategies have proceeded in similar phases, reflective of broadly similar conditions, but given the differences in regimes, at each phase Egyptian reform has gone further. *Initial liberalization* was accompanied and shaped by major transitions in leadership in each state. Sadat's power consolidation needs led to the transformation of the regime's social base: lacking Nasser's popular support, he sought support from the bourgeoisie – a strong social force prepared to follow a leader promising a populist rollback and a substantial *infitah*. Asad, however, sought alteration, not transformation of the regime, in order to increase his autonomy and continue the struggle against Israel in a more realistic way. A mini-*infitah* was meant to win support from the bourgeoisie to balance the left-wing Ba'th party's ability to constrain Asad's foreign policy.

Slowdowns and reversals in liberalization resulted from similar mounting costs. In Egypt, the 1977 riots and the post-Sadat backlash against the excesses of the *infitah* slowed liberalization, rent relieved growing IMF pressures for it, and the public sector remained the main engine of investment. Mubarak sought to consolidate his power by balancing liberalizing and statist/populist forces. In Syria, rent allowed Asad to combine continuing selective economic liberalization with investment in the public sector. The Islamic uprising forced him to fall back further on his populist alliance, which retarded liberalization.

A second wave of liberalization, however, followed after a period. In Egypt, debt and vulnerability to IMF leverage plus conditional Gulf war rent stimulated a second *infitah* while buffering its political costs. A major elite conversion to economic liberalism followed as Mubarak embraced once-scorned IMF prescriptions, including privatization. But Egypt still receives enough rent to ward off pressures for shock liberalization. In Syria, renewed liberalization was precipitated by a politically dangerous economic stagnation and geopolitically-dictated realignment toward the West which required some further liberalization and also provided an opportunity to appease the bourgeoisie more thoroughly and reduce Asad's dependence on the army and party. But Syria's rent windfall, not being conditional, and its ability to evade IMF pressures, have allowed it to tailor a carefully selective, more modest, second *infitah* than in Egypt.

Assessing Reform Strategies in Egypt and Syria

Although under intense external pressures, both Egypt and Syria have successfully insisted that the pace and scope of economic reform be compatible with political stability. From a conventional economic point of view, their strategies were not always optimal. But, far from being the products of an economically irrational political culture, they resulted from a partially rational balancing of external and indigenous pressures and opportunities. Thus, for example, when rent was available, it made sense to use it to cushion a risky and precipitous dismantling of the public sector otherwise likely to leave an economic black hole, while when opportunities to attract investment mounted, it made equal sense to liberalize investment and tax laws. Despite the predictions of liberal economists, *infitah* brought costs, such as import booms and debt, while the benefits, notably new investment, were sluggish in materializing. Political leaders in these states have also had to be sensitive to the social class implications of economic policies so often ignored by international economic institutions: at least initially, liberalization hurts the mass public which Middle East republics initially mobilized to build their power while strengthening a bourgeoisie historically hostile to them. State autonomy and survival depends on tailoring economic policy to minimize the growth of class inequalities or at least the worsening of conditions for those at the bottom. In international perspective, Egypt and Syria appear less like the Russian than the Chinese model where the indigenous state's political-economy needs and persisting capabilities shaped an incremental economic liberalization. Arguably, too, these states have done well to avoid the Russian path where the hasty and uncritical imposition of liberal formulas, especially ill-considered privatization, led to economic collapse, social inequity, and political instability. Although the story of Middle East economic liberalization is really only just beginning, the current bottom line is that in both cases, incremental liberalization has, so far, revitalized economies without jeopardizing stability.

REFERENCES

Amin, Galal (1982) 'External Factors in the Reorientation of Egypt's Economic Policy,' in Kerr and Yassin (1982: 285–315).

Ayubi, Nazih (1992) 'Withered Socialism or Whether Socialism? The Radical Arab States as Populist-Corporatist Regimes', *Third World Quarterly*, vol. 13, no. 1: 89–105.

—— (1993) 'The "Fiscal Crisis" and the "Washington Consensus": Towards an Explanation of Middle East Liberalisation', in Blin (1993: 21–33).

—— (1995) *Overstating the Arab State: Politics and Society in the Middle East*, London: I.B. Tauris.

Bahout, Joseph (1994) 'The Syrian Business Community, its Politics and Prospects', in Kienle (1994: 72–80).

Barkey, Henri (1992) *The Politics of Economic Reform in the Middle East*, New York: St. Martin's Press.

Blin, Louis (ed., 1993) *L'Economie Egyptienne: liberalisation et insertion dans le marche mondial*, Paris: Editions L'Harmattan.

Dessouki, Ali E. Hillal (1982) 'The New Arab Political Order: Implication for the 1980s', in Kerr and Yassin (1982: 319–47).

Ehteshami, Anoushiravan and Emma C. Murphy (1996) 'Transformation of the Corporatist State in the Middle East', *Third World Quarterly*, vol. 17, no. 4: 753–72.

Heikel, Mohammed (1978) *The Sphinx and the Commissar*, New York: Harper & Row.

Heydemann, Steven (1992) 'The Political Logic of Economic Rationality: Selective Stabilization in Syria', in Barkey (1992: 11–39).

Hinnebusch, Raymond (1985) *Egypt Under Sadat: The Post-Populist Development of an Authoritarian-Modernizing Regime*, Cambridge: Cambridge University Press.

—— (1990) *Authoritarian Power and State Formation in Ba'thist Syria: Army, Party and Peasant*, Boulder, CO: Westview Press.

—— (1993a) 'Syria', in Niblock and Murphy (1993: 177–202).

—— (1993b) 'The Politics of Economic Reform in Egypt', *Third World Quarterly*, vol. 14, no. 1: 159–71.

—— (1995) 'The Political Economy of Economic Liberalization in Syria', *International Journal of Middle East Studies*, 27: 305–20.

—— (1997) 'Syria: the Politics of Economic Liberalisation', *Third World Quarterly*, vol. 18, no. 2: 249–65.

Keinle, Eberhard (1994) *Contemporary Syria: Liberalisation Between Cold War and Cold Peace*, London: British Academic Press.

Kerr, Malcolm and El Sayed Yassin (eds, 1982) *Rich and Poor States in the Middle East: Egypt and the New Arab Order*, Boulder, CO: Westview Press.

Niblock, Tim (1993) 'International and Domestic Factors in the Economic Liberalisation Process in Arab Countries', in Niblock and Murphy (1993: 55–87).

Niblock, Tim and Emma Murphy (eds, 1993) *Economic and Political Liberalisation in the Middle East*, London: British Academic Press.

Owen, Roger (1992) 'Economic Restructuring', in *State, Power and Politics in the Making of the Modern Middle East*, London: Routledge.

Perthes, Volker (1991) 'The Bourgeoisie and the Ba'th', *Middle East Report*, no. 170, vol. 21, (May–June): 31–37.

—— (1992a) 'The Syrian Private Industrial and Commercial Sectors and the State,' *International Journal of Middle East Studies*, 24, 2 (May): 207–30.

—— (1992b) 'The Syrian Economy in the 1980s,' *Middle East Journal*, vol. 46, no. 1: 37–58.

—— (1995) *The Political Economy of Syria Under Asad*, London: I.B. Tauris.

Richards, Alan (1991) 'The Political Economy of Dilatory Reform: Egypt in the1980s', *World Development*, vol. 19, no. 12: 1721–30.

Richards, Alan and John Waterbury (1996) *A Political Economy of the Middle East*, Boulder, CO: Westview Press.

Springborg, Robert (1989) *Mubarak's Egypt: Fragmentation of the Political Order*, Boulder, CO: Westview Press.

Sukkar, Nabil (1994) 'The Crisis of 1986 and Syria's Plan for Reform', in Kienle (1994: 26–43).

Sullivan, Denis (1990) 'The Political Economy of Reform in Egypt', *International Journal of Middle East Studies*, vol. 22, no. 3, (August): 317–34.

Waterbury, John (1983) *The Egypt of Nasser and Sadat: The Political Economy of Two Regimes*, Princeton, NJ: Princeton University Press.

—— (1992) 'Twilight of the State Bourgeoisies?', *International Journal of Middle East Studies*, vol. 23, no. 1, (February): 1–17.

Chapter Six

Economic Reform and the State in Tunisia

Emma C. Murphy

INTRODUCTION

In the past two decades, many states in the Middle East and North Africa have come to view economic liberalization as an appropriate strategy to retrieve the region from its economic difficulties. In doing so, they have followed what amounts to a near-global consensus, led by the international financial institutions and their neo-liberal faith in the supremacy of market forces. Yet, while the strategy is based on what are believed to be universally relevant economic principles, these reforms cannot be properly understood as a set of corrective policies without reference to the political contexts within which they are introduced and implemented. Experience has shown that there is no universally appropriate blue-print for the transformation from a centrally-planned or state-managed economy to one in which the market is supreme. In every case, there is a unique combination of history, culture and political system which impacts upon both the stimulus for economic change and its political fall-out. Clearly, this must be taken into consideration when devising reforms or evaluating their results.

The state is perhaps the single most critical player among the myriad of political forces at work in these complex equations. Economic liberalization arises from the failure of the state to successfully determine production and resource allocation in an increasingly international context. It cannot take place without the compliance of the state; indeed the state is required to initiate the process. Yet, ironically, the state appears at first glance to be the single political force with the most to lose. After all, economic liberalization

135

is all about the retreat of the state from certain economic activities, threatening both its power and its reach. The state itself is not a monolithic actor, but comprises a variety of interests which may find themselves at odds with one another as the impact of economic reforms is felt unevenly among them. For instance, the determination of the regime's political figures to advance economic liberalization can threaten the power, if not the very jobs, of the bureaucracy. Also, party officials may find themselves marginalized and redundant as technocrats take over their places in the decision making process. Any examination of the role of the state in supporting and implementing economic liberalization must therefore consider these multifarious dimensions and conflicting relationships.

This chapter examines the case of Tunisia, one of the region's most successful liberalizers. Although the country abandoned socialism and began a gradual process of reform as early as 1969, the real transformation has only taken place since the coming to power of President Zine el Abidine Ben Ali in 1987. In the absence of a strong private-sector industrial class, it has been the regime which has pushed for economic liberalization, usually pre-empting rather than responding to demands of external actors such as the World Bank or IMF. The regime has been driven by its own needs to reconstruct a power-base following the failures of populist and socialist policies in the post-independence era. The chapter will examine the way in which the regime came to adopt the economic reform strategy, and the political tactics which it used to reshape the structures of state and society to accommodate those reforms. I will argue that the old corporatist state of Bourguiba has been reformed into a new multi-party version of corporatism that allows the regime to act with relative autonomy from both its own party and the bureaucracy. An ongoing process of stage-managed democratization has concealed the reality of a retreat into an authoritarian mode of government, giving the regime the ability to implement economic liberalization and compensating for the consequent loss of direct economic control by increasing its political powers through a re-structured state apparatus.

Finally, the chapter addresses the question of the extent to which the political manoeuvrings of the Tunisian regime can be credited with achieving the relative success of the economic reforms. The political strategies of Zine elAbidine Ben Ali find a familiar resonance elsewhere in the MENA region, even where economic liberalization packages have neither advanced as far nor achieved as much. The particular advantages favouring the Tunisian experience must be considered, including a number of social, historical, geographic, resource and cultural features. Thus, we may attempt an assessment of the relevance of this specific regime's strategy, in terms of re-shaping the state and the role that it plays, for other regional players undergoing economic liberalization.

THE OLD CORPORATIST STATE IN TUNISIA

Independent Tunisia's first president, Habib Bourguiba, was the principal architect of the new state form. Following the first general election in 1959, his own nationalist Neo-Destour party was allocated the task of establishing rule and order in the country. Alternative political parties were banned and an organic linkage was established between the higher party echelons and the state machinery which revolved around Bourguiba's own position as president of both. The party itself espoused a nationalist and populist agenda, although once in power it rapidly became clear that it had neither a monolithic ideological position nor an homogeneous membership. Bourguiba sought as much to crush challenges from within the party to his own rule, as to prevent the ascendance of alternative political forces to the party. In order to mobilize the population behind his regime, popular organization and representation was allowed through national associations and organizations, bodies which were in effect vertically or 'functionally' stratified unions. These represented social interest groups – farmers, industrial workers, women, youth, craftsmen, etc. They should not be confused with more conventional trade unions since Bourguiba perceived class-based interests as being essentially hostile to the state, introducing social struggle rather than collabora-tion. Even Neo-Destour support for the Union Générale des Travailleurs Tunisiens (UGTT) has its origins in the former's efforts to draw support away from the French Communist-supported Confédération Général des Travailleurs (CGT) in the 1940s. Once the party had infiltrated the union's organization and membership, it was rapidly transformed into a support base for the party rather than an independent trade union.

Bourguiba believed strongly that the key to effective government lay in his own personal control of a strong and disciplined party. Neither unions nor national organizations were allowed to challenge his policies; rather, they should seek to negotiate with the state through the party on behalf of their constituencies. Equally, challenges to Bourguiba's own supremacy from within the party were swiftly dealt with. His populist policies were derived from what he perceived to be the national consensus: where ideology threatened to splinter that consensus it was abandoned, hence Bourguiba's reputation for moderation and pragmatism (at least in the first decade of his rule).

Such a quintessentially corporatist political system was not wholly alien to Tunisian political culture. Bourguiba, in playing the role of the national patriarch, was in many ways replicating the rule of the Beys under the French administration. His personalized and patrimonial rule resulted in extended lines of patronage, in the division of elites that sought constantly to advance their positions relative to one another, and in the tight control of access to power and resources (Larif-Béatrik 1988: 116–8). He continued a tradition of reformism rather than revolution which had been evident in centuries of Tunisian political history and which recognized that the military had to be subordinated to the civilian rulers in order to preserve social harmony. Moreover, Tunisian society was sufficiently homogeneous to comfortably accommodate notions of consensus and solidarity. Without a large urbanized proletariat, and with a substantial middle class having grown up around olive production in the rural *sahel*, there was little real sympathy with notions of class struggle. Finally, the Tunisian colonial experience had not been as traumatic as that of Algeria and independence was by and large negotiated rather than won at the point of a gun. Consequently, post-independence politics were neither militarized nor particularly radicalized, with the unity of the nation occupying greater status as a motif than any more developed and potentially divisive ideological positions.

FROM CORPORATISM TO REFORM

Given Bourguiba's preference for avoiding ideological extremes which threatened the harmony of the party and the society it was supposedly representing, it is hardly surprising that the socialist experiment in Tunisia was relatively short-lived. The drive for collectivization was conducted under the supervision of the Minister for Finance and Planning, Ahmed Ben Salah. As Ben Salah gathered more power into his own hands, influential members of the party elite grew jealous, joining forces with those sections of the national organizations whose interests were threatened by the diminution of private property. Together (and not without some help from the

World Bank), they convinced Bourguiba that collectivization was of dubious economic value and that Ben Salah was using it to build himself a power-base within the UGTT that could threaten the president's own authority. In 1969, just five years after the Neo-Destour had changed its name to the Parti Socialiste Destourien (PSD), socialism was, to all intents and purposes, abandoned as a guiding economic strategy. What was left was an essentially mixed economy but one in which the state had almost incidentally assumed control of the major economic activities, leaving an unsupported private sector to struggle as best as it could in a maze of state-controlled prices and distribution networks.

Bourguiba had originally been sympathetic to the private sector, favouring western investment and trade with Europe. His priority, however, had been the initial decolonization of the economy, expropriating colonial assets and 'Tunisifying' administration. The early years after independence saw him trying to balance strategic nationalization of public utilities with a desire to reassure foreign investors and the domestic private sector. The socialist experiment had resulted from the weakness of the latter and Bourguiba's perception that industrialization would require the helping hand of the state. When that failed, he turned to international finance to fund his development programmes, relying on an abundance of oil revenues, migrant labour remittances and cheap loans. To some extent, the private sector was able to benefit from tax incentives and credit facilities which enabled it to become more export-oriented but not income-generating. With insufficient attention being paid to the state's own burgeoning role in price supports, controls and subsidies, Tunisian manufacturing industry and hydrocarbons exports grew impressively on paper; however, this growth was neither competitive nor sustainable. Production was over-concentrated in both geographic and product-type terms, exacerbating regional inequalities and changing the structure of employment. Urban migration and a preference for industrial investment led to the neglect of agriculture and a growing food import bill. The government was meanwhile injecting cash into the growing number of loss-making State Owned Enterprises (SOEs) and attempting to offset the problems of poverty created by rural-urban migration, a high birth rate and growing unemployment by handing out subsidies through the Caisse Général de Compensation (CGC). Wage pressure in the hydro-carbon industries spread through the economy, increasing the public sector wage bill and in turn boosting demand for imports. By the early 1980s the economy was in serious trouble, overly-dependent on oil revenues, over-extended in foreign borrowings and unable to develop a domestic base that could either absorb the labour or export a diverse and competitive range of goods.

This tale of woes, it must be said, was not unique to Tunisia and, more generally, affected the developing world pursuing early import substitution industrialization policies (including those in the Arab world). For Tunisia, however, the economic crisis was accompanied by political stagnation that derived from the combination of corporatist structures and Bourguiba's personalized rule. The Ben Salah episode had exposed the conflicting interests of the national organizations and their representatives in the party itself. While the UGTT felt aggrieved over the diminution of its influence, the Union Tunisienne de l'Industrie, du Commerce et de l'Artisanat (UTICA), which approximates to an employers' federation, saw new opportunities in government policies to undo the socialist measures through a limited economic liberalization. The same party old-guard which had seen Ben Salah's socialism as a threat, now perceived a new generation of economic liberals to be challenging their position. When Bourguiba arranged to be elected as President for Life in 1975, there emerged a growing section of the party hierarchy which demanded political reforms and a reduction in the personalization of power. Since open opposition was not tolerated, unofficial opposition bodies such as Ben Salah's *Mouvement de l'Unité Populaire* (MUP) and Ahmad Mestiri's *Mouvement des Démocrates Socialistes* (MDS) began to spring up in exile or as semi-underground organizations.

Bourguiba's response was double-edged. On the one hand, he allowed the security forces to ruthlessly track down, harass, arrest and imprison known opposition personalities who operated outside the PSD. On the other, and to control the party itself, he centralized power still more firmly in his own hands, playing the various factions off against one another, acting as arbiter in their disputes, and issuing edicts in an ever more unpredictable manner. In particular, he chose to keep the succession issue high up on the agenda. By the 1980s, he was already in his eighties and it was clear that a designated successor, or at least a clearly established way of appointing such a person, was needed to preserve stability during any change of regime. Bourguiba was fearful, however, that any appointed successor would be able to build up a power-base to rival his own. Thus, he repeatedly built up personalities from the party, only to undermine and replace them later. Consequently, potential successors became wary of pushing themselves forward in case they should be wooed and finally wasted by the increasingly senile president.

By 1986 the corporatist system had decayed into political immobilism and growing authoritarianism. The national organizations had begun to recognize and develop their contradictory interests and, when the PSD failed to mediate those interests adequately with the state, opposition to the regime began to surface in the open. Workers' strikes in 1977 and riots in 1978 had brought some minor political concessions, including the formal end of the one-party state (the Parti Communiste Tunisien becoming the only other party allowed to operate legally). But the lack of any real channel through which dissatisfaction could be voiced had added to the frustrations of consolidating class interests (notably the UGTT on the one hand and middle-class business interests on the other) and liberal intellectuals who demanded political reform. The party old-guard were equally dissatisfied with reformist tampering of the economy which threatened to erode their own status. Within the party, internal dissent was rife over the direction which policy should take to resolve the economic crisis. In any case, the party was incapable of achieving anything of substance without Bourguiba's own approval. To add to its woes, the PSD was faced with a rising tide of Islamist opposition. The party's ideological bankruptcy, corruption and immobilism stood in sharp contrast to the alternative 'authentic' agenda for social reconstruction proposed by the unrecognized Mouvement de la Tendance Islamique, whose membership figured prominently in the 1978 general strike and the bread riots of 1984.

Bourguiba's subsequent persecution of the Islamists was ruthless. He attempted to avert the instability caused by the economic crisis by closing in on the opposition and staging show trials against their leaders. His timing proved to be abysmal. In 1986, a stand-by agreement was agreed with the IMF and the World Bank which committed the country to a Structural Adjustment Programme (SAP) that included further tough and inevitably unpopular austerity measures. Foreign reserves had fallen to dismal levels and, in return for an IMF compensatory fund facility and stand-by credit to support the budget, the government agreed to reduce the budget deficit significantly, restrain growth in the money supply, and embark on a programme of whole-sale economic reform. With tensions rising and with a government that was too weak to advance convincingly on the road to reform, it would only be a matter of time before Bourguiba was displaced.

THE ONSET OF REFORM

President Zine el Abidine Ben Ali came to power in Tunisia via a constitutional coup on the night of 6 November 1987 and launched a new era for the country characterized by profound economic liberalization and a corresponding process of political change.[1]

The structural adjustment programme in Tunisia has been implemented over the course of three development plans. The Seventh Development Plan (1987–1991) was intended to achieve macro-economic stability and to put in place initial structural changes that would pave the way for consolidating deeper liberalization measures in the Eighth Plan (1992–96). Thus a sharp reduction in the budget deficit, the control of inflation, financial sector reform and trade liberalization would be followed by legislative arrangements to encourage foreign investment, an accelerated privatization programme, development of capital and equity markets, and closer integration of Tunisian trade into world, and especially European, markets. The Eighth plan also focused on developing human resources, among other things improving the educational and skills base of the labour force. The Ninth Development Plan (1997–2001) is intended to all but complete the liberalization process and take Tunisia to developed nation status by the turn of the century.

Broadly speaking, Tunisia's SAP has been a success, at least if one judges it in terms of economic growth, increased diversity of production and exports, rising living standards and the restored financial credibility of the government. By 1996, the country ranked 69th on the UN's Human Development Index, way ahead of neighbours Algeria (85th) and Morocco (117th), and 37th on the Economic Freedom index. The American Heritage Foundation declared the country to be in the category of 'wholly liberalized economies', along with France, Germany and Italy among others (*Conjuncture* 1995). GNP per capita, at over $5000, is within the realms of Europe's poorer periphery, and less than 6 per cent of the population live below the official poverty line. The Seventh Development Plan saw an average annual growth rate of 4.3 per cent, despite the problems created by the Gulf War, poor agricultural performance and declining oil-sector output. Exports grew at an average of 9 per cent per annum; non-energy exports by more than 10 per cent per annum and demonstrated increasing diversity (manufacturing exports grew by 13.4 per cent per annum) (Nsouli *et al.* 1993: 39–41). The budget deficit was reduced from 5.3 per cent of GDP in 1986 to 3.5 per cent in 1991, and some progress was made in terms of debt reduction and public sector reform. However, overall levels of external debt remained a problem[2], as did low investment rates, high unemployment levels and bureaucratic obstruction to privatization. Overall, a 1992 study concluded that the Tunisian economy was 40–50 per cent liberalized (Larbi 1993: 14–23).

The Eighth Development Plan accelerated the pace of structural reform, despite growing public awareness of its pitfalls inside Tunisia. Urgency was added by the fact that in 1994 the country became a net energy importer for the first time in many years. Privatization still proceeded much more slowly than hoped, although sixty public enterprises had been wholly or partially privatized by 1995. The pace flagged in 1996 and was only revived in 1998 after intense pressure from the IMF and World Bank. Likewise, financial reforms inspired a much enlivened bourse to expand its operations, only to become overheated in 1996 and to suffer a subsequent period of stagnation. To broaden its trading operations, Tunisia joined the GATT and GATS, and signed an Association Agreement with the EU, opening its markets to free competition and abolishing import controls and tariffs such that, by 1997, the government could claim that trade was 96 per cent liberalized (Merdassi 1997). The dinar has been made almost fully convertible, prices are almost fully deregulated, the country has been fully rehabilitated as a debtor nation and has returned successfully to the international capital markets, and the budget deficit has been kept to below 3 per cent of GDP.

If all this seems just a little too good to be true, it is. There have been substantial social costs for this macro-economic success, despite government efforts to provide social transfers that mitigate against the worst side effects of the reforms. Official unemployment rates hover around 15–17 per cent, although unofficial figures are much higher. Education has become increasingly selective, with social connections and ability to pay playing an ever more important role (Simon 1996: 20), the population with access to health care has fallen (World Bank 1996) and, while wages have risen faster than prices, so too has taxation. Nonetheless, during the decade to 1995, real per capita income rose by 1.8 per cent per annum (compared to a regional average of −2 per cent).

THE ROLE OF THE STATE AND THE SAP

One may legitimately ask why Ben Ali's regime has been so much more successful than Bourguiba's in implementing reform. Although the extent of the crisis in 1987 would suggest that there was little option but to finally and wholeheartedly embrace full-scale reform, the answer lies much more in the political reconstruction carried out by Ben Ali which ensured that a reduction in the economic prowess of the state did not equate to political reduction: in fact, Ben Ali consolidated the power of the state relative to other political forces, enabling him to then put the weight of the state behind the economic reforms, to quash any social or political opposition, and to nurture the industrial and commercial bourgeoisie such that they could finally play their full role in developing the private sector.

The new president was not alone in recognising that economic reform was vital if his regime was to survive. Economic liberals in both the PSD and the state machinery were convinced that the combination of excessive and inefficient state interference in the economy, and Bourguiba's legacy of persistent and arbitrary political intervention in policy-making both had to be eliminated. They were opposed, however, on three fronts: by the PSD party old-guard, by the legal and illegal opposition parties and by an alienated section of the population represented not least by the Islamist MTI.

Ben Ali began by reforming the PSD in such a way as to undermine the power-base of the party old guard while establishing his own. His own roots were not in the party but in the army and the Interior Ministry and he could ill-afford to have the party lined-up against him. In fact, his choice of a constitutional rather than a bloody route to power, his promises of national political reform and renewal, and his strong leadership after the vacillations of Bourguiba, gave him tremendous initial popular appeal and the younger and liberal elements of the party were easily brought on board. Ben Ali immediately assumed the chairmanship of the PSD political bureau (the party 'cabinet' which had run parallel to the government cabinet). He reduced its size, excluding most of the old Bourguibists, and introducing his own ex-military or interior ministry and technocratic personnel. By contrast, he increased the membership of the next tier of party organization, the central committee, from 90 to 200 members, 125 of whom were appointed by himself. Only 22 members of the 1986 central committee remained in office by August 1988.

The president also initiated a recruitment drive to introduce young Tunisians to the party who were unencumbered with any out-dated ideological baggage. He changed the party's name, abandoning the word 'Destour' in all but the Arabic translation. The new name, the Rassemblement Constitutionnel Démocratique (RCD), emphasized the commitment to a new political era. Opposition personalities were encouraged to defect to the RCD with promises of position and status. Finally, and perhaps most importantly, Ben Ali cut the official party representation in the government cabinet, even though he arranged for his own election to the party presidency.

This last move began the process of reducing the influence of the party on the state while simultaneously retaining the party's own dependence on the beneficence of the presidency. Thus Ben Ali advanced the relative autonomy of the state from class interests other than its own. The taming of the party continued after the 1989 national and presidential elections. With an overwhelming mandate for himself,[3] Ben Ali was able to now enlarge the political bureau, bringing in pro-liberalization technocrats like Mohammed Ghannouchi and even political independents like Hamouda Ben Slama and Habib Boulares. The highest organ of the party was now packed with Ben Ali's men, while the party cells at the bottom of hierarchy were made up of as much as 60 per cent new pro-reform members. The middle and low-level management ranks were to remain loyal to the old guard, but the president had behind him both the most senior bodies and the tide of popular appeal.

The second area of political change introduced by Ben Ali, which also ultimately served to reinforce the autonomy of the state, was wider political and electoral reform. In May 1988, a new law authorized the establishment of new political parties. In a deliberate attempt to exclude the only mass-based movement which might represent a genuine challenge, the law stipulated that no party could organize on the basis of race, religion, language or region, thereby preventing the MTI from being formally recognized. The introduction of the multi-party system was followed by piecemeal reforms of the electoral code, designed to chip away at the inevitability of comprehensive RCD victories in national and municipal elections. The reforms had not proceeded far enough in 1989 to prevent the RCD from winning all 141 seats in the national assembly, but new measures, which were introduced in time for the 1994 elections, allowed the opposition parties to divide 19 seats among them on the basis of their proportion of the national vote. Needless to say, the RCD again won all 144 constituency seats in a system which was basically rigged to ensure that no party could achieve a position that would challenge the regime but that the image of multi-party democracy was maintained as opposition parties fought one another rather than the RCD.

This image was crucial for Ben Ali. The third part of his strategy was to recreate the illusion of national harmony and consensus that had under-pinned Bourguiba's early corporatist legitimacy. To this end he had sponsored the National Pact in 1988, a document derived from widespread consultation between the government, the opposition, national organizations, and pressure groups. Even the outlawed MTI was included in the debate which preceded the publication of the pact, and all the organizations and parties subsequently committed themselves to it, including the RCD and the government itself. The document confirmed the Arab and Islamic character of the state, the liberal Code of Personal Status (which enshrined the legal emancipation of women), and asserted that the constitution provided for free elections, freedom of organization and association, the separation of powers, the rule of law, protection of human rights and basic liberties, and the locating of sovereignty in the people. It stated that this constitution had been violated by the practices of the previous regime but that, under the new president's leadership, the country would be returned to the democratic and pluralist system originally intended. The document was Ben Ali's attempt to re-incorporate all the organizations and institutions of the country into a political consensus. The Islamists committed themselves to the secular nature of government and the legal emancipation of women, while the Communists accepted the Islamic character of the country. Continuity with a corporatist past was apparently reconciled with changes that introduced democracy. The government promised a multi-party political system while the opposition parties were placed in the position of seeming to be unpatriotic and destructive if they opposed government policies.

The National Pact ultimately proved to be the illusory political tool that it was. Despite efforts to revive it in subsequent years, it all but collapsed under the weight of Ben Ali's refusal to accelerate genuine political reform and his ultimate resort to using the internal security forces to control the opposition. At the time that it was devised, however, it did serve to reunite the country temporarily at a time when the succession could have proved to be destabilizing.

The essential point here was that the introduction of multi-party politics was not intended to equate with full-scale democracy.

146

Rather, the collectivity of legal parties would replace the single party of the PSD era. The RCD would become increasingly dependent on the state to retain its privileged position and its ability to distribute patronage. Any complacency on the part of the party old-guard would be knocked out by the need to compete with the other smaller parties. However, while these could compete with one another, and to a token extent with the RCD, they could not challenge the state itself. The smaller parties were themselves divided between, on the one hand, leftist and communist parties whose appeal had declined rapidly in the wake of the collapse of the Soviet Union and the blow to their ideology, and on the other, liberal, bourgeois parties whose economic interests fell broadly in line with those of the government. Such centrist parties were generally offshoots of the Neo-Destour, built around disgruntled individuals and without mass appeal or national organizational structures. Any party which had a genuine capacity to mobilize mass support, such as the MTI, remained banned. Equally, the government sought to prevent elements of the UGTT from breaking away to form a class-based party. When Islamists standing as independents won at least 13 per cent of the vote in the 1989 national elections, Ben Ali's response was to launch a violent and vicious attack, arresting, imprisoning and torturing the membership. Likewise, as the leadership of the secular opposition have perceived the fraudulent nature of the president's reforms, they too have been increasingly subjected to the harsh hand of the security forces.

With the RCD and the secular opposition engaged in competition with one another, albeit weighted heavily in favour of the president's own party, the state was able to rise above the fray and move ahead with its economic liberalization. The limited political reforms served to deflect the most intense grievances and to buy popular support for the president as he tried to introduce the potentially traumatic economic reforms. Ben Ali used successive cabinet reshuffles to ease the remaining RCD old-guard and conservative Bourguibists out of the government and to move in his own technocrats and political allies from the security forces and the Interior Ministry. Thus he backed-up his 'change-management team', including reformist figures such as Ahmed Smaoui, Sadok Rabah, Mohammed Ghannouchi and Ismail Khelil with military colleagues such as Abdallah Kallel, Chadli Neffarti, Abdelhamid Escheikh and Habib Ammar. The highest levels of government had become a virtually autonomous coterie of pro-economic liberalization figures who carried with them control over the coercive capacities of the state and who, equally, dominated the highest tiers of the RCD organization.

Ironically, it was not the uncomfortable side-effects of economic reform which revealed the true nature of this political change, but the popular, and specifically the Islamist response to the Gulf War of 1990–91. Until then, observers had noted approvingly the very limited new press freedoms, the release of political prisoners and the minuscule improvements in the electoral laws. The promise of further political liberalization was believed by many to be evidence that economic reform inevitably brought with it new standards of political accountability and transparency. There had been little serious popular opposition to the SAP due to a number of factors. Firstly, Ben Ali's commitment to the programme brought a new certainty and clarity of direction to economic policy-making that was a relief after the uncertainty of previous years. Second, the programme had been introduced as a result of domestic decision-making and was not strictly-speaking an imposition of the IMF. For this reason, it did not carry the stigma of being an act of 'neo-imperialism' as did similar programmes elsewhere. Thirdly, Tunisia began its SAP with a relatively large middle class and a small proportion of the population already living in poverty. The programme was designed, especially in its later stages, to protect the poorest elements through targeted social transfers at the expense of squeezing the middle classes. To some extent, the effects of increased and regularized taxation, the lifting of price subsidies, and the loss of job security caused by reform of the *Code de Travail* were offset by new investment opportunities for the small saver, greater choice of consumer products, and the generally freer and rapidly modernising economic environment. Fourthly and finally, the government made it clear that, while greater public debate over many issues was desirable, the direction of economic policy was not to be challenged. Careful compromises were made over public sector wage increases, and the UGTT was included in consultations over labour policy, but serious challenges were not to be tolerated.

The ugly face of this new state-civil society relationship became evident when the Islamists, who had reformed themselves into a still illegal party, *Nahda*, led demonstrations objecting to the government's failure to support Saddam Hussein against 'Western aggression' in the Persian Gulf. Ben Ali had initially attempted to placate popular opinion but when his ministers pointed out how this was damaging economic relations with the developed world, the government proceeded to ban critical newspapers and use the opportunity to clamp down on Islamist activity. Over the following three years, *Nahda* was all but destroyed, its membership imprisoned and, in some instances, executed, the justification being that a radical wing of *Nahda* had adopted a violent strategy of its own. The secular oppositions soon realized that they too were vulnerable to the arbitrary exercise of force on the part of the internal security forces and that the government was implementing a reversal of political reform even as it continued to promise piecemeal electoral changes. Today, the Tunisian government is a frequent target of criticisms from international human rights organizations for its persecution not just of Islamist leaders, but also of legal, secular opposition figures who dare to speak out against the regime. Far from introducing democratization, the government is accused of reconstituting the authoritarianism of Bourguiba's final years, although in a possibly more effective and thus more sinister form.

For its part, the president has claimed that the state has a principal responsibility to preserve the political stability of the country during a period when profound economic transformation could easily be disrupted by vested interests and subversive forces. There has been some sympathy for this argument from the middle classes and bourgeois forces which can benefit from economic reform and which view the Algerian scenario as being frighteningly close to home. The argument can only hold, however, for as long as the economic reform process continues to bring opportunities and economic growth to offset its more painful aspects.

This brings us back to the issue of the success or failure of the economic reform process, upon which the future of Ben Ali's regime must to a large extent rest. In order to differentiate his regime from that of his predecessor short of introducing genuine power-sharing, Ben Ali must at least provide the economic dividend. Yet it seems that some of the most difficult tests are still ahead of him.

The Association Agreement with Europe represents a severe challenge for the economy, despite the *mise à niveau* arrangements to prepare Tunisian products for the competition. It has been estimated that as many as 2,000 Tunisian firms are likely to fold (*Middle East Economic Digest* 1995: 3), placing heavy strains on employment figures, the balance of trade and public support for free trade. The EU is applying strong pressure on Tunisia to clean up its human rights record and to introduce appropriate levels of transparency, financial accounting and good governance. Tunisian firms still lag behind their European counterparts in publishing regular, independently audited accounts; banks still carry burdensome capital to loan ratios and the government has a long way to go before the EU endorses its political accountability.

There is also evidence that the reform process is now meeting retrenched opposition from those bureaucratic and party elements which can stand little further erosion of their own positions. The Association Agreement with Europe has tied the country into a set of political conditionalities which aim to introduce criteria of good governance and accountability as well as requiring the technocratic upgrading of management at both the firm and national level. Not only do the party old guard find it hard to swallow being upbraided by their EU counterparts, they also recognize that the technocratization of the management of resources threatens their own powers and position. Until now, for example, the privatization and public sector reform processes have been managed without massive lay-offs. As foreign competition digs in, however, it is likely that the employment profiles of companies will have to be considerably slimmed down, inevitably bringing serious opposition from the trade unions, but also quite possibly from the party old guard as well. If the pressures of association are felt too strongly in an economy which has otherwise survived the liberalization process quite well, elements within the party may yet regroup, with public support, and take on the government openly.

Patronage remains an issue for party and state alike. Although the state has disengaged from some areas of economic activity, it has retained its right to control others and has redefined, rather than reduced, its interventionary role. Government financial supports and shelters are awarded on a discretionary basis, maintaining a dependency linkage between the state and the private sector. Business associations and trade unions are tightly, if informally, controlled, and areas of economic autonomy are not allowed to translate into political contest. Profitability in the market is enhanced by constructive relations with the state and political contacts retain their usefulness in accessing licences, subsidies and contracts (a phenomenon known as *copinage*). Eva Bellin has described this as the state retaining a 'gate-keeping' function (Bellin 1995: 144) which incidentally serves to mobilize the growing entrepreneurial class behind the state. One might also argue that, while the RCD is allowed to act as one channel for the distribution of patronage, smaller parties must first earn their spurs of loyalty to the regime before they can do likewise. Consequently, the smaller parties have little of tangible worth to offer the public, reducing their chances of drawing support to challenge the regime and again reducing the efficacy of the multi-party system.

A final point in this state/economic reform equation relates to the impact of liberalization on civil society and its relations with the state. Advanced communications and interaction with Europe and the rest of the industrialized world are bound to have an impact upon civil society's aspirations and expectations. Equally, the missionaries of democracy and good governance have Tunisia's trading and lending partners on their side. Modern technology makes it increasingly difficult for the regime to control access to ideas or the linking up of organizations and associations within the country with their counterparts elsewhere. It is difficult to see how the regime can delay political liberalization indefinitely, given its current economic strategy.

TUNISIA IN COMPARATIVE PERSPECTIVE

The Tunisian experience offers us a number of insights into the political mechanisms of economic reform, although, inevitably, there are some features of the liberalization process which have been specific to Tunisia. There is little doubt that Tunisia started its structural adjustment with a number of advantages relative to some of its MENA neighbours. Firstly, it had a small population (around 9 million), of which only a small proportion lived in poverty. Bourguiba's liberal social policies had enabled the country to keep population growth rates low and urbanization had not resulted in the sprawling slum-lands typical of Algiers or Cairo. Secondly, Tunisian society was relatively homogeneous, with a large middle class able to absorb the belt-tightening pressures of austerity programmes, and even to see opportunities for itself in privatizations and the opening of financial markets. Thirdly, geographical proximity to Europe, and a political culture that absorbs rather than rejects the influences of the developed world, have sustained exports of goods (and labour) and imports of technology and modern business practices. Moreover, hydrocarbon exports have continued to cushion the budget, although with less effect as domestic energy needs have risen.

All these factors have smoothed the way for Ben Ali and his technocrats, while others have had to contend with widespread and endemic poverty, ethnic or sectarian challenges to the territorial integrity, rapidly expanding populations, chronic resource scarcity and even proximity to the running-sore of the Arab-Israeli conflict.

However, one can see echoes of Ben Ali's political strategy across the region. The emasculation of single parties by increasingly autonomous states has been evident, for example, in Syria (with Assad's creation of the Progressive National Front), Egypt (when Sadat divided the Arab Socialist Union into three competing parties), and Algeria (where Chadli Ben Jedid trimmed the higher organs of the FLN and legalized alternative political parties). Limited and tightly-controlled political liberalization across the region has not resulted in democratic government. It has, however, incorporated new business elites and political liberals into the public perception of *government*, thus implicating them in responsibility for economic strategies over which they have little real control. This political tactic on the part of an elevated *change management team* (Nelson 1993: 436) relies on the weakness of organized liberal, bourgeois and even leftist opposition groups. Parties and movements which have genuine mass appeal, notably Islamist groups, are not simply excluded from these new *democratic bargains* (Brumberg 1989), they are ruthlessly pursued and eliminated in the name of national security, national interest and the preservation of national unity during a time of crisis. The party old-guards who would otherwise resist economic reforms in order to maintain their own political and economic rent-accruing status, are disempowered by the need to compete in a political arena with alternative parties, not only for public support but, more importantly, for the patronage of the regime itself.

Political liberalization across the region has, as in Tunisia, relapsed into authoritarianism in moments of popular resistance to the economic reforms themselves and their impact, as well as to the selective nature of meaningful political enfranchisement. Bread riots, so-called austerity protests (Seddon 1993: 88–112) and other forms of social unrest in Morocco (1980, 1981 and 1984), Algeria (1988), Egypt (1977, 1984), Jordan (1989 and 1996) and Sudan (1985) led the regime to draw on the military, with which it is organically integrated, to enforce its authority. Ironically, the Algerian example illustrated that when Chadli ben Jedid's political and economic reforms began to take on a life of their own, threatening the heart of the regime itself, the military actually stepped directly into the arena and removed the ill-fated President. Equally, when Bourguiba proved unwilling to implement the necessary reforms at all, the military still stepped in to remove him and replace him with its own man. The Turkish experience in 1997 similarly saw the military stepping in to remove an Islamist government which strayed from the path laid out by the ruling military-industrial alliance. In other words, the political manoeuvrings of the Middle Eastern regimes amount to a delicate balance between economic and political reform, the guarantor of which is ultimately, and in the absence of democratic forms of accountability, the military. In Tunisia's case, the army's job in preserving a stable political environment in which economic liberalization can take place unheeded, has been made easier by a political culture that abhors the extremism of the more militant Islamists and by a relatively large middle class which has more to lose by the overthrow of the system than by its reform.

CONCLUSION

Ben Ali's corporatism, like that of his predecessor, is based around the state-party-civil society relationship. Unlike Bourguiba, however, he has been able to release the state from its dependence on what had become a reactionary, immobile and ideologically stale party. He has done this by introducing competition at the level of political parties, even while preventing competition at the level of real power-holding. Bourguiba's regime relied on a party power-base while Ben Ali's depends upon a convenient alliance of the technocratic and entrepreneurial bourgeoisie on the one hand, and the military and security apparatus on the other. Despite his attempts to dress this up as a revived corporatism and an effort to restore the triangular harmony, his multi-party corporatism is fraught with contradictions. His limited political opening generated new, and revived old, expectations of greater freedom and rapid democratization. His regime's repression of genuine competition for power undermines his efforts to reconstitute a national consensus and makes it look ever more akin to simple authoritarianism than to any modernized form of the populist state (Ehteshami and Murphy 1997, Murphy 1999).

The resemblance of Tunisia's fragile experiment with political liberalization to those of its MENA neighbours is clear. Democratization has failed to take root in the face of the unwillingness of regimes to cede genuine power lest it disturb the route to economic reform. Economic liberalization itself is subject to delicate equations that seek to preserve the security of the regime in power and sustain its access to rent. Thus, the reformulation of the state itself is necessary, with redefinition of its role, its component parts and its relationship to the ruling elites.

NOTES

1 As the old president slept, Ben Ali called a group of doctors to declare Bourguiba mentally incapable of performing the functions of office. As recently-appointed Prime Minister, Ben Ali was then able to step into his shoes and his office.
2 As a proportion of GDP, external debt was reduced from 63 per cent in 1986 to 51 per cent in 1991, and the debt servicing ratio fell from 28 per cent of current receipts to 20 per cent. Total debt, however, increased from $6 billion to $7.5 during the same period (Nsouli *et al.* 1993).
3 Ben Ali was the only candidate, unsurprisingly winning 99 per cent of the vote. While observers were inevitably cynical about the 'fairness' of the election, they could not deny that Ben Ali was enjoying a political honeymoon which meant that no opposition candidate could have hoped to match his popularity. Even the opposition conceded that the election gave the president a vote of confidence.

REFERENCES

Bellin, E. (1995) 'Civil Society in Formation: Tunisia', in Norton (1995).

Brumberg, D. (1989) 'Democratic Bargains and the Politics of Economic Stabilization', *MESA Annual Conference Paper*.

Conjuncture (1995) 'La Tunisie à L'heure du Libéralisme Economique', no. 192.

Ehteshami, Anoushiravan and Emma C. Murphy (1997) 'Transformation of the Corporatist State in the Middle East', *Third World Quarterly*, vol. 17, no. 4: 753–72.

Larbi, E. (1993) 'Tunisia's Approach toward the Advanced Developing Country Threshold', *Finances et Développement au Maghreb*, no. 12.

Larif-Béatrik, A. (1988) *Édification étatique et environnement culturel: Le personnel politico-administratif dans la Tunisie contemporaine*, Paris: Publisud.

Merdassi, F. (1997) Secretary of State for International Co-operation and Investment at the Royal Institute for International Affairs. RIIA/UK Government/EC conference, *Opportunities for Investment in the Mediterranean Region*, London.

Middle East Economic Digest (1995), 19 May, London.

Murphy, Emma C. (1999) *Economic and Political Change in Tunisia: From Bourguiba to Ben Ali*, Basingstoke: Macmillan.

Nelson, J. (1993) 'The Politics of Economic Transformation: Is Third World Experience Relevant in Eastern Europe?', in *World Politics*, vol. 45, no. 3.

Niblock, T. and E. Murphy (eds, 1993) *Economic and Political Liberalization in the Middle East*, London: British Academic Press.

Norton, A.R. (ed., 1995) *Civil Society in the Middle East*, vol. 1, Leiden: E.J. Brill.

Nsouli, S., S. Eken, P. Duran, G. Bell and Z. Yücelik (1993) The Path to Convertibility and Growth: The Tunisian Experience, *Occasional Paper* 109, Washington D.C.: International Monetary Fund.

Seddon, D. (1993) 'Austerity Protests in Response to Economic Liberalization in the Middle East', in Niblock and Murphy (1993).

Simon, C. (1996) 'Maghreb Nations on a Steep Learning Curve', *Le Monde International*, (20 June).

World Bank (1996) *World Development Report*, New York: Oxford University Press for World Bank.

Chapter Seven

International and Regional Environments and State Transformation in Some Arab Countries

Mustapha Al-Sayyid

INTRODUCTION

There has been a radical shift in public perceptions of the economic role of the state in most Arab countries in recent decades. In its *World Development Report* of 1997, the World Bank identified five main roles for the state: direct producer, partner, catalyst, facilitator, and regulator in the economy (World Bank 1997a). In recent years, there has been a movement away from the first of these roles (direct producer) and in favour of the others. This shift of emphasis has been noticeable in radical or revolutionary Arab regimes as well as in conservative or moderate ones.[1]

The common explanation for this shift in public policies is the combination of the 'fiscal crisis of the state' brought about in the 1980s by a drastic fall in external resources (petroleum exports, workers' remittances and foreign aid), and the determination of advanced capitalist countries to resolve their accumulation crisis through increased exports of capital and consumer goods to developing countries. The debt crisis in the South and the later fall of Socialist regimes gave the North, arguably, an opportunity to reshape the economies of both the South and the East in such a way as to integrate them more tightly into the global capitalist market. One basic condition for the success of such integration was to limit the role of the state in these countries to the bare minimum required for guaranteeing the free movement of capital, goods, and services and promoting the interests of transnational corporations as the new dominant actors in the international economy (Frank 1984). Leaders of Arab countries, faced by the spectre of a serious debt crisis or

156

declining oil revenues, thus found themselves constrained in their choice of economic policy. Lacking much enthusiasm for a policy of 'disengagement' of the state, they had to accept recommendations of international financial institutions, supported by the advanced capitalist countries, in order to avoid further hardship for their population with potentially severe internal consequences (Ayubi 1995). Other explanations of this shift of policy have stressed, in particular, the economic interests of the state bourgeoisie, which has found in the encouragement of the private sector and joint ventures with foreign enterprises an effective strategy to perpetuate its privileges and to move away from simple control to direct ownership of the means of production (Mursi 1976, and Waterbury 1993 for another view).

This chapter examines those external political influences that have contributed to the shaping of the economic policy choices of the ruling groups in Arab countries since the 1970s. It draws examples from three countries, namely, Egypt, Tunisia and Jordan, which have been committed to a policy of economic liberalization for some time now. It argues that both the international and regional environments have impacted in several ways on this shift: by offering inducements; highlighting success stories; or even placing constraints on the implementation of certain development strategies. However, it suggests that both these (regional and international) environments contributed also to the adoption of the state-led model of development in the 1950s and 1960s, but reversed their directions after the mid-1980s in favour of a more liberal model.

In order to examine the impact of changing international and regional environments, first the shift in the economic roles of the state will be outlined, followed by a reference to the manifestations of this shift in the changing social backgrounds of senior state officials and their adoption of a new discourse. A detailed examination of the contribution of the external environment to this shift takes up the substantive part of the chapter. The chapter then concludes by suggesting that a rational choice model provides the best way of interpreting choices made by the policy-makers in this regard.

This task is fraught with methodological difficulties. State leaders, for instance, rarely admit that external forces unduly influence their decisions.[2] It is also hard to gain access to documents which might suggest the impact of such external forces.[3] Naturally, the governments of the countries in the South treat negotiations with foreign actors over domestic economic policies as sensitive and are concerned that disclosure of information about such negotiations could have an adverse effect on public opinion. Reflecting these difficulties, gauging the external political influences that might cause a transformation of the state is – at best – based on guesswork. This chapter is, therefore, limited to identifying external political conditions that were associated with a perceived shift in economic functions of the states in some Arab countries during the last two decades.

The three countries chosen for the purposes of this chapter represent important countries from three sub-regions in the Arab world, namely, the Arab Orient (or the Mashreq), the Nile Valley and the Maghreb. One of these, Egypt, had gone the farthest in the Arab world along the path of what was called a version of the socialist model of development, and was among the first to move away from it in the 1970s. The second, Tunisia, did not go that far during its socialist phase, but its former head of state was perhaps the first to declare the failure of the socialist model. By contrast, the third country, Jordan, was committed to free enterprise since its inception. The fact that it too experienced a transformation of its state functions supports the observation that the conditions which were associated with the adoption, and later abandonment, of the statist model, are common to a variety of countries in the South, despite their diverse histories of statehood, social background of their leaders and foreign policy alliances.

SIGNS OF A SHIFT

A brief examination of the economic history of the three countries indicates their espousal of a strategy of development assigning to the state and its public sector a leading role as early as the 1950s, with this strategy reaching its climax in the 1960s. The story of this strategy was detailed elsewhere (Owen 1992: 139–65; Ayubi 1997: 289–394), but it is important to note that such a strategy made sense at the time it was adopted.

Despite differences in their social backgrounds, political experience and foreign policy positions, the political leadership in all three countries agreed on the importance of the public sector and assigned a direct role to the state in providing economic growth. Some causes of this stance were unique to each country, while others were common to all three. The private sector was perceived to be incapable of shouldering the major responsibility for development. This is understandable in the case of Jordan, with its small market and short history of statehood (Ayubi 1997: 144–45). In the case of Tunisia, prior to independence, the private sector was dominated by French settlers (Harik and Sullivan 1992: 211). There were also signs of the weakness of the private sector in Egypt, long before army officers seized power in July 1952. Liquidity problems faced by Bank Misr, the major grouping of a nascent Egyptian capitalist class, were resolved only at the cost of the resignation of its founder (*Tal'at Harb*) in 1939 and the appointment by the government of his successor, in return for its support of the Bank at that difficult moment (Davis 1983). The Free Officers, as it is well-known, were not opposed in the 1950s to the growth of the private sector, but were convinced that the state had to step in, to help with the establishment of basic industries and to direct the development of the country (Mabro 1974: 110–15; Mursi 1987: 391).

It is important to bear in mind that, at the time, many other developing countries including several ex-colonies of the European powers in Asia, Africa and Latin America were pursuing similar state-led development paths. This applied not only to Algeria, Syria and Iraq in the Arab world, but also to Ghana, Guinea, Mali in Africa, Vietnam and North Korea in Asia, and Cuba in Latin America. Even regimes with a strong anti-leftist reputation such as those in South Korea, Brazil and even the conservative Arab monarchies of the Gulf region resorted to extensive state intervention in directing their course of economic development in the 1970s and the 1980s.

In general, state intervention in the economy between the 1950s and 1970s was justified on grounds of the modest size of the private sector, or its perceived incapacity to mobilize sufficient resources to generate and sustain growth and to improve the welfare of the masses. This general trend in what was then called the 'Third World' was enhanced in some countries by the positive view their leaders took of the performance of the socialist economies, which were believed to have outperformed growth in capitalist countries. The example of the Soviet Union, in particular, or even that of China, impressed a number of leaders in Middle Eastern, African, Asian and Latin American states. They credited socialism for its ability to transform Russia from an agrarian and backward society to that of a superpower in less than three decades following the Bolshevik Revolution. It was also fashionable, among leftist intellectuals in the countries of the South at the time, to compare China favourably with India. The former seemed to suffer no famines and enjoyed political stability, while the

159

latter continued to rely on international help in the 1960s to feed its population, and witnessed intense infighting among its Congress Party leaders. Although China, with its Cultural Revolution, was not immune from such intra-elite conflicts, the leadership (including Mao-Tse Tung, the Chairman of the Communist Party, and Chou En Lai, its Prime Minister) seemed firmly in command of the Chinese state (Karol 1973).

While acknowledging the difficulties encountered by the state-led model of economic development in the South in the 1970s, intellectuals and political leaders in the three countries under study (or more generally in the South) did not necessarily view it as a lost cause that should be abandoned.[4] The negative assessment of the state-led model of growth did not, in fact, herald in the 1980s any significant contraction of public sector in either of the three countries, notwithstanding the *infitah* or 'economic opening' rhetoric in Egypt and Tunisia and the proclaimed commitment to the development of the free entreprise in Jordan's five year plans (HKJ, various years).

The declared intention of moving to a different model of development was not therefore translated immediately into concrete measures to dismantle the public sector. In fact, the perceived shift in the economic role of the state in Egypt and Tunisia went through two stages. The first, extending from 1969 to 1986 in Tunisia and from 1974 to 1987 in Egypt, was marked mostly by a change in the rhetoric of public officials. In this phase, there was a general move away from extolling the leading role of the public sector to an admission of its shortcomings and articulation of the need to make the transition. Aware of the unpopularity of this transition, the state officials avoided calling the alternative model by its true name – capitalist model of development – to avoid also any of its negative connotations. Rather, the alternative model was described in most Arab countries, including Egypt, Tunisia and even Algeria in the 1980s as an *infitah*, or an economic and political opening, as though the discarded model could have loosened its ties to the international 'capitalist' market on which all these countries remained heavily dependent during their so-called socialist phase. During this period, some pieces of legislation were enacted in both countries with the specific purpose of encouraging the private sector and foreign investments, but their states remained, as before, the owners of productive enterprises and continued to assume some welfare functions (Fahmy 1988; Lawless and Findlay 1984). Public outrage at the impact of the early market reform measures, vividly expressed in Egypt in the January 1977 uprising and in Tunisia in the January 1978 and 1984 riots, was perhaps responsible for the slow progress of the *infitah* in practice. Since Jordan was committed since its establishment as a state to a free enterprise economy, there was no need for such rhetoric there. In fact, there are many indications that the role of the public sector was expanding in both Tunisia and Jordan in the 1970s. In Egypt, the absolute size of the public sector remained very large despite an impressive growth of the private sector in nearly all branches of economic activities.

The second phase in this 'transition' process came in the latter half of the 1980s in Jordan and Tunisia when more concrete measures were adopted to reduce the role of the state in resource management. These were followed in the 1990s by specific measures to privatize state owned enterprises. Although the Egyptian government committed itself to a similar approach in 1987, the move to a liberalized economy acquired more momentum in the 1990s. The landmark for the beginning of a shift in the state's macroeconomic management methods was the signing in all three countries of standby agreements with the International Monetary Fund and structural adjustment accords with the World Bank. In the case of Egypt, the first standby agreement of 1987 was followed, four years later, by a more comprehensive package with the IMF, called the Economic Reform and Structural Adjustment Program, together with an agreement on a structural adjustment loan with the World Bank in May 1991. Both Jordan and Tunisia have signed several agreements with the IMF and the World Bank. Closer cooperation between the two countries and these two international financial institutions accelerated in Tunisia after 1986 and in Jordan after 1990.[5] All three countries have received considerable support from the World Bank Group in particular, with Egypt receiving over five and a half billion US dollars during the period 1970–1997, and Tunisia getting over four billion dollars during the period 1985–1997 (World Bank 1996a: 188, 190). As for Jordan, the total financial flows from the World Bank Group have been estimated at just under 1.4 billion dollars during the period 1979–1996 (World Bank 1996b).

While the five roles suggested in the 1997 World Development Report (see above) are still very relevant in all three countries, there has been a shift in the relative importance of these functions. In particular, the role of the state as a direct provider of growth has been receding in favour of its role as a facilitator and regulator. Weakest of all, perhaps, is the state's role as a catalyst and partner for the private sector, trade unions and professional syndicates.

From an alternative perspective, it can be argued that, in fact, the states under discussion have been abandoning direct methods of capital accumulation in favour of private accumulation while doing little to increase their social legitimacy. By reducing their involvement in the direct provision of welfare, and not substituting similar arrangements for it, these states have, arguably, relinquished some of the foundations of their legitimacy.

Privatization programmes and falling public sector investment in the three countries are the most important signs of the gradual abandonment by the state of its role as a direct provider of investment. But privatization has not proceeded in any of the three countries at a pace that would be satisfactory to international financial institutions. It is hard to find many examples of the private sector-government partnership in Tunisia and Jordan due to the lack of sufficient data. In the case of Egypt, there are many examples of the partnership between state and private and foreign enterprises.[6] Moreover, the government's policy regarding the so-called strategic projects is predicated upon such partnerships.[7]

As mentioned earlier, the three states have expanded their function as facilitator and regulator in their respective economies by reducing bureaucratic hurdles for investment by the private sector and simplifying procedures for the conduct of import and export activities.

Finally, Tunisia presents a good example of the state as a catalyst in its attempt to promote a new kind of collective bargaining between workers and employers. Following the ousting of Habib ben Ashour, the historical leader of the General Federation of Tunisian Workers, known under its French acronym UGTT,[8] the Tunisian government strove to adapt the Federation to the new liberalized economic environment. In essence, this involved discouraging the old practice of centralized collective bargaining and replacing it with a sector-level and more decentralized system of negotiation with the Tunisian Union of Commerce, Trade and Handicrafts (UTICA).[9] In this way, by encouraging 'societal corporatism' in industrial relations, the state in Tunisia aimed at achieving and maintaining industrial peace during the tough period of adjustment (Christopher 1996: 177–201).

To sum up, this section has argued that the role of state as a direct provider of economic growth has been on the decline in Egypt, Tunisia and Jordan in recent years, while its other functions have become more prominent. In particular, the state has expanded its roles as a facilitator and regulator of economic activities. Simultaneously, however, the nature of regulation has changed as the state has at times removed restrictions on economic activity and substituted new ones for them.[10]

TRANSFORMED STATES?

Important though these changes were, they were not the only type of change these states experienced. In fact, they reflected a new kind of alliance at the top of the state, which replaced the old ones under the state-led development phase, and made state officials adopt a new discourse at variance with the one they used during the earlier period.

No detailed data is available on the social background of policy-makers in any of these three countries. However, it is probably safe to assume that the nature of the ruling coalition in Jordan has not experienced any major change. The royal family continues to rely on the Bedouin tribes and leaders of the major East Jordanian communities for grassroots support, despite the fact that economic reforms have taken their toll on the Bedouin areas in which some of the food riots took place. However, in contrast to the Jordanian cabinets of the 1950s and 1960s, formed mostly of politicians, the Jordanian cabinets of the 1980s and the 1990s are dominated by technocrats, many of whom hold doctorates in scientific disciplines from Western universities (particularly the UK and USA). Different communities are still represented in cabinets, like the Bedouins, Palestinians and other religious and ethnic groups, and the educational level of ministers has risen, as evidenced by the increase in the number of cabinet ministers who hold PhDs.[11] Moreover, premiership continues to be occupied by figures from families known for their support for the King.

In contrast to Jordan, Egypt and Tunisia have experienced notable changes in the relative positions of both labour and business groups in their ruling coalition. Trade unions were a principal partner of the bureaucratic bourgeoisie that ruled Tunisia after independence. Relations between these two partners suffered in the wake of worker unrest in 1978, 1984 and 1985. Powerful leaders were evicted from the UGTT and were replaced by others who were more willing to acquiesce to the new policies of structural adjustment. In the meantime, there has been a marked increase in interpenetration between the bureaucratic bourgeoisie and private entrepreneurs as the size of the Tunisian private sector has grown and the involvement of foreign enterprises in Tunisian economy has increased. As in Jordan, the presence of a good number of highly educated technocrats has been a major feature of the Tunisian governments since the 1980s, compared to the immediate post-independence period.

The changing composition of the ruling coalition has been even more remarkable in the case of Egypt. Workers provided Nasser's regime in the 1960s with an important social base, although their presence in the ruling coalition, made up principally of former military officers and civilian experts, was a ceremonial one. Under Sadat and more particularly under Mubarak, the position of trade unionists within the ruling coalition has become even more marginalized, specially in the aftermath of the demise of Sa'd Mohammed Ahmad, the powerful trade unionist who had combined the two posts of the head of the General Federation of Trade Unions of Egypt and the Minister of Labour (Posusney 1992: 29–98). On the other hand, businessmen have made their entry into the ruling coalition with the bureaucratic bourgeoisie as members of the cabinet and partners in policy-making, and are closely consulted on matters related to the economy and even some foreign policy issues. Constant interpenetration between government posts and leading positions in the private sector has created a symbiotic relationship between these two partners. Examples abound of former Prime Ministers and Ministers who have subsequently found lucrative jobs in major banks and big private sector or joint venture firms after they quit office. This interpenetration is also manifested in family and social links as sons of senior members of the government are usually powerful figures in the expanding private sector (*Al-Hay'a al-'amma li al-Este'lamaat* 1992).

The composition of the bureaucratic bourgeoisie itself in both Egypt and Tunisia has undergone important changes. This class had always included some radical members who were in favour of maintaining the state-led model of development, and who used a type of populist discourse. Those like Ben Saleh in Tunisia, Aziz Sidqi and leftist ministers under Sadat in Egypt, were gradually eliminated and replaced either by liberal-minded technocrats or by those who managed to perfect their metamorphosis from supporters of state socialism to ardent advocates of structural adjustment and liberalization of the economy. Hadi Nouira and Mzali in Tunisia and Atef Sidqi and Kamal Al-Ganzouri in Egypt are prominent examples in this respect.

The changing social background of the ruling coalition accompanied the shift from the state-led model of development to the more liberal model. It came gradually to reinforce the new policy choices. The elimination of the more radical elements from this coalition coincided with moments of strain experienced under the first model when it seemed to be running out of steam. This happened with the failure of the agricultural cooperative scheme in Tunisia and the sluggish growth of the Egyptian economy in the early 1970s, although the removal of the Nasserites in Egypt in May 1971 was provoked rather by their opposition to the late President Sadat's foreign policy initiatives. The constant element in the ruling coalitions in all three cases was the head of state who must have found it more expedient to bring to the government technocrats whose sympathies coincided with his new liberal positions on the economy.

Such changes in the composition of the ruling coalitions have also been duly reflected in the kind of public discourse they have adopted. In Tunisia, senior government officials started, in the 1980s, to emphasize the incapacity of the state to fulfil all citizens' aspirations, and highlighted the importance of individual initiative and responsibility. Their definition of state functions simply echoed conceptions of the international financial institutions.

The Egyptian ruling coalition adopted a similar discourse. President Mubarak moved away from his public commitment not to sell off the public sector and his denunciation of the IMF as a 'quack doctor' killing the patient with too strong a medicine. He later defended privatization of electric power stations and recognized reports of the IMF on the Egyptian economy as a testimony to the 'soundness of the government's economic policy' (Al-Ahram 2 May 1998; Wahba 1993: 51–62).

The new vocabulary, stressing individual initiative, flexible planning, economic reform and coping with changes in the international environment, is to be seen also in the introductory statements to the economic and social plans of Jordan signed by both the late King Hussein and the former Crown prince Hassan ben Talal (HKJ 1993).

REGIONAL AND INTERNATIONAL ENVIRONMENT

The preceding sections of this chapter have demonstrated the transformation in some Arab states, not only in terms of their economic policies, and the discourse their leaders have adopted, but also in the composition of their ruling coalition and alliances with different social groups and classes. This transformation has taken place within specific international and regional environments, which influenced the emergence among the state elite of a new perception of the role of the state, particularly with respect to the management of the economy, and facilitated in some cases (and obstructed in others) the implementation of these policies.

This section examines the concrete ways in which these two environments have helped or constrained state action during the last four decades. The regional environment of these states includes both the Arab and the Mediterranean regions. The latter links Arab states, particularly the three under study, to the countries of the European Union which have a major share in the foreign trade of both Egypt and Tunisia and, to lesser extent, Jordan. The following discussion suggests that, while the regional and international environments favoured the state-led strategy of development in the 1950s, 1960s and even 1970s, by the 1980s, changes in both international and regional environments made it almost impossible to continue with such a strategy. The discussion begins with an examination of the international environment which the Arab states faced in recent decades.

The International Environment

Stephan Haggard and Steven Webb have emphasized the importance of international influences in the process of economic adjustment. In particular, they identified three relevant factors: the conditionality bargain with international financial institutions; the existence of export opportunities; and external ideas and advice about policy (Haggard and Webb 1994: 25). The first and third of these influences will be examined in this section, the second will be dealt with in the context of the direct and indirect implications of oil price changes for the economies of the three countries.

Several actors in the international environment have influenced the perceptions of Arab state officials of the proper economic role of the state, offering them opportunities to carry out specific development strategies or setting constraints on the possibility of pursuing such strategies. The opportunities and the constraints were related, in particular, to the availability of economic and technical assistance which encouraged and facilitated the adoption of certain strategies instead of others. These actors included other states (with a positive or negative demonstration effect on Arab states), aid donors and international financial institutions.

Demonstration Effects

The choice of a particular development strategy and a specific model for the management of the economy is determined not only by factors such as the degree of state autonomy vis-à-vis other social classes and groups, and past experiences of the ruling groups and their foreign policy alliances, but also by the success or failure stories and experiences of development policies in other countries. The state-led model of economic and social development was seen by intellectuals in the South and by several of the leaders of newly-independent countries in the 1950s and the 1960s to be a more effective way of attaining structural changes in the economy and enhancing economic independence. Central planning and public ownership of the means of production, including cooperatives and collective farms, were considered basic elements of this model. Thus, the countries which first adopted this model exercised a positive demonstration effect on the leaders and intellectuals of other countries in the South. Arab countries were no exception to this. Mohammed Hasanein Heikal, who was a close confidant of the late President Nasser, recalled a long conversation between Gamal Abdel Nasser and Jawahar Lal Nehru, the then Prime Minister of India, about Indian planning, when they first met in 1954. He also spoke of Abdel Nasser's strong admiration for the Chinese model of development. Furthermore, Abdel Nasser was a close friend of Tito, the first President of Yugoslavia, and some observers have noted similarities between the structure of the Arab Socialist Union, Egypt's single mass organization in the 1960s, and the Socialist Alliance and its League of Communists in Yugoslavia (Heikal 1971: 275–338).

Difficulties of the state-led model became apparent in the 1970s with stagnation in the Soviet economy and society, the beginning of instability in Eastern Europe and India and the power conflicts within the Chinese leadership. By the 1980s, in fact, an alternative 'model' started to exercise a positive demonstration effect on Arab leaders. This was the model of the newly-industrialized countries in East Asia, which was portrayed to the Arab public as a free enterprise system, despite the strong role played by the state in South Korea, Taiwan and Singapore. Thus, writings abound in the Arab world about the Asian miracle (Mahboub 1993; Al-Sayyid 1991a and 1991b; Handoussa, 1997). Simultaneously, contacts with the East Asian governments at high official levels were growing.[12] There is little doubt that these contacts expanded largely out of convictions, formed over the years,

about the relevance to Arab countries of the development experiences
of these economies.

Inducements

The international environment had been quite favourable to the state-
led model of development in the 1950s and the 1960s. The Soviet
Union offered support to countries that were willing to pursue the so-
called 'non-capitalist path of development'. On the other hand,
Western countries, as well as the World Bank, were willing to offer
different types of assistance in a bid to dissuade developing countries
from closely allying themselves with the foreign policies of the
Socialist countries. Inspired by the economic history of modern
Germany, Italy and Japan, they were even led by the genuine belief
that the economic role of the state had to be large in the early stages of
development. Thus, Egypt was getting economic assistance from the
USSR and Germany and food aid from the United States. Tunisia
received considerable economic assistance from France, the United
States and other members of the European Community. Finally,
Jordan was the beneficiary of substantial amounts of US and British
aid. Hostility to public ownership was not as fierce then as all aid
donors currently maintain (OECD 1984).

With economic stagnation in Eastern Europe, followed by the fall
of the Socialist regimes, sources of foreign aid became largely limited
to advanced capitalist countries, and increasingly, to member
countries of the Development Assistance Committee (DAC) within
the OECD. Economic assistance offered by these countries became
tied to the implementation of Stabilization and Structural Adjustment
Programmes. In the 1980s and 1990s, economic assistance was
offered for a variety of reasons, but assistance in the implementation
of the so-called 'economic reform' programmes, which called for a
drastic reduction in the role of the state in the economy, became a
strong component of these aid flows. This was particularly the case of
loans offered by the World Bank Group, whether of concessionary or
non-concessionary nature, and of credit provided by the International
Monetary Fund. Aid donors did not always share the same assessment
of the soundness of economic policies of recipient countries or the
particular pace of stabilization or structural adjustment in any of
them. By virtue of their strategic importance to the more powerful
advanced capitalist countries, a few recipients could play donors off
against one another or use diplomatic influences to get more lenient

treatment from the IMF or the World Bank. While there were relatively few such cases, Egypt is reputed to have been one of the more fortunate ones.

The Egyptian government was able to continue to insist on a slower pace in the implementation of some reform measures. For instance, it resisted calls for the devaluation of the Egyptian pound, faster privatization of the public sector, or aligning energy rates to those of the international market. This ability arose from its so-called 'strategic rent', which gave rise to close ties with some major aid donors, particularly the United States, France and, to a lesser extent, Germany. Some observers have noted that divergences over the course of the reform programme in Egypt existed even within the administration of one single aid donor, the USA. Denis Sullivan has argued that Egypt could exploit differences of assessment between USAID, on the one hand, and the US State Department or Department of Agriculture, on the other, in order to lessen pressures to move fast along the path of liberalization. According to Sullivan, Department of State officials were particularly concerned that a fast pace of economic liberalization might trigger an angry popular reaction, similar to what happened in January 1977 (Sullivan 1992: 26–33). Another observer has maintained that – relying on its 'strategic rent' – the Egyptian government used dilatory tactics in its negotiations with both the IMF and the World Bank. It was quite customary for the Egyptian president to pay short visits to important capitals of the Group of Seven, particularly Paris, Bonn and London prior to any crucial round of negotiations between Egypt and the IMF (Richards 1992).

While Jordan was not in a position to do so in the 1980s, its strategic importance to the US increased after it signed a peace treaty with Israel in 1994. Thanks to this new relationship with Israel, it is probably getting more lenient conditions from all aid donors and both Bretton Woods institutions.

As for Tunisia, it does not seem that its government has actually put up much resistance to the demands of these institutions (see Chapter 6 in this book where Emma Murphy elaborates this point). Domestic opposition to structural adjustment, although present, was not as strong as in Egypt following the removal of powerful leaders of the UGTT and introduction of strict controls over the media (Christopher 1996: 177–201; Pfeifer 1996: 42–52).

Aid donors were quite crucial in encouraging countries to shift to different models of economic management. Economic assistance could ease the social burden resulting from stabilization and adjustment measures and technical assistance could be necessary to introduce certain institutional innovations with which recipient countries might not be very familiar, like the establishment of capital markets or the setting up of new schemes for managing food subsidies.

Aid donors can also allocate funds to encourage the adoption of risky reform measures likely to incur heavy social or political costs. One can find examples of funds offered by the World Bank or USAID in the three countries in order to cover the costs of the valuation of public sector enterprises to be offered for sale, or to enable their employees to acquire equity in the would-be privatized enterprises. Supported by the collective efforts of the donor community, one institution – the Social Fund for Development – was established in Egypt with the specific purpose of dealing with the unemployment and poverty problems that would potentially be aggravated in the wake of the implementation of stabilization and structural adjustment programmes (Sullivan 1992: 32).

Constraints

The international environment could also act as an impediment to the emergence of a particular model of the state-economy relations. For instance, a drop in the price of a major export commodity, reluctance to cancel or reschedule heavy foreign debts, or to offer external assistance, can trigger or aggravate internal unrest. Under such conditions, the likelihood of a change of government, either through the ballot box or violence is increased. Economic destabilization may, in fact, be a deliberate objective of foreign action. Both Chile under President Allende and Nicaragua under the Sandinistas have experienced such pressures from the US government. The downfall of both regimes (the former by a military coup and the latter through electoral defeat) paved the way for US-friendly regimes that subsequently adopted economic models based on free enterprise with the strong blessing of international financial institutions. Of course, external economic pressures cannot, on their own, provoke the fall of any regime unless accompanied by powerful internal opposition movements. Nor are such pressures used only to cause a shift in state-economy relations in any country. They might also be rooted in disagreements over the foreign policies of the country in trouble or its treatment of certain groups of the population.

In the Arab world, of the three countries in question, the perception of such pressures was present in the minds of many Egyptians as negotiations between Egypt and the IMF continued throughout the late 1970s and 1980s. Such perception was probably absent in the two other cases, as commitment to the state-led model was not as ideologically charged as in the case of Egypt. Many Egyptians still remember vividly the events of 1956, when the World Bank, under instructions from both the US and the UK governments, refused to finance the building of the Aswan High Dam, which proved later to be so important for the protection of the country against hazards posed by the River Nile. This memory is refreshed every summer, when the Nile floods its banks and the potential for natural disaster in Upper Egypt is heightened. This perception was revived more recently in the 1970s and 1980s, when there were protracted negotiations with the two Bretton Woods institutions over reform of the Egyptian economy. Many Egyptians believed that the IMF, supported by members of the Paris Club, was trying to pressure the Egyptian government to accelerate the pace of privatization and to devalue the Egyptian pound. A change of cabinet in January 1996 was followed later by a favourable report by the IMF on the state of the Egyptian economy and the Paris Club's agreement to drop the last tranche of the cancelled part of the Egyptian debt and to reschedule the rest. The Egyptian government promised to accelerate the pace of privatization, and the IMF accepted its point of view on the devaluation of the pound.

This last instance demonstrates that pressures by international financial institutions or even by some donor countries do not always succeed in immediately bringing about the required changes in the management of the national economy when they are dealing with a big country or one that enjoys some strategic rent. The country concerned could do without this aid, as was the case of India for some time, or use its strategic rent to get some major donors to apply pressures instead on the international financial institutions themselves to soften conditionalities (Richards 1992).

The Regional Environment

The regional environment can either enhance the net impact of the international environment or dilute it. It can produce a snowballing effect if the number of the countries that follow a certain model of economic management increases over a short period of time. It can also generate forces that may encourage the adoption of this model or constrain it. The final outcome of forces operating in both the regional and international environments depends on the relative strength or weakness of each.

The snowballing effect was manifest in the 1960s. The shift to the state-led model of development in Egypt inspired partly similar developments in Syria and Iraq in the early 1960s, and in the Sudan and Libya in 1969 and 1970. When the shift to liberalization was announced in Tunisia and Egypt in the early seventies, it failed to produce similar effects, with the exception of weak echoes in Syria which started to ease restrictions on the private sector in the 1970s (Hinnebusch 1995). It is doubtful that President Sadat's decision to announce an 'Open Door Policy' was inspired by the same move in Tunisia two years earlier. Liberal economic policies became fashionable in the Arab world in the 1980s, but this reflected other difficulties in the regional environment, rather than the snowballing effect originating in Egypt or in Tunisia (Harik and Sullivan 1992; Handoussa 1997).

One could observe that the Arab regional environment acted in two contradictory ways in the 1970s and 1980s. It endowed the three countries in the 1970s with additional resources that enabled them to maintain the state-led model of development, although it was discredited in Tunisia and denounced by President Sadat in Egypt (Kerr and Yasin 1982: 1–15). The value of Tunisia and Egypt's petroleum exports went up after the first and second price hikes of 1973 and 1980. Remittances of expatriate Egyptian, Tunisian and Palestinian workers in the Arab petroleum exporting countries and in Europe provided another source of funding imports and stimulating private investments, which mitigated the effects of the poor finances of state-owned companies.

Thus, while governments in Tunisia and Egypt were aware of the necessity to deal with their growing fiscal deficits and escalating foreign debts, the availability of these revenues, combined with considerations of the social costs of stabilization measures, encouraged them to delay the adoption of any corrective measures.

The situation was reversed in the mid-1980s. Oil prices went down in international markets, and recession started in the petroleum exporting countries. Oil revenues decreased sharply, workers' remittances shrank significantly, and the burden of servicing foreign debt rose substantially. As mentioned before, the second half of the 1980s was the period of crucial decisions in all three countries.

Tunisia started its Structural Adjustment Programme in 1986, Egypt signed a stand-by agreement with the IMF in 1987, and Jordan followed suit with an 18-month stand-by agreement with the IMF in 1989 (World Bank 1996b).

Relations with the European countries, on the other hand, worked completely in one direction, pushing the three countries to liberalize their economies. The three countries are parties at present to different arrangements with the European Union. Tunisia has concluded a partnership agreement with Europe, and Egypt is in the process of concluding one. Moreover, all three countries are parties to the Barcelona Declaration. This declaration calls for economic liberalization and the lifting of all barriers to foreign trade among all its parties with a view to establishing a free trade area between countries of the Eastern and Southern Mediterranean and the European Union by the year 2010.[13]

The European Union has been an important aid donor to the three countries and its aid policies have been consistently geared to the promotion of economic reform in all of them – as understood by EU members (Vandewalle 1996).

CONCLUSION

This chapter has examined external influences that have shaped the model of state-economy relations in the three Arab countries of Egypt, Tunisia and Jordan. While setting out the broader context in which the orientation of state policy has been changing in these countries in recent decades, it has focused on the external influences – both in regional and international contexts.

There is little doubt that, in deciding the nature and direction of the state-economy relations, the state elites are guided by their understanding of state interests. Maximization of the political power of the state and social and political stability are parts of this understanding. In fact, they are not rigidly committed to any ideology. In this way, their conduct befits the description by the Chinese leader, Deng Hsiao Ping, who once remarked that 'the colour of the cat does not matter so long as it can catch mice'. Indeed, one can find the same senior officials who promoted state-led development in the Arab countries in the 1960s and 1970s, working with no less enthusiasm to push market-oriented reforms in the 1980s and the 1990s. They strive to operate in regional and international environments in ways that do not diminish their powers or risk destabilizing the social and political order over which they preside. This is why their 'commitment' to a free-market economy, in which the state only sets the rules and avoids direct involvement in production, or to a liberal political order, will always be a highly qualified one.

NOTES

1 In fact, gone are the days when public ownership of the means of production, central comprehensive planning and 'liquidation' of class differences were exalted by Arab ruling groups in countries like Egypt, Syria, Iraq, Algeria, Sudan, Yemen and, to a much lesser extent, Tunisia. By contrast, the same rhetoric was not fashionable in countries with conservative regimes (such as Morocco or the Gulf countries), where state intervention was at least partially accepted as complementary to the development of the private sector. Nevertheless, the change in perception has affected both sets of countries.

2 Even on rare occasions when they may admit to such influences, their admission of such influences may be shaped by considerations broader than those guiding the historian's quest for truth. For instance, they may be intended for domestic consumption, or to identify scapegoats, or to place elsewhere the responsibility for adopting policies that entail heavy social costs.

3 The texts of standby and structural adjustment accords concluded with the International Monetary Fund and the World Bank are rarely published, although their general contents might be disclosed by the media. Despite much emphasis on transparency in recent years, one cannot even dream of having access to the minutes of such meetings between state officials and the representatives of international financial institutions and aid donors.

4 In Tunisia, for instance, this was probably the belief of President Bourguiba in the late 1960s following the collapse of the agricultural cooperatives schemes, which was supported by Ben Saleh (Tunisia's long-time Secretary of State for Finance and Planning, 1962–1969). In Egypt, it was definitely a matter of faith for President Anwar El-Sadat, and was certainly not shared by the Nasserites and leftist intellectuals whom he persecuted in the first year of his presidency and again, along with others, in the last months of his rule and life in 1981.

5 An Investment and Trade Adjustment programme was signed with Tunisia in 1986 and an Industry and Trade Adjustment loan was concluded with Jordan in 1990.

6 For instance, Egyptian businessmen have responded favourably to calls by the President and Mrs Mubarak to participate with the government in the building of schools in different parts of the country and in areas heavily hit by natural disasters, such as an earthquake in 1992 or flooding the following year.

7 There are four such national projects: the National Project for the Development of South Egypt (known in the press as the Toshki project); Resettlement of Sinai; East of Port Said; and North of the Gulf of Suez.

8 Union Générale des Travailleurs Tunisiens; see also the chapter by Emma Murphy in this volume.
9 Union Tunisienne de l'Industrie, du Commerce et de l'Artisanat.
10 A good example of this is the Jordanian laws of 1987, which limited employment of foreign workers and ordered businessmen and schools to hire national engineers and physicians. This by-law, in particular, could be considered an exceptional measure called for by growing unemployment among Jordanian citizens (Brand 1992: 177–8).
11 In the last cabinet in Jordan before the death of King Hussein, which was in office in 1998, the number of highly educated ministers was no less than eleven – or exactly half the cabinet members (JR 1998: 1068). The first cabinet formed under King Abdallah on 4 March 1999, following the death of his father, did not depart from this pattern (*Al-Hayat* 5 March 1999).
12 For instance, it is reported that Dr Kamal Al-Ganzouri, the Prime Minister of Egypt since 1996, made a state visit to Malaysia and Singapore 'to learn about the secret of this East Asian success quite closely.' (*Al-Ahram* 1997)
13 The second chapter of the Declaration defines the principles on which the free trade area should be based, including, in particular:

'– The pursuit and development of policies based on the principles of market economy and the integration of their economies taking into account their respective needs and levels of development;
– the adjustment and modernization of economic and social structures, giving priority to the promotion and development of the private sector, to the upgrading of the productive sector and to the establishment of an appropriate institutional and regulatory framework for a market economy. They will likewise endeavour to mitigate the negative social consequences which may result from this adjustment, by promoting programs for the benefit of the neediest population'. (European Union 1995: 4)

REFERENCES

Al-Ahram, Daily, Cairo, several issues.
Al-Hayat, Daily, Cairo and London, several issues.
Al-Hay'a al-'amma li al-Este'lamaat (State Information Authority – Arab Republic of Egypt, 1992) *Mawsou'at al-shakhseyyat al-misriyyah (Encyclopaedia of Egyptian Personalities)*, Cairo: Al-HAE.
Al-Sayyid, Mustapha (1991a) 'The Question of Privatization: The Egyptian Debate', *Cairo Papers in Social Science*, vol. 13, monograph 4, Cairo: American University.
—— (1991b) 'Al-Dowal al-sena'eyya al-jadidah wa al-nizaam al-dawli-Newly-Industrialized Countries and the International System', *Al-Fikr al-Estratiji al-'arabi*, no. 36, (April).
Ayubi, Nazih (1995) *Over-Stating the Arab State, Politics and Society in the Middle East*, London: I. B. Tauris.
—— (1997) 'Etatisme versus Privatization: The Changing Economic Role of the State in the Middle East', in Handoussa (1997).

175

Brand, Laurie (1992) 'Economic and Political Liberalization in a Rentier Economy: the Case of the Hashemite Kingdom of Jordan', in Harik and Sullivan (1992).

Christopher, A. (1996) 'State, Labour and the New Global Economy in Tunisia', in Vandewalle (1996: 177–207).

Davis, Eric (1983) *Challenging Colonialism: Bank Misr and the Industrialization of Egypt, 1920–1941*, Princeton: Princeton University Press.

European Union (1995) 'Euro-Mediterranean Partnership: Barcelona Declaration–Work Program', Barcelona: Euro-Mediterranean Conference, (27–28 November).

Fahmy, Khaled Mahmoud (1988) 'Legislating *Infitah*: Investment, Currency and Foreign Trade Laws', *Cairo Papers in Social Science*, vol. 11, monograph 3, Fall, Cairo: American University.

Frank, Andre Gunder (1984) 'Global Crisis and Transformation', in *Critique and Anti-Critique: Essays on Dependence and Reformism*, London: Macmillan.

Haggard, Stephan and Steven B. Webb (1994) *Voting for Reform, Democracy, Political Liberalization and Economic Adjustment*, Oxford and New York: Oxford University Press.

Handoussa, Heba (ed., 1997) *Economic Transition in the Middle East – Global Challenges and Adjustment Strategies*, Cairo: The American University in Cairo Press.

Harik, Iliya and Denis J. Sullivan (eds, 1992) *Privatization and Liberalization in the Middle East*, Indiana University Press: Bloomington.

Hashemite Kingdom of Jordan (HKJ) *Economic and Social Plan*, for the periods 1981–1985, 1986–1990, 1986–1990, and 1993–1997, Amman: National Planning Council.

Heikal, Mohammed Hasanein (1971) *Les Documents Du Caire*, Paris: Editions J'ai Lu.

Hinnebusch, R. (1995) 'State, Civil Society and Political Change in Syria', in Norton (1995).

JR (1998) *Al-Jarida Al-Rasmiyya*, (February), Amman.

Karol, K.S. (1973) *La Deuxiéme Révolution Chinoise*, Paris: Editions Robert Lafont.

Kerr, John and Sayyid Yasin (1982) *Rich and Poor States in the Middle East: Egypt and the New Arab Order*, Cairo and New York: The American University in Cairo Press.

Lawless, Richard and Allan Findlay (1984) *North Africa, Contemporary Politics and Economic Development*, London: Croom Helm.

Mabro, Robert (1974) *The Egyptian Economy, 1952–1972*, Oxford: Clarendon Press.

Mahboub, Abdel-Hamid (1993) 'Men Ehlaal al-waaredaat ela al-tasnee' li al-tasdeer, 'awamel al'nagaah al-kouri (From Import-Substitution to Industrialization for Export, Factors of Success in the Korean Model)', *Kurrasat Estratigiyyah*, Cairo: Al-Ahram Centre for Political and Strategic Studies, (May).

Mursi, Fou'ad (1976) *Hathda al-Infitah al-Eqtesaadi – This Economic Opening*, Cairo: Dar Al-Thaqafa Al-Jadidah.

—— (1987) Maseer al-Qeta' al.'am Fi Misr (Destinty of the Public Sector in Egypt), Cairo: Markaz Al-Bohouth A-'Arabiyyah.

National Bank of Egypt, *Economic Bulletin,* Cairo, several issues.

Norton, Augustus Richard (ed., 1995) *Civil Society in the Middle East,* Leiden: E.J. Brill, vol. 1.

Organisation for Economic Cooperation and Development (OECD) (1984) *Development Cooperation: Efforts and Policies of Members of the Development Assistance Committee,* Paris: OECD.

Owen, Roger (1992) *State, Power and Politics in the Making of the Modern Middle East,* London and New York: Routledge.

Posusney, Marsha Pripstein (1992) 'Labour as an Obstacle to Privatization', in Harik and Sullivan (1992).

Pfeifer, Karen (1996) 'Between Rocks and Hard Choices: International Finance and Adjustment in North Africa,' in Vandewalle (1996: 25–65).

Richards, Alan (1992) 'The Political Economy of Dilatory Reform: Egypt in the 1980s', *World Development,* vol. 9, no. 12.

Sullivan, Denis (1992) 'Extra State Actors and Privatization in Egypt,' in Harik and Sullivan (1992: 24–45).

Vandewalle, Dirk J. (ed., 1996) *North Africa, Development and Reform in a Changing Global Economy,* New York: St. Martin's Press.

Vandewalle, Dirk J. and Karen Pfeifer (1996) in Vandewalle (1996: 3–25).

Wahba, Murad Magdi (1993) 'The Nationalization of the IMF: The Nature and Evolution of the Official Discourse on Economic Reform in Egypt (1987–1991)', in *Cairo Papers in Social Science,* The Economics and Politics of Structural Adjustment in Egypt, Third Annual Symposium, vol. 6, monograph 3 (Fall), Cairo: American University.

Waterbury, John (1993) *Exposed to Innumerable Delusions, Public Enterprise and State Power in Egypt, India, Mexico and Turkey,* London and New York: Cambridge University Press.

World Bank Middle East and North Africa Economic Studies (1996a) *Tunisia's Global Integration and Sustainable Development, Strategic Choices for the 21st Century,* Washington D.C.: TGI.

World Bank (1996b) *Al-Ordon aw al-bank al-dawli- Jordan and the World Bank,* Washington D.C.: World Bank.

World Bank (1997a) *World Development Report,* Washington D.C.: World Bank.

World Bank (1997b) *Al-taqrir al-sanawi* (Annual Report), Washington D.C.: World Bank.

Chapter Eight

Restructuring the Public Sector in Post-1980 Turkey: An Assessment

*Oktar Türel**

INTRODUCTION

As in many other countries, the public sector has been playing important roles in the Turkish economy, both as a *spending agent* (which appropriates a sizeable part of national income net of redistribution, and purchases goods and services for current consumption and investment) and as a *producer of goods and services* (which involves direct *provision of employment*). The first function is mainly concerned with the allocation of resources in the economy, and the second, with production and efficiency issues. There is, of course, some, but not complete, overlap between these two functions.[1]

The aim of this chapter is to assess the change in the role of the public sector as a major spender and producer in line with the structural adjustment experience of the Turkish economy in the last two decades. Since the nature and the extent of the structural transformation in the macroeconomic and sectoral spheres are well documented elsewhere (see, *inter alia*, Boratav *et al.* 1994, 1995; Celasun 1994; Şenses 1994; Togan 1996; and Yeldan 1995, to cite

*This chapter was finalized in August 1999 before the conclusion of a 3-year standby agreement between Turkey and the IMF in December 1999. This agreement confirms a strong commitment by the Turkish government to 'structural reforms' and an extensive privatization programme, which will further reduce the extent of public sector involvement in the economy. Thanks are due to Hassan Hakimian and Cem Somel for their helpful comments and to Ms Pervin Seven for her meticulous assistance in producing the script. Errors are the writer's own responsibility.

only a few contributions in the last five years), our interest here will be focused on the activities of the public sector alone.

The structure of the chapter is as follows. The next section provides evidence for, and discusses, the pattern of public spending over the period 1980–97 and the way it has been financed. After that, we offer a review of the public sector in its role as a producer. In this substantive part of the chapter, we shall first briefly comment on the human capital stock in the public sector; second, we examine the state-owned enterprises (SOEs) operating in manufacturing industry and public utilities, together with the effort to privatize these establishments; and third, we consider provision of services in education and health. The review on the social security network (which is almost entirely administered by the government and quasi-governmental organizations today) is also considered in this section, given its intimate connection with the provision of health service in Turkey. The final section concludes the chapter.

PUBLIC SECTOR FINANCES IN THE LAST TWO DECADES

An International Comparison

The evolution of the Turkish public spending pattern exhibits some interesting parallels with both middle income developing countries and the developed economies since the early 1970s. Data for G-7 show that from 1970 to 1996 (i) total public spending as a proportion of GDP has been rising (albeit very slowly in the UK and the USA); (ii) current plus capital expenditures relative to GDP (which is a reflection of the proportion of claims on goods and services and thereby on economic resources of society) has been falling or stagnating in the UK, the USA and Canada, while it has been slowly rising in Japan, Germany, France and Italy; and (iii) in all of the countries 'other public spending' (which is mostly made up of income transfers and interest payments) has been rising (see OECD Historical Statistics and National Accounts Statistics). Turkey fits well into the first and third of these trends and her experience as regards consumption plus investment expenditures has been closer to that of the Anglo-Saxon countries.

For developed economies some kind of levelling off, and later a modest fall, in public spending/GNP ratio should not be surprising, as long as the ideologically motivated drive against the involvement of public agents in economic life continues to be strong. Furthermore, a reduction in the share of interest payments can be expected, following the increased preference for balanced budgets. However, the fall in spending on some goods and services may in due course be offset by greater spending on the environment. In the case of social security, a radical change will be difficult to realize in the medium- and even the long-term, in view of the demographic transition in developed societies and strong public support for the 'welfare state'; hence no big jumps or breaks in the spending pattern.

The Turkish case, however, is more difficult to predict. In the closing years of the century, expenditure on public investment and consumption has been falling to what may be regarded as bare essentials in a civilized society. Even in the unlikely event of a further fall, this will not be sufficient to make room for ever-rising transfers, which have turned the public sector in Turkey of the late 1990s into a vast and complicated machinery, the essential function of which is not the provision of goods and services, but rather to realize income and capital transactions of a redistributive nature.

Waterbury is right in his assessment that '(t)he public sector in its broadest sense has not diminished its weight in the Turkish economy; rather it has regrouped' since the early 1980s (1992: 50). The regrouping which has been taking shape in the Turkish economy cannot be projected into the future without bringing questions of social harmony and even political legitimacy into the foreground. Hopefully, the scope for securing modest increases in the gross tax burden offers an opportunity to accommodate rising spending and hence the growing 'weight' of the public sector in Turkey.

Expenditure and its Composition

The patterns of change in public sector finances from 1980 to 1997 can be examined under the following four periods, which are based on political developments in the country over this period (see Table 1):[2]

   (i) 1980–3 (the military interregnum).
 (ii) 1984–8 (the heyday of Mr Özal's Motherland Party government).
(iii) 1989–92 (from weakened Motherland Party rule to coalition governments).
(iv) 1993–7 (various endeavours to prevent a slide into chaos under coalition governments).

Limited space precludes an extensive commentary on the distinct characteristics of each sub-period, and only the general trends will be noted here. From 1980–3 to 1993–7, a 6 percentage point fall in net tax

TABLE 1: Public Revenue, Spending and Deficits Relative to GNP,
1980–97 (%)

Sub-periods	Yg	Cg	Sg	Ig	DEF	PSBR
1980–3	15.5	9.1	6.4	9.5	3.1	5.3
1984–8	14.0	6.9	7.1	9.2	2.1	4.7
1989–92	12.4	10.4	2.0	7.6	5.6	8.4
1993–7	9.6	10.6	−1.0	5.3	6.3	8.3

Legend:
Yg	:	Net tax revenue of the government,
Cg	:	Public current consumption,
Sg	:	Public saving (= Yg − Cg),
Ig	:	Public investment, including changes in stocks,
DEF	:	Public sector I/S gap (= Ig − Sg),
PSBR	:	Public sector borrowing requirement,

all *relative* to GNP.
Source: Calculated from SPO (1997: 69–70); SPO, *Annual Programme*, (1999: 174, 199).

revenue was observed, which was partly offset by a 4 percentage point fall in the average propensity to invest of the public sector. The overall rise in the current consumption/GDP ratio by about 1 percentage point meant that deficits (as saving/investment gaps) had to rise by about 3 percentage points above the level prevailing in 1980–3.

The fall in the public current expenditure/GNP ratio in the second sub-period is essentially related to a fall in the price of goods and services bought by the government relative to the GNP deflator, and this was engineered by a squeeze on real wages and salaries of public sector employees.[3] The rise in that ratio in the third sub-period is the outcome of both price and quantity effects. While real wages and salaries rose as a reaction to the wage repression of the 1980s and more than compensated the past deterioration in real incomes, national security expenditures also increased substantially, even to the detriment of the provision of other public services.[4]

Notwithstanding occasional deviations, the secular downward trend in the public investment/GNP ratio is strong and apparent. This trend was also associated with a radical reorientation of public investment across sectors (see Table 2). The government retreated from manufacturing industries and mining in favour of transport, communication, education, health and other public services. The share of agricultural investment also had a general tendency to rise (this was mostly in infrastructure with insufficient profit motives for the private sector). Investment in energy, once a preserve of the public sector, has, to a large extent, been left to private enterprise in the

TABLE 2: Distribution of Public Investment by Sectors, 1980–97 (%)

Sectors	1980	1985	1990	1995	1997
Agriculture	7.9	7.0	9.6	12.0	10.9
Mining	7.6	9.8	3.4	2.1	1.6
Manufacturing	26.3	12.6	4.5	5.7	2.5
Energy	21.3	22.0	21.7	12.3	12.8
Transport and Communication	20.8	28.0	34.0	31.7	33.6
Tourism	0.5	0.9	1.2	2.2	0.8
Housing	2.4	2.6	4.0	1.7	1.5
Education	4.1	4.2	6.9	7.7	12.6
Health	1.8	1.2	2.8	4.7	4.4
Other Services	7.2	11.6	11.9	20.0	19.2
TOTAL	100.0	100.0	100.0	100.0	100.0
Memo items: Indices of real public investment in fixed capital (1980 = 100)					
– Total sectors	100.0	120.2	115.3	78.4	127.2
– Manufacturing	100.0	51.3	16.1	13.3	9.7

Source: SPO (1997: 28–30); SPO, *Annual Programmes* (various issues).

1990s on the expectation that investors may respond positively to 'build-operate-transfer' or 'build-operate' schemes proposed by the government (see below). In any case, high capital/output ratios in energy investments were highly prohibitive for the government operating under financial strain.

The data on the functional distribution of Turkish central government expenditure are plagued with definitional breaks and inconsistencies; hence neither the changes in functional shares over time nor comparisons with those of other countries seem very reliable.[5] Spending on defence, and to a lesser extent, spending on 'general public services & public order' perhaps are the only cases with which international comparisons are legitimate.

The share of defence expenditures in Turkey, narrowly defined, seems to be around 12 per cent of central budget outlays and 2.5 per cent of GNP, respectively. There are indications that this is an underestimate, since some security expenditures under the 'public order' category are defence-related, and the shadow wage costs of the armed forces, composed mainly of conscripts, are not taken into consideration. After making allowance for these facts, and judging in terms of budgetary proportions, the Turkish case is somewhat similar to those of some the Middle Eastern and Asian countries where perceived external threats and/or ethnic conflicts are more frequent in comparison to most of the

G-7 member countries. Clearly, the major military powers like the USA, the Russian Federation and China stand as outliers. As a proportion of GNP, Turkish defence spending in the early 1990s seems to be near the G-7 average, excluding the USA (Table 3). The unduly swollen general public service category in IMF records is partly due to excessive involvement of the central administration in local affairs and possibly also because some interest payments appear under that item.[6]

TABLE 3: Central Government Expenditure on General Public Services and Public Order and Defence: Turkey and other Countries, 1980–96

| Country | Year | Share of Central Government Expenditure on | | Central Government Expenditure/ GDP, % |
		General Pub. Ser. and Public Order	Defense	
Turkey[a]	1980	26.7	15.2	20.6
	1985	54.0	10.9	15.1
	1990	25.2	11.7	16.9
	1995	45.9	9.7	22.0
	1996	49.2	8.4	26.6
G-7				
Canada	1994	10.7	5.8	24.0
France	1993	7.8	5.4	47.2
Germany	1991	8.6	6.4	30.2
Italy	1988	7.5	3.6	46.3
Japan	1993	3.6	4.1	23.7
UK	1995	7.1	7.9	41.7
USA	1995	9.7	16.8	22.7
Eastern Europe & Asia				
Russia[b]	1995	14.1	12.2	24.7
Poland	1995	8.0	4.4	43.4
China	1995	8.0	13.1	8.1
India[b]	1995	7.0	14.7	16.1
Indonesia	1995	9.9	7.2	14.7
Korea	1995	10.9	17.8	17.7
The Middle East				
Egypt	1994	7.1	8.2	37.4
Iran	1995	4.8	7.6	32.7
Israel	1995	5.2	17.9	47.4
Syria	1995	3.4	28.5	25.7

[a] The last column is based on SPO (1997: 7, 74 5)
[b] Provisional.
Source: Calculated from IMF, *Government Finance Statistics Yearbooks*, 1991–7; OECD, *Historical Statistics* and OECD, *National Accounts Statistics*, various issues; SPO (1997).

Public Revenue, Deficit and Deficit Financing

The constituent parts of the net tax revenue were more volatile than the net tax revenue itself, which has shown an almost secular decline up to the present (see Table 4). Raising the gross tax burden and SOE contributions by about 3 and 1 percentage points from 1980–3 to 1993–7 could not relieve the negative impacts of growing deficits in social security institutions and soaring income transfers (by 2 and 8 percentage points, respectively), leading to an almost 6 percentage point fall in the net tax revenue of the government.

The contribution of external sources in financing the PSBR was substantial over 1980–3 and 1984–8 (see Table 5). Turkey's creditors provided much support for her structural adjustment programmes in

TABLE 4: Components of Net Tax Revenue and Deficits, 1980–97 (% GNP)

Sub-Periods	T	SEC	SOE	TR	Yg	DEF	INT	NIDEF
1980–3	16.6	0.2	2.3	3.6	15.5	3.1	1.0	2.1
1984–8	15.4	..	5.5	6.9	14.0	2.1	2.7	0.6(s)
1989–92	17.3	−0.2	2.1	6.8	12.4	5.6	3.7	1.9
1993–7	19.5	−1.6	3.1	11.3	9.6	6.3	7.7	1.4(s)

Legend:

T	:	Tax revenue, including non-tax normal revenue and excluding taxes on wealth
SEC	:	Operating surplus of social security institutions
SOE	:	Operating surplus of state-owned enterprises
TR	:	Current transfers, including interest payments
Yg	:	Net tax revenue of the government (= T + SEC + PES − TR)
DEF	:	Public sector I/S gap
INT	:	Interest payments
NIDEF	:	Non-interest deficit ((s) indicating a surplus).

Source: Same as Table 1.

TABLE 5: Sources of Financing PSBR, 1980–97 (%)

	Percentage Shares of Sources (OECD)			% Share of External
Periods	Central Bank	Other Domestic	External	Financing (SPO data)
1980–3	13	46	41	36
1984–8	18	42	40	18
1989–92	9	80	11	10
1993–7	15	98	−13	−13

Source: OECD, *Economic Surveys – Turkey, 1991/2–1997/8*; SPO, *Annual Programmes* (various issues).

the 1980s, while the government gradually moved toward bond financing from deficit financing, which had characterized the 1970s. Since the late 1980s, official external assistance has receded in importance. After the liberalization of the capital account in 1989, bond finance has turned out to be almost the single most important component of financing deficits. The contribution of external sources became negative in the period 1993–7, although indirect funding through domestic financial intermediaries continued (Ekinci 1997). This has been a very lucrative business for both external creditors and the Turkish banking system, as real borrowing rates of interest have risen to very high levels, alongside rates of inflation, which has settled onto a higher plateau of about 80 per cent per year. Although the rate of inflation started to slow down after the early months of 1998, real interest rates did not follow *pari passu*. The exorbitantly high real interest rates over most of the 1980s and the 1990s in public sector borrowing have usually been attributed to asset holders' growing risks, associated with the variability of inflation and exchange rates (see, *inter alia*, Berument and Güner 1997). However, the weakened bargaining position of the Treasury vis-à-vis the private banks and their foreign creditors, who hold more than four-fifths of the government paper, has clearly played a part in this story.[7]

The spectacular rise in public deficits in the sub-period 1989–92 demonstrated the unsustainability of fiscal policies (Özatay 1994) and from 1994 on, the government started to produce consecutive primary surpluses. However, high real interest rates led debt/GNP ratios to escalate from 11.4 per cent in 1990 to 21.4 per cent in 1997. To describe the current situation as 'an internal debt trap' is not much of an exaggeration. What orthodox wisdom (as reflected in the recent staff monitoring agreement with the IMF) suggests is that even greater primary surpluses be produced and the tempo of privatization be accelerated, as a precaution against unpalatable eventualities such as default on debt or a levy on financial assets.

PUBLIC SECTOR PRODUCTION AND EFFICIENCY

Human Capital in the Public Sector

Public sector employment between 1980 and 1990 increased by 34 per cent, surpassing the overall rate of employment generation (26 per cent), but falling substantially behind the growth in non-agricultural private sector employment (51 per cent).[8] There are indications that the rate of growth of employment in local administrations was higher than that in the central administration, in line with rapid urbanization and its attendant problems of urban management, and changing perceptions on the functions of state in the 1980s. Moreover, the expansion of employment in local administration (especially in municipalities) was in line with changes in the rules of sharing government revenue in 1984 in their favour.

The public sector in Turkey employs an educationally more qualified workforce than the private sector, as seen in greater proportions of high school and university graduates employed in the sector, and higher average schooling years of its employees (9.5 and 6.6 for the public and private sectors, respectively, in 1990). Over the period concerned, the share of junior high and high school graduates in public sector employment did not change much, while the fall in the share of illiterates and primary school graduates was balanced by a rise in the share of university graduates. By contrast, the fall in the share of less educated segments of private sector employees was offset by a rise in the share of junior high and high school graduates; the proportion of employees with higher education rose only marginally.

Such a pattern of upgrading manpower may have implications for the future growth and pattern of public sector employment. Intense competition for highly qualified and well-paid positions in the private sector will put pressure on the government to enlarge employment opportunities in the public sector and/or downgrade university graduates to less challenging tasks.

SOEs

The folklore is that (i) the Turkish economy has a very large SOE sector and that (ii) SOEs, in general, are less efficient than private establishments. The first of these claims is simply incorrect; and the second is not convincingly supported by evidence.

As of 1995, the value added shares of SOEs in the three major sectors of the economy (agriculture, industry and services) were 0.5 per cent, 29.0 per cent and 7.4 per cent, respectively. In total this accounted for 10.9 per cent of GDP and just 2.8 per cent of all employment. Furthermore, these shares (in GDP and employment) were on the decline throughout the 1980s and 1990s. For example, the respective figures were 12.8 per cent for GDP and 4.0 per cent for employment in 1985 (Boratav *et al.* 1998: 15–7). This is not surprising in view of the declining pace of capital accumulation in the public sector over the last twenty years and the public sector's withdrawal from 'directly productive' activities (see Table 2, especially the first three rows).

SOE activity within non-agricultural sectors exhibits considerable diversity. In the energy and mining sectors, SOEs accounted for 78 per cent and 65 per cent, respectively, of the total value added in 1995. A similar share in manufacturing was only about 21 per cent. In services, public sector involvement seems to be important in the case of communication, air and rail transport and banking, in addition to historical preserves like education and health services. Within manufacturing, SOEs were active principally in petrochemicals and oil refineries (within ISIC 35) and in iron and steel (the major item under ISIC 37). Next were industries either important for their contribution to public revenues (alcoholic beverages and tobacco industries within ISIC 31) or related to the legacy of the import-substituting industrialization of the pre-1980 years (like pulp and paper under ISIC 34) (see Table 6).

Even under the three-digit ISIC classification, manufacturing industries are very heterogeneous; hence, the SOEs' average labour productivity relative to private establishments, presented in Table 7, is not very illuminating. Low (and even worsening) relative productivity performance is not surprising in the case of 'retreats' like food, textiles and apparel, wood products, non-metallic products and metal products and machinery, most of which are characterized by low

TABLE 6: **Share of State-Owned Enterprises in Large Manufacturing Value Added, 1980–1996 (%)**

Sectors (ISIC Codes)	1980	1985	1990	1995	1996
All Manufacturing (3)	40	39	32	23	22
Food, beverages and tobacco (31)	55	61	47	23	15
Textile, apparel and leather products (32)	14	10	7	3	2
Forestry products (33)	33	50	25	6	5
Paper and printing (34)	37	39	23	18	12
Chemicals, oil refining, rubber and plastics (35)	59	62	60	53	54
Non-metallic products (36)	17	15	12	4	3
Metallurgy (37)	62	43	33	29	44
Metal products, machinery and vehicles (38)	17	12	6	4	4
Memo Item:					
SOE share in total manufacturing VA	37	34	28	23	21

Source: *SIS Manufacturing Surveys*, various years.

TABLE 7: Labour Productivity in State-Owned Enterprises vis-à-vis
Large Private Manufacturing, 1980–96[a]

Sectors (ISIC Codes)	1980	1985	1990	1995	1996
All Manufacturing (3)	120	135	136	142	167
Food, beverages and tobacco (31)	78	131	105	53	38
Textile, apparel and leather products (32)	70	59	59	47	46
Forestry products (33)	110	178	71	34	52
Paper and printing (34)	57	68	45	55	38
Chemicals, oil refining, rubber and plastics (35)	364	372	419	363	449
Non-metallic products (36)	86	76	71	40	39
Metallurgy (37)	84	44	35	54	100
Metal products, machinery and vehicles (38)	74	50	37	40	47
Memo Item:					
Public sector wages in manufacturing relative to private wages (:100)	151	118	142	170	155

[a] Labour productivity in each respective private industry is taken as 100.
Source: SIS Manufacturing Surveys, various years.

capital and/or technology intensity. The structural change observed in Table 6 positively contributed to the secular rise in average labour productivity in SOEs vis-à-vis the private sector.

Empirical studies undertaken for comparable branches of manufacturing (e.g. cement, paper and fertilizer) industries show that size, location and vintage of technologies employed are more meaningful variables than ownership in explaining deviations from the stochastic efficiency frontier (Boratav *et al.* 1998: 34–66).[9] In none of these sectors do ownership variables appear statistically significant. Boratav *et al.* also test the impact of privatization on productivity in the cement industry, in which a complete divestiture of public sector plants was realized between 1989 and 1997, and find no evidence of improvement in productivity attributable to transfer of ownership (1998: 43–8).

Although SOEs have not been operating much nearer to the technical efficiency frontier, this does not necessarily preclude productivity improvement over time. Uygur's findings suggest that manufacturing SOEs as a whole were not inferior to private manufacturing establishments in the period 1965–88 in terms of labour, capital and total factor productivity growth (1993: 42–6).[10] The deterioration in the financial position of SOEs in the late 1980s and early 1990s indicated in Table 4 can largely be attributed to high interest charges on short-term borrowing from commercial sources, the real wage hike in the period 1989–92, intensification of international competition due to trade liberalization after the late 1980s, and appreciation of the Turkish Lira. The SOE system responded to these challenges by: shedding labour (which brought the number of SOE employees from 648 thousand in 1987 down to 467 thousand in 1997), effectively preventing real wage increases, and recourse to subcontracting and downsizing, whenever possible, since technological improvements to be introduced by rebuilding, modernization and expansion were ruled out by an effective check on investment.[11] Judging by the extent of reduction achieved in the combined operational deficits of the five 'problem' enterprises (i.e. Hardcoal Corp., State Railways, Iron & Steel Works, Sugar Factories and Electricity Authority), these responses were successful to a certain extent (their deficit went down from 2.3 per cent of GDP in 1992 to 0.2 per cent of GDP in 1997).[12] Thus, the alarmist tone observed in the World Bank report on SOEs prepared in 1991 may be an overreaction to a conjunctural low in SOE profitability (World Bank 1991).

A note may be added here on the educational qualifications of the SOE employees vis-à-vis those employed in the private sector. As shown in Table 7, not only are average productivities of labour on aggregate, but also average wages in SOE manufacturing establishments are higher than their private sector counterparts. Clearly, wages in the public sector are influenced by factors such as degree of unionization (which has been higher in SOEs compared to private industry) and politicization of the wage bargaining process. Nevertheless, if wages are positively related to human capital embodied in labour, the wage differential in favour of SOE workers may reflect skill differentials, and therefore, the differences in educational attainments.

Since there were no compelling reasons for the divestiture of SOEs on financial or efficiency grounds in the 1980s, privatization then was largely a non-issue, occasionally brought to the fore by international financial institutions and some ardent supporters of the idea of 'a lean state' within the political and administrative cadres.[13] In the first half of the 1980s, interest in the SOE system seemed to be focused essentially on putting forward new legislation and administrative regulations so as to regroup and reorganize them and to design best practice rules for improving their management. However, some contingencies were also incorporated into Decree-by-Law No.233

(1984), the basic piece of legislation concerning SOEs, for their eventual privatization.

The drive for privatization gained momentum by the preparation of a 'Privatization Master Plan' by Morgan Guarantee Trust & Associates, which was financed by the World Bank and issued in 1986. This plan classified SOEs with respect to the ease of and priorities for their full or partial divestiture and suggested some measures other than divestiture to improve their performance without clear prospects for sale. The government received the plan favourably and the second half of the 1980s witnessed the preparation of the legal framework and administrative set-up and procedures for privatization. As Kilci (1998) shows, these rules and regulations were subject to frequent revisions up to 1997.[14] Throughout the 1980s, the aims and priorities of privatization were not unambiguously spelled out by the political authorities and revenue from this source remained at modest levels (Table 8).[15]

Events took a dramatic turn in the early 1990s with a rapid deterioration of state finances and a virtual disappearance of SOEs' operational surpluses (Tables 1 and 4). The rising cost of government borrowing made privatization a possible escape route from a fully-fledged fiscal crisis, given the government's apparent unwillingness or inability to raise tax revenue as an alternative way to deficit reduction. Businessmen and their powerful organizations, facing a substantial increase in real wages from 1989 to 1992, joined the bandwagon to exorcise the spectre of increased taxation. A very effective campaign in the mass media, fuelled by the government and the private sector, eventually built up a large constituency for privatization.[16] However, the Turkish privatizations during the period 1985–98 can rightly be called a failure, judged from the point of view of transfer of ownership.

First, the proceeds from the sale of SOE assets over this period amounted to only about one-third of the SOE equity still under public ownership during the mid-1980s and about 60 per cent of the proceeds were obtained from the sales of equity participations of SOEs in other companies, where the share of the public firm is less than 50 per cent. Second, divestiture was fully, or almost fully, realized in a few industries like cement, forestry products, dairy products, meat and fodder; revenue from privatizations in the cement industry alone accounts for 26 per cent of the total proceeds from 1985 to 1998 (June). The major problem areas, as far as financial and efficiency considerations are concerned, remained intact. Third, the

TABLE 8: Privatization – Revenues and Expenditures, 1985–97 ($ million)

Items	1985–9	1990–7	1985–97	1998
		Total		
Revenues	293	4658	4951	1064
– Privatization gross revenues	183	3381	3564	1020
(Block sales)	(136)	(1608)	(1744)	(289)
(Public offering)	(13)	(420)	(433)	(241)
(International offering)	(–)	(330)	(330)	(392)
(İSE sales, net)	(10)	(514)	(524)	(2)
(Asset sales [a])	(24)	(509)	(533)	(96)
– Interest earnings, net	–	2	2	–109
– Dividend income	110	1265	1375	152
– Other income	–	10	10	1
Expenditues	–47	–512	–559	–43
– Payments to brokers	35	–347	–382	–5
– Consulting, auditing & P.R.	–12	64	–76	–10
– Social assistance supplements [b]	–	–101	–101	–28
Surplus of Revenue over Expenditure	246	4146	4392	1021
– Transfers to the Treasury	–97	–1317	–1414	–163
– Transfers to administrative budget	–	–11	–11	–22
– Participation to capital increase	–176	–1857	–2033	–348
– Borrowing, net [c]	–	–192	–192	–108
– Privatization account balance [d]	27	–769	–742	–380

[a] Includes sales of work in progress.
[b] Includes compensation and/or severance payments to personnel after privatization, and early retirement bonuses.
[c] Net borrowing outside the Privatization Administration + loans extended to establishments under privatization programme, net of repayments.
[d] Largely accounted for by the difference between gross sales revenue and actual cash proceeds.
Source: Kilci (1998: 28–30, 56) and records of the Privatization Administration.

fiscal strains of the public sector made aims other than revenue-raising (i.e. deepening the stock markets and broadening the equity ownership base in society, enhancing efficiency, reducing industrial concentration) irrelevant. As seen in Table 8, the preferred method of divestiture has been block sales and public offerings (the latter literally meaning the sale of SOE equity to firms or persons applying to the Privatization Board) and only 12 per cent of net sales were realized through the İstanbul Stock Exchange. Lack of transparency in procedures and absence of strict rules of conduct for negotiating the transfer of ownership frequently led to serious allegations of political interference, favouritism and corruption.

This failure is better attributed to inherent weaknesses in the privatization policy than to legal disputes, bureaucratic inefficiencies and even resistance by organized labour, which, in the event, turned out to be local and relatively mild. Given the deterioration in public sector balances and the rising cost of government borrowing, prospective buyers could try to negotiate an unacceptably low price and/or wait for a better bargain in the future. On the other hand, the government's refusal to allow SOEs to invest in order to reach optimal capacities and/or to upgrade them technologically, subjected most of the SOE plants and equipment to obsolescence. This in turn discouraged not only buyers, but also the seller, who was unwilling to accept an offer well below the book value of equity.

Public Utilities

As far as the privatization of public utilities is concerned in post-1980 Turkey, two cases deserve special attention. These pertain to the production and distribution of electricity and telecommunication services.

Various Turkish governments tried to manage the privatization of electricity by means of three pieces of legislation promulgated in 1984, 1986 and 1997. The first one of these put forward the principles for the private provision of service and for franchising, but did not envisage the transfer of public ownership. The second dealt with the sale or transfer of equities and assets through reorganization of the Turkish Electricity Authority (TEK), of which the production and distribution branches were separated in 1993.[17] The last one set out the rules and procedures for franchising to private producers and distributors of electricity (colloquially known as 'build and operate' or the BO model).

Legal provisions for the so-called 'build, operate and transfer' (BOT) scheme were formulated in 1994. These were later amended in 1994 and 1996. Under this legal framework, the BOT schemes can also be applied to all infrastructure investments and public utilities subject to private law (Kilci 1998: 19–20).[18]

The case of the telecommunication services is more complex. The parent company, the General Directorate of Postal, Telegraph and Telephone Services (PTT), started privatizing its participations in firms producing telecom equipment (TELETAŞ and NETAŞ) in stages, from 1986 to 1993. The following major steps were taken:

- the separation of Türk Telekom (the last T of the PTT) from the parent company (1993)
- contracting out to or forming joint ventures with private firms for the establishment and/or construction of cable TV networks (from 1991)
- data transmission network (1988)
- production and launching of communication satellites (1995)
- satellite ground stations (from 1991)
- links with the Internet (1996), and
- franchising Global System for Mobile Communications (GSM, from 1994) (Başaran and Özdemir 1998: 76–107).

The privatization of the telecommunication services in the 1990s was almost always complicated from a legal point of view, due to the Constitutional Court's rulings that telecommunication was essentially a 'public service' (a different notion from that of the economists' conception of a 'public good'). Thus, although private provision of such services *is* allowed, franchising it requires the approval of the Court of State, which examines the franchise from the point of view of its 'public benefit'. Further, settling disputes between private service providers and the franchising authority currently falls under the jurisdiction of the Turkish law courts. Prospective international investors in energy and telecommunication and their Turkish partners vehemently object to this legal arrangement, lobbying very actively for it to be replaced with international arbitration.[19]

Economically, three related issues are at stake: (i) How can efficiency be secured in the use of a national electricity grid or telecommunication infrastructure under a system of multiple service providers, whether public or private? (ii) How should a franchise be regulated in the case of a monopoly? and (iii) What is the proper way to institutionalize the regulatory body or bodies? Experience suggests that, at present, the Turkish public authorities are not well-prepared, informed and organized for regulatory tasks.[20]

It should be noted that the debate over the provision of public services by private agents is not confined to these two sectors alone. The growing Turkish urban settlements have been facing complex problems concerning water supply, mass transportation, sewage and waste disposal and treatment, and environmental protection. Local authorities which lack the finance and/or expertise to solve these problems have started to rely increasingly on BO or BOT models of some kind (for a detailed recount of attempts in this direction, see KİGEM-Genel İş 1998: 30–75).

Education and Health

A significant and substantial rise in enrolment ratios at all levels, combined with continued fiscal stringency over the past two decades, has raised new challenges in the education sector, which along with health is traditionally considered a public sector stronghold. Despite the rise in enrolment rates and the need for quality improvements, total central government spending relative to GNP has been stagnant: 2.5 per cent in 1983, rising to 3.2 per cent in 1990 before falling back again to 2.2 per cent by 1997. Against this general background, a number of important developments have taken place, which are summarized below:

(i) The time-honoured tradition of free education in Republican Turkey is threatened by budgetary stringency. Although the practice is illegal, the majority of parents with children in primary and secondary schooling age are asked to make 'voluntary' contributions to the current expenses of schools at present. Parents have to bear the additional costs of 'preparation courses for the universities', which are quite widespread among secondary school students. Tuition fees in higher education (albeit modest by developed country standards) have also been raised substantially. Moreover, the government frequently appeals to and encourages charitable persons to contribute to investment in education.

(ii) Poor funding of education raises the issue of quality of education. Student-teacher ratios, which are crude but useful indicators of overcrowding and hence of lack of guidance and care, have been rising since the early 1980s. Parents and the Ministry of Education have responded to this erosion of quality in various ways. First, the number of private, fee-paying schools, especially at the high school level, has been growing. Although the percentage of pupils in private secondary schools was a modest 4.3 per cent in 1996/7, this ratio has been rising continually. Second, the Ministry of Education introduced a new category of secondary school with better training facilities (known as Anatolian High Schools) in the early 1980s. This type of school, which attracted about 11 per cent of pupils at secondary school level by 1998/9, has further accentuated discrimination against 'ordinary' secondary schools.

(iii) A highly selective entrance exam for the universities has led to the proliferation of the preparatory courses mentioned above, creating a parallel and mostly duplicative tier in the last two years of secondary education, and leading to the inefficient use and even waste of human and physical resources. The number of the pupils enrolled in and the teaching staff of these private establishments are not known exactly; however, a reasonable estimate is that about one-sixth of the relevant population age-group attends these courses. Leaving aside the benefit of improved entry chances, the contribution of this tier to the mental and productive capabilities of pupils is questionable. The proportion of pupils under vocational training at the secondary school level has consistently been lower than that of the pupils under general training; this brings pressure on public authorities to open up new universities and faculties without adequate facilities and proper research and teaching staff, just to offer a new chance to secondary school graduates who are otherwise barely employable due to a lack of productive skills.

Prior to the major reorganization of the higher education system in 1982, there were 19 universities in the country. Their number rose to 58 by 1996/7, seven of which are private establishments. The number of university enrolments (including open education) almost quadrupled from 335 thousand to 1290 thousand in the period 1983/4–1996/7 while the number of academic staff increased by a factor of 2.6. Thus, far from being an indicator of success, the rising enrolment rates in higher education are a reflection of unresolved problems at the secondary level, i.e. poor quality and absence of vocational orientation. Similar to the case of secondary education, the percentage of students in private higher education establishments is really minor (1.6 per cent and 1.4 per cent at undergraduate and postgraduate levels, respectively, in 1996/7), but has a clear tendency to rise. Low pay, poor inducements to work and associated problems of staff recruitment in public establishments, together with insufficient funding, leave little doubt that what has been observed at the secondary level will be replicated at the level of higher education in the near future.

The public sector has been facing similar challenges in the health sector. Current expenditure on health in Turkey as a proportion of GNP has been generally stable since 1980. However, the share of public expenditure within the total has been rising, mainly due to an increase in the coverage of social security schemes (see below). In the period 1992–6, about two-thirds (66–71 per cent) of public health outlay were financed out of the general budget and the rest by the social security premia earmarked for health.[21] Over the same period, 56–59 per cent of services were provided by the public sector and the rest by the private sector; these shares remained fairly constant, indicating that the public sector purchases a high and even increasing proportion of services from the private sector (Table 9). As the figures in this Table imply, the supply of private services was essentially concentrated in medical examinations, dental care and provision of medication (see also Ministry of Health 1998: 58).

As of 1996, 92 per cent of GPs and 76 per cent of specialists (including part-timers) had a working relationship with the public sector. For full-time MDs in the public sector, the figures come down to only 27 per cent and 29 per cent, respectively (Ministry of Health 1998: 49). These figures show that a greater proportion of MDs are

TABLE 9: Health Expenditure and its Financing, 1992–6 (%)

Percentage Shares of ...	1992	1993	1994	1995	1996
Expenditure by					
– Public sector	67	66	69	71	71
– Private sector	33	34	31	29	29
Source of financing by					
– General budget	46	47	46	43	43
– Social security premia [a]	23	22	24	27	25
– Private individuals [b]	31	31	30	30	32
Provision of service by [c]					
– Public sector	59	57	56	57	58
– Private sector	41	43	44	43	42
Nature of the service provided [c]					
– Preventive health care	2	2	1	1	1
– Out-patient departments	63	65	66	63	64
– In-patient health care	25	26	27	29	29
– Other (training, medico-social expenditures, etc.)	9	7	6	7	6
Memo Item:					
Health expenditure relative to GNP, % [d]	3.8	3.7	3.6	3.3	3.7

[a] $\frac{1}{4}$ of the premia paid by the active members of the Retirement Fund (ES) are included; all other payments by ES are treated as subsidies paid out of the general budget.
[b] Includes private health insurance schemes.
[c] Calculated on expenditure basis.
[d] Ministry of Health estimates.
Source: Calculated or taken from Ministry of Health (1997: 59–63, 68, 71).

engaged both in public sector work and in private practice, and MDs who are exclusively in private practice are mostly specialists.

The number of hospital beds per thousand of the population has not changed much since 1980 either, while the percentage distribution of hospital beds among major institutional groups has shown rather small variations (Table 10). Hospital beds administered by the Ministry of Health and by hospitals affiliated with the Social Insurance Institution have continued to account for about two-thirds of the total. Other ministries, SOEs and local administrations have been losing their shares to medical faculties and private establishments. Although rising in proportion, private hospitals account for a modest part of the total number of hospital beds, a picture similar to that of education.

Over the last ten years, issues of efficiency and financing in Turkey's health sector have become the focus of much attention and work on health reform has been intensified since the late 1980s. An initial study by the World Bank in 1988 was followed by a master plan prepared by the State Planning Organization in 1990. Later, the Turkish government concluded three credit agreements with the World Bank in support of health reform in 1990, 1994 and 1997, totalling $240 million. By the end of 1998, about 40 per cent of this

TABLE 10: Selected Health Indicators for Turkey, 1980–97

Items	1980	1990	1995	1997
Total no. of hospital beds (thousands)	114.2	137.7	152.0	159.3
No. of hospital beds per thousand population	2.54	2.42	2.44	2.53[a]
Distribution of hospital beds by institutions, %				
– Ministry of Health	50.0	50.5	50.7	50.2
– Other ministries & SOEs	16.5	13.7	12.3	11.8
– Social Insurance Institution (SSK)	16.1	17.4	16.7	16.1
– Universities	11.8	13.1	13.7	14.5
– Local administrations	2.2	0.8	0.8	0.8
– Private establishments [a]	3.4	4.4	5.9	6.7
Memo Items:				
Total no. of doctors (thousands)	27.2	50.6	69.7	73.8[b]
No. of doctors per thousand population	0.61	0.89	1.12	1.17

[a] Foreign hospitals, hospitals administered by charitable bodies and private clinics.
[b] Figures refer to 1996.
Source: Ministry of Health, *Health Statistics* (various issues); SPO, *Supporting Studies for the Annual Programmes*, 1997–9.

sum was disbursed. These credit agreements envisaged joint contribution by the Turkish government of some \$126 million in domestic currency. The aims of the reform were defined as improving access to, and the quality of, basic health services (essentially in the preliminary stages of health care) and improving the efficiency and technical and administrative capability of the Ministry of Health.

The health planners of this Ministry identify the main problems as follows (Engiz 1996: 23–30):

  (i) The health insurance system currently in effect finances a small part of the spending, especially in the case of the Retirement Fund; and the low amounts of premia collection leads the Social Insurance Institution to consider budgetary constraints more than users' satisfaction.

 (ii) Only 15 per cent and 20 per cent of current spending by the Ministry of Health goes to preventive health care and preliminary stages of health care, respectively. This is claimed to be inequitable since this type of health care affects large segments of society.

(iii) Indirect subsidization of health expenditure through funding institutions – and not individuals – is also claimed to be inequitable, since most beneficiaries of the service are relatively better-off, i.e., the insured population as against the low-income, uninsured strata of society.

So the solution is sought in separating the health insurance system from the old age/retirement insurance scheme, establishing an extensive health insurance system and turning hospitals into autonomous bodies which offer health services competitively on the basis of agreements made with the health insurance institutions. This Thatcherite model of 'user pays' reform has strong supporters within the government, political parties and some members of the medical profession, mostly those in private practice. It constitutes a radical break from the socialization of health services and free medical care which had been the guiding principles of governments' health policy prior to 1980. Insured workers (mostly organized labour and civil servants) are unlikely to have much sympathy for the pro-reform arguments noted above, since in terms of income distribution they have been on the losing side of the structural adjustment measures of the 1980s and 1990s. It is unlikely that the suggested efficiency gains will be enough to compensate for their relative income losses. It remains to be seen whether some kind of compromise can be reached in the coming years between the 'reformers' on one hand and the large masses of the working population, on the other, who feel that they are destined to foot the bill under the proposed measures.

The Social Security Network

Thanks to urbanization and the growth of non-agricultural activities, Turkey has succeeded in substantially increasing the proportion of population covered by her social security network over the last twenty-five years. A very large section of people covered by the system benefits from health services that are financed partly by premium payments. As in any maturing social security system where the number of pensioners starts to outgrow the number of those actively insured, the Turkish social security system too has become financially squeezed in the 1990s. The situation has been aggravated by the inability of the public administration to react to the crisis in a timely and desirable manner (Table 11). The social security institutions

TABLE 11: Some Characteristics of Turkish Social Security System, 1970–96

Items	1970	1980	1990	1996
Actively insured/pensioners ratio for				
– ES	4.6	2.5	1.9	1.9
– SSK	9.1	3.5	2.4	2.3
– BAĞKUR	–	8.0	4.7	2.4
Combined financial surplus of public social security institutions relative to GNP, %	n.a.	0.2	0.1	−2.0
Index of real pension payments per retired person (1980: 100) [a]				
– ES	79	100	113	101
– SSK	122	100	114	97
– BAĞKUR	–	100	90	96
Memo Items: Popn. benefiting from health service/Total population, %	27	38	54	67
Popn. covered by social security system/Total population, %	27	49	73	84
Popn. benefiting from health service/Popn. covered by social security system, %	100	79	75	80

[a] Pensions plus allowances for social security assistance per retired person, deflated by İstanbul Chamber of Commerce wage earners index.
Source: Calculated from SPO (1997: 150–1) and records of social security institutions.

themselves bear most of the responsibility for this situation. Throughout the 1980s and the 1990s, they failed to assess their actuarial position correctly, were soft in premium collection and tolerant of low or negative rates of return on their assets. The combined operating surplus of the social security system, which was about 1.1 per cent of GNP in 1978, was reduced to almost zero in the early 1990s and rapidly went into the red (2.0 per cent and 2.3 per cent of GNP, respectively, in 1996 and 1998).

The social security institutions reacted to their worsening financial situation not only by demanding support from the general budget, but also by becoming rather niggardly towards pensioners: the real value of payments per retired person did not change much between 1980 and 1996, and actually fell in the 1990s in a society where per capita real GNP rose by about 48 per cent between 1980 and 1996. Not surprisingly, the deterioration in the finances of social security institutions created a strong backlash in influential circles; the well-known business association TÜSİAD was quick to follow the lead taken by the World Bank (1994) and produced its own blueprint for reform (TÜSİAD 1996). Since then, social security reform has been part of the so-called 'structural reforms' repertoire of the government, and has been included in the list of policy measures promised to the IMF since 1994 (both during negotiations of stand-by credit as well as in staff monitoring agreements). Without necessarily absolving the public authorities from their past mismanagement, a student of the Turkish economy will have difficulty in understanding the fuss over the budgetary transfer of about 2.3 per cent in 1998 to the social security system, while the government remains silent on the magnitude of interest payments on public debt in the same year (11.7 per cent of GNP, about a third being real interest payments). As in the case of health reforms, a reasonable compromise between the government and the participants in the social security system may be an alternative to an IMF-conditioned reform from above.

THE CHANGING BOUNDARIES OF THE PUBLIC SECTOR: PROSPECTS

Over the last twenty years, the state in Turkey has experienced a combined process of retreat and repositioning in the economic sphere. The proportion of current public consumption and investment in GNP has fallen by about 3 percentage points, reducing the proportion of human and physical resources claimed by the public sector.

Simultaneously, total transfers (including interest payments) have risen by about 8 percentage points, bringing the overall rise in the outlays/GNP ratio to about 5 per cent. By the late 1990s, almost one half of total government expenditure has been earmarked for transfers plus interest payments, a proportion comparable to those prevailing in developed economies.

This precocity is the outcome of the preferences of successive governments since 1980 to *borrow* rather than to *tax* private agents. The tax reform of 1998 is not expected to change this course in the medium term since this reform envisaged a redistribution of the tax burden rather than raising it substantially. The reform will probably make minor contributions to the tax collection effort and raise the gross tax burden by two percentage points to around 22 per cent in the foreseeable future.

One may be tempted to construct a steady-state configuration based on past trends such that gross tax burden and seigniorage (in the neighbourhood of 22 per cent and 2 per cent, respectively) can finance public consumption, investment, non-interest transfers and real interest payments, which are around 11, 4, 4 and 5 per cent of GNP, respectively. The implicit assumptions in this exercise are that (i) the public debt burden (domestic and international) will stabilize at around 70 per cent of GNP; (ii) there will be no factor income, since there will be no SOEs; and (iii) public investment outlays can only compensate for the wear-and-tear in the capital stock of the public sector, which will now be limited to those in infrastructure and public services.

The assumption about the complete divestiture of SOEs in the next decade or so may seem rather unrealistic in view of both Turkish and international experiences. Over the past fourteen years (1985–98), just about one-third of the SOEs' equity in Turkey has been transferred to private hands and employment in this sector has been brought down only by a quarter. On the international front, too, evidence suggests that the zeal behind privatization has been waning (Ramamurti 1999). However, a number of factors may lead to a rapid dissolution of the SOE sector in Turkey. First and foremost, a government which has been in financial distress for a long time will be inclined to the urgent sale of SOE assets (see Yarrow 1999: 158). Second, all SOEs, which are candidates for privatization today, are corporate structures with no serious institutional obstacles to their divestiture. Third, privatization in Turkey has gained a momentum of its own, which will be carried over into the next decade. Finally, if the SOEs are deprived of investment in the next decade, as they have been in the 1990s, both their equity and aggregate operational surpluses are likely to diminish due to technological obsolescence and the erosion of their human capital stock in qualitative as well as in quantitative terms. In fact, both managers and better-placed workers will be tempted to move to private jobs rather than stay put in their respective SOEs, doomed to death. While moving forward to such an eventuality 'the relative paucity of general, positive theorizing on privatization' (Yarrow 1999: 161) becomes irrelevant for the public administration in Turkey.

The same fate awaits most of the public utilities. Recently, the state enterprises which produce and distribute electricity (TEAŞ and TEDAŞ) and the State Hydraulic Works (DSİ) have been so desperately short of investible funds that only the successful conclusion of some ongoing 'BOT' or 'BO' negotiations can avert electricity shortages in the next decade. Similar shortages of funds also hinder Türk Telekom from expanding its services. In the next decade, therefore, the retreat of the public sector from 'directly productive' activities will be more or less completed. This will leave practically no scope to use public investment as an instrument of regional development policy, a disturbing prospect given the apparent unwillingness of private entrepreneurs to invest in underdeveloped regions of Turkey, notwithstanding very generous incentives offered in the 1980s and 1990s.

The advocates of orthodoxy may prefer to franchise a private monopoly rather than a state-owned one, because of the alleged abilities of the former to innovate and its greater responsiveness to market signals. They may also argue that the regulatory measures used to check the detrimental effects of monopoly are similar, anyway. However, in the context of a developing country like Turkey, where the state bureaucracy has weakened considerably, and become politicized and infiltrated by business interests over the last two decades, it would be folly to expect regulatory bodies to work effectively and to the advantage of large segments of the population. There have been indeed allegations of bribery and corruption with almost each and every act of privatization and franchising in post-1980 Turkey. This suggests that the efficiency-centred arguments put forward by the international institutions have been used by politicians and some top-level administrators as a cover for securing private advantages. Moreover, these abuses of power could not have been checked by the judiciary or by the fledgling organizations of civil society. If 'crony capitalism' is the expression coined to describe East

Asian cases, it would be rather difficult to coin a more appropriate one to characterize the Turkish case. Clearly, it is inconsistent to assume that the state bureaucracy is too incapable and corrupt to manage SOEs and public utilities, yet it is capable and honest enough to administer sophisticated systems of regulation not for private advantage, but for public benefit.

In the realms of education and health, relatively low per capita incomes can be expected to act as a brake on the commoditization of these services, as the very low proportions of facilities like private secondary schools and private hospitals within the total establishments suggest. The poor funding of public education and health facilities has been leading to a situation where some vestiges of the precept of 'free education and health for all' still exist, but the services offered are so low in quality that the relatively well-off either purchase private services and pay for it in full or in part, and/or the government differentiates the services according to 'ability to pay'. In addition to a wasteful use of resources, such a development will have serious social consequences in a country that already suffers from blatant inequalities in income distribution. The solutions offered as alternatives to the present systems (such as the World Bank-inspired proposals for health and social security reforms) remind us of a similar problem encountered in the case of regulating franchises. Administrative designs which sound reasonable on efficiency and even on equity grounds (e.g. separating the management of the health institutions from social security issues, establishing health insurance, emphasis on preventive health services, etc.) all involve the risk of commoditization of services and can ultimately lead to greater inequalities. Apparently, Turkey will go a long way towards downsizing and even crippling her public sector institutions before realizing that '(a) market-friendly approach ... need not be government-unfriendly' (Ramamurti 1999: 137).

CONCLUSIONS

An examination of the April 1999 general election manifestos of the six major parties (three centre-right, two centre-left and one Islamist), which garnered about 90 per cent of the votes, clearly shows that they are all committed, in varying degrees, to a 'leaner' state, no additional tax effort, privatization, and social security and health reforms of a 'market-friendly' kind. This looks like the ultimate triumph of the gospel according to the Bretton Woods twins: at no time in Turkish economic history since the 1960s have the economic platforms of the parties likely to be in power and in opposition been so convergent.

Can this near-unanimity be taken as an indication of the social and political feasibility of further 'reforms', basically at sectoral level, in the public sector from now on? Although the trends observed in the 1980s and 1990s are, to some extent, irreversible in the medium-run and Turkey currently seems to be committed to the letter of her orthodox policy approach in the next decade, the present course is likely to meet with greater resistance ahead.

First, further cuts in public spending together with reductions in, and/or the commercialization of, public services will start to erode both the legitimacy of governments and the credibility of the political system. It will lead the impoverished segments of society to seek refuge in communal clusters of kinship, neighbourhood, ethnicity and religion rather than in established and formal social safety nets. Dissatisfaction with inequalities will not necessarily be channelled into organized mass movements or autonomous class organizations, but may assume violent forms which the political establishment will find hard to contain. Perhaps recent Turkish governments have been aware of dangers of this kind, as indicated by their occasional slippages into 'populism', a word which is currently used in a derogatory sense by advocates of the Washington consensus.

Second, the current Turkish practice of introducing 'reforms from above' (i.e. to let a problem which can be solved earlier by a reasonable compromise fester for a long time and later try to impose a 'solution' on the unwilling but exhausted masses in a time of a crisis) does not seem to be an acceptable method of problem-solving. If repeated many times, this method of 'management by crisis' (which has already been applied in the cases of social security and health reforms and the revamping of the agricultural subsidy system) will ultimately result in a loss of trust in, and credibility of, public administration such that all reform proposals will be strongly resisted, irrespective of their aims and instruments, i.e., whether they are benevolent or not. The alternative method of management by consent and cooperation should not be very difficult to envisage and implement, while the costs of ignoring it may be too high.

NOTES

1 For instance, it is possible to consider cases where the public sector spends on the goods and services it produces, while, in other instances, the

products of state-owned enterprises (SOEs) are used up by private agents in the economy. Even pure public goods may be produced by private firms.

2 Unless otherwise stated, all percentage shares and percentage points given below are with reference to GNP.

3 It must be noted that about three-fourths to four-fifths of government current spending in Turkey consists of payments of salaries and wages of government employees.

4 However, conversion of ratios calculated in current prices (as those in Table 1) to those in constant (1987) prices suggests that public consumption as a proportion of GNP is smoother in Turkey, lying in a narrower band of 6–9 per cent of GNP for the entire period of 1980–97.

5 Further, some categories like social security and welfare which are usually under the responsibility of central (or federal) organs are handled by such institutions in Turkey which are, formally, SOEs operating in the financial sphere. Conversely, some spending which is generally made through regional or local bodies in many countries (e.g., education and health) is disbursed by central budgets in Turkey.

6 For example, SPO data for 1996 put the share of interest payments in central budget at 38.0 per cent, while the corresponding figure in IMF Government Finance Statistics is a mere 12.5 per cent.

7 The average maturities of new issues, on the other hand, fell from 233 days in 1989 to 119 in 1994 (when financial crisis hit the economy), and later rose to about 238 days in 1998 due to attempts by the Treasury to gain a breathing space in its operations, apparently at the cost of accepting higher long-term borrowing rates.

8 The public sector figure excludes employment by SOEs. Including them, however, does not change the overall picture as it brings down the percentage increase in total public sector employment to 31 per cent.

9 In addition to these variables, some sector-specific explanatory variables like the level and growth of regional and international demand (for cement), the degree of product specialization (for pulp and paper, and fertilizer) and composition of the workforce (for pulp and paper) turn out to be important in that study.

10 Özmucur and Karataş (1994), employing data for the 500 largest firms for the period 1983–8, also find evidence for total factor productivity growth in public enterprises, albeit at a slower pace than the private sector. They are highly critical of technical inefficiencies and the lack of cost-reducing efforts in the SOEs, however.

11 It should be noted that the SOE employment figure in 1987 includes 67 thousand people working for establishments that were privatized later, while the figure for 1997 does not.

12 The splitting-up of the Turkish Electricity Authority (TEK) into power-generating (TEAŞ) and distribution (TEDAŞ) branches in 1993 shifted operational deficits onto the power-generating branch, making the distribution branch highly profitable.

13 Even the late Mr Koçman, the then president of the Turkish Industrialists' and Businessmen's Association (TÜSİAD) made it clear in 1982 that the Turkish private sector has no claim on the ownership of SOEs and the

problem of SOEs is not the problem of ownership, but of productivity, management and finance.

14 Some of these revisions were hasty and ill-conceived attempts to fill the void created by annulments of some pieces of legislation by the Constitutional Court, thus creating serious problems of legality in privatizations. There were even cases of ignoring court rulings or injunctions by the privatizing administration on the pretext of 'unenforceability' of delayed adjudications (Boratav *et al.* 1998: 123–9). On the other hand, the government seems to have preferred the attrition of the SOE workforce due to 'normal' causes (e.g., leaving for another job, retirement, death, etc.) rather than facing the problems of labour unrest, high amounts of severance pay and other forms of compensation. This policy has turned out to be quite effective in bringing down the number of the SOE workforce by more than a quarter in seven years.

15 This is line in with international experience. Shirley (1999: 116–7) notes that there were five times as many transactions in developing countries during 1988–93 as in the previous period of 1980–7. Evidence suggests that the value of these transactions also increased dramatically after 1988. For a highly informative account of privatization experience in Turkey in the 1980s, see İlkin (1994).

16 270 leading officials of the Confederation of the Turkish Labour Unions (TÜRK-İŞ) responded to an opinion survey in 1998 in the following manner: (i) more than 90 per cent of respondents believe that privatization led to the creation of private monopolies, opened up possibilities for corruption, reduced job security and contributed to deunionization; (ii) more than 95 per cent of the respondents do not want to see privatization of the establishments in which their union is active; (iii) the respondents who are definitely against privatization of any SOE make up 64 per cent of the sample (TÜRK-İŞ 1999: 252—5)

17 Some writers consider this separation as a prelude to privatization – of distribution networks first and power plants later (see EMO 1998: 103).

18 The BOT system had been tried in the 1980s in an *ad hoc* fashion without much success.

19 The recent amendments in the constitution in August 1999 cleared the ground for such a legal procedure.

20 A draft bill prepared by the government under the advice of consultants Goldman Sachs and presented to the Parliament in 1998 envisages the establishment of an administratively and financially autonomous Telecommunication Authority, for which technical staff can be recruited from the related departments of the Ministry of Transport. Two members of the five-strong top level decision-making body of the proposed Telecommunication Authority are supposed to represent the interests of private service providers and consumers. It remains to be seen whether this set-up for a regulatory body will be accepted by the Parliament and, if so, whether it will function successfully. The history of regulatory bodies in the telecommunication sectors of developing countries (e.g., those in Chile, Argentina and Mexico) leaves little room for optimism that these bodies can be strong enough to resist the demands of powerful private firms and transnationals, and clear the

ground for genuine competition (Başaran and Özdemir 1998: 63–7; Sinha 1995).

21 Public sector outlays do not precisely match the sum of financing from general budgets plus social security sources. The difference is accounted for by transfer items and errors leading to some double-counting.

REFERENCES

Başaran, F. and Ö. Özdemir (1998), *Privatization in Telecommunication Sector: Claims, Examples and Realities*, Ankara: KİGEM (in Turkish).

Berument, H. and N. Güner (1997), 'Inflation, Inflation Risk and Interest Rates: A Case Study for Turkey', *METU Studies in Development*, 24(3): 319–27.

Boratav, K. *et al.* (1998), *An Economic Assessment of the Turkish SOE System: Quantitative Analysis, Problems of Privatization and Policy Options*, Research Report, Ankara: KİGEM (in Turkish).

Boratav, K., O. Türel and E. Yeldan (1995), 'The Turkish Economy in 1981–1992: A Balance Sheet, Problems and Prospects', *METU Studies in Development*, 22(1): 1–35.

—— (1994), 'Distributional Dynamics in Turkey under the "Structural Adjustment" of the 1980s', *New Perspectives on Turkey*, 11 (Fall): 43–69.

Celasun, M. (1994), 'Trade and Industrialization in Turkey: Initial Conditions, Policy and Performance in the 1980s', in G.K. Helleiner (ed.), *Trade Policy and Industrialization in Turbulent Times*, London: Routledge.

Ekinci, N. (1997), 'Public Deficits and "Hot" Money', *Economic Conditions*, 2 (Winter): 158–66 (in Turkish).

EMO (1998), *Law and Energy: Proceedings of a Symposium*, Ankara: The Chamber of Electrical Engineers (in Turkish).

Engiz, O. (1996), 'Problems of Financing Health Expenditures in Turkey and the Search for Solutions', in *Toplum ve Hekim*, 72: 22–31 (in Turkish).

İlkin, S. (1994), 'Privatization of the State Economic Enterprises', in M. Heper and A. Evin (eds), *Politics in the Third Turkish Republic*, Boulder, CO: Westview Press.

IMF *Government Finance Statistics Yearbooks*, 1991–7, Washington D.C.: International Monetary Fund.

KİGEM-Genel, İş. (1998), *Local Administrations: Localization, Privatization and Alienation*, Ankara: KİGEM (in Turkish).

Kilci, M. (1998), *Privatization in Turkey (1984–98)*, Ankara: State Planning Organization (in Turkish).

Ministry of Health (1997), *Health Expenditures in Turkey and Their Financing, 1992–6*, report of a study group under Dr M. Tokat's supervision, Ankara: Ministry of Health (in Turkish).

Organization for Economic Co-operation and Development, *Economic Surveys – Turkey*, 1991/2–1997/8, Paris: OECD.

——, *Historical Statistics*, various issues, Paris: OECD.

——, *National Accounts Statistics*, various issues, Paris: OECD.

Özatay, F. (1994), 'The Sustainability of Public Sector Deficits: The Case of Turkey', *Central Bank Research Paper* no.9402, Ankara: The Central Bank of Turkey.

Özmucur, S. and C. Karataş (1994), 'The Public Enterprise Sector in Turkey: Performance and Productivity Growth', in F. Şenses (ed.), *Recent Industrialization Experience of Turkey in a Global Context*, Westport, CT: Greenwood Press.

Ramamurti, R. (1999) 'Why Haven't Developing Countries Privatized Deeper and Faster?' *World Development*, 27(1): 137–55.

Shirley, M. (1999), 'Bureaucrats in Business: The Roles of Privatization versus Corporatization in State-Owned Enterprise Reform', *World Development*, 27(1): 115–36.

Sinha, N. (1995), 'Regulatory Reform: An Institutional Perspective', in B. Mody, J.M. Bauer and J.D. Straubhaar (eds), *Telecommunication Politics*, New Jersey: LEA Publishers.

State Institute of Statistics (SIS), *Economic and Social Characteristics of Population*, 1980, 1985 and 1990, Ankara.

——, *Manufacturing Industry Surveys*, various issues, Ankara.

State Planning Organization (SPO) (1997), *Economic and Social Indicators (1950–98)*, Ankara: SPO.

——, *Annual Programmes*, various issues.

——, *Supporting Studies for the V., VI. and VII. Plans.*

——, *Supporting Studies for the Annual Programmes*, 1997 and 1998.

Şenses, S. (1994), 'The Stabilization and Structural Adjustment Program and the Process of Turkish Industrialization: Main Policies and Their Impact', in F. Şenses (ed.), *Recent Industrialization Experience of Turkey in a Global Context*, Westport, CT: Greenwood Press.

Togan, S. (1996), 'Trade Liberalization and Competitive Structure in Turkey During the 1980s', in S. Togan and V.N. Balasubramanyam (eds), *The Economy of Turkey Since Liberalization*, London: Macmillan.

Türk-İş (1999), *State Economic Enterprises and Privatization: Claims and Realities*, Ankara: Türk-İş Research Centre (in Turkish).

Turkish Industrialists' and Businessmen's Association (TÜSİAD) (1996), *Retired and Happy: Problems of Turkish Social Security System, Proposals for their Solution and the Initiatives for Private Social Insurance*, Pub. No. Tüsiad – T/96-1/193, İstanbul: TÜSİAD (in Turkish).

Uygur, E. (1993), 'Liberalization and Economic Performance in Turkey', *UNCTAD Discussion Paper* no.65 (August), Geneva: UNCTAD.

Waterbury, J. (1992), 'Export-Led Growth and the Center-Right Coalition in Turkey', in T.F. Nas and M. Odekon (eds), *Economics and Politics of Turkish Liberalization*, Bethlehem: Lehigh U.P.

The World Bank (1994), *Averting the Old Age Crisis: Policy Options for a Graying World*, New York: Oxford University Press.

——, (1991) Turkey-State Owned Enterprise Review, Report no. 10014-TU, Washington D.C.: The World Bank Country Operations Division.

Yarrow, G. (1999), 'A Theory of Privatization, or Why Bureaucrats are Still in Business', *World Development*, 21(1): 157–68.

Yeldan, E. (1995), 'Surplus Creation and Extraction under Structural Adjustment: Turkey, 1980–1992', *Review of Radical Political Economics*, 27(2): 38–72.

Part III

Rethinking the State and Global Change

Chapter Nine

States, Elites and the 'Management of Change'

Charles Tripp

INTRODUCTION

Much of the debate on the state in the Middle East and particularly on its role in the economy has been coloured by a number of ideas which need rethinking. In the first place, from the perspective of political economy, the state has often been portrayed primarily as an apparatus for the accumulation of capital, more or less well adapted to the conditions under which capital accumulation is possible in the present international system. This view, privileging the economic aspects of state capacity, has been heavily influenced by the structural-functionalist assumptions underlying most writing on political economy, whereby states, as integral parts of this assumed system, are represented as actors responding with varying degrees of effectiveness to the pressures and attractions of the system itself. In this respect, not only have the economic functions of the state been highlighted and assigned a determining part in any explanation of state behaviour, but the state has been transformed from a particular framework for action into an actor for and of itself, playing its part as the shaper and executor of policy, divorced in some important senses from the individuals and groups which in fact hold the power of decision within any state.

The 'economist' view of the state, whether promoting free market capitalism or highly critical of it, comes out of the same broad tradition and experience of Western state building and societal differentiation. In both there is a shared belief in the primacy of a certain kind of rationality, largely instrumental in nature and thus intimately entwined with the developing discourse of economics.

211

Economic reason or reasoning is thus assigned a privileged place in the determination of state behaviour, both by virtue of the fact that it is assumed that such reasons or interests are universal to humanity and because it is thought that such factors form the substructure underlying the organization of power in the world. This has enabled those with a concern for political economy to elide in certain important ways the decision-making of specific groups of people with the remorseless logic of the economic state.

In addition to a conception of interests and rationality predicated upon economic advantage which comes out of a distinctive Western tradition of thought, a substantial part of the debate has revolved around the notions of the public, as distinct from the private sphere. From this perspective, the Middle Eastern state (like states elsewhere) has been portrayed as a public authority which, depending upon the epoch and the circumstances, has been either more or less tolerant of an active private sphere wherein citizens pursue their interests in social interactions that largely escape state surveillance, regulation or intervention. In the Middle Eastern case the argument is often made that the state, having occupied the prime position in the economy in the wake of independence, has been obliged through fiscal crises and external pressures, to pull back in some fashion, opening up areas of the economy for private enterprise and initiative. The developmental, broadly socialist, welfare state of the mid-century which based its strategies on public ownership of the means of production is thought to be giving way to a less ambitious state project which acknowledges the importance of private initiative and, accordingly, appears likely to open up the private sphere to some degree, with consequences of a distinctive kind for the political realm (Ayubi 1995: 196–209, 329–32, 382–9).

It is assumed in much of the neo-liberal debate that these consequences are both predictable and desirable and, furthermore, that the setting for them can be created through institutional and administrative ingenuity. Thus, a model of 'good governance' has been established, founded not only on the institutions of the dominant states of the international system, but also on the philosophical assumptions associated with them, with an ontology in which structures, intentionally established, play a key role in creating the conditions of possibility whereby the relationship between public and private can be decisively regulated. According to this thinking, the reorganization of the state's administrative capability and the regulated enlargement of the private sphere jointly create both the conditions and the incentives for further reform along similar lines (see, for example, The World Bank 1997: chs 1, 2, 9 and 10). In part this is premised on the universally assumed recognition of the material benefits to be achieved and thus a willing acceptance of certain norms of efficiency. In part, however, there is a more impersonal functionalist assumption that the adaptation of particular state institutions to the larger systems or structures dominating the global economy is both necessary and inevitable. Underpinning this is the belief that the parts obey a logic derived from the given ends of the system itself, restructuring themselves to conform or risking disintegration by failing to do so.

These twin poles of state conformity or state collapse have been much in evidence in debates about the nature of the state in the Middle East, especially insofar as the restructuring of economies and of state capacity are concerned (see Hirst's critique in Hirst 1997: 206–215; see also Waterbury 1998: 159–77). However, this chapter intends to argue against the presuppositions underlying such a view, as well as to question the validity of the assumptions of economic primacy and structural-functionalism that shape a number of apparently antithetical perspectives. In this instance, the states of the Middle East and North Africa will form the chief focus of examination, but the suggestion is not that they are unique or exceptional. Rather, it may be supposed that theories with universal pretensions that demonstrate gaps or inadequacies in one region will also need revision elsewhere.

As a way of escaping from the circular logic and teleological difficulties of the structural-functionalist approach, with its prescriptivist bias, as well as to return the focus to human agency (without nonetheless succumbing to the connected and similarly situated logic of rational choice theory), it is important to stress the shaping of policy and of the states that emerge from these distinctive forms of structuration. Rather than treating states as if they were actors, working within given parameters with greater or less success, they will be treated as settings for the courses of action pursued by elites or decisive groups. It is the latter who develop strategies, who act within the structure of a state that is in part received as their inheritance – the accumulation of past actions, encountered consciously and sometimes unconsciously as structures, habitual processes, norms and practices – in part imagined as a model, in part shaped by their own actions. In this sense, therefore, in the Middle East, as elsewhere, the state becomes both the site of conflict and contestation, but a site that is itself shaped by previous conflicts and by the variety of outcomes that they may have produced.

In order to bring this understanding of the state into focus and incidentally to 'bring the political back in', the intention here is to look at three aspects of the state, corresponding to key sites of conflict and issues of contestation in which it is argued that far from retreating, the state emerges as a defining structure shaping people's lives and to a large degree bounding their imaginations. The aspects of the state in question are: the state as community, the state as hierarchy, and the state as coercive apparatus. These are not exhaustive – the state as an abstract idea and any given state may have a multitude of other aspects – but they serve to underline the political, rather than the economic, features of the state. In doing so, they will provide an understanding of the political forces working upon the formulation of economic and other policies. None is likely to be unaffected by economic calculations broadly conceived. Indeed, in certain circumstances economic calculations may be the dominant ones, bringing motives and discourse into the purview of considerations of material resources, their distribution, ownership and production. However, this will always be conjunctural and contingent, never determinant or necessary as some of the political economy literature may suggest. The intention is, therefore, to fragment the 'economic' and integrate it into the political in its fullest sense, allowing for reciprocity and for a view of the 'economic' that is shaped not by some impersonal set of given criteria, but rather by particular hegemonic practices and languages of power (Foucault 1986: 21–30; 37–49; 64–70; and Tribe 1978: 20–47; 145–148). This counters the tendency to separate the 'economic' analytically in any understanding of the state, whilst simultaneously undermining the claim that it is in some sense privileged, driving and defining the state in an autonomous or determining manner.

THE STATE AND THE POLITICAL IN THE MIDDLE EAST AND NORTH AFRICA

There is clearly a difficulty in seeking to make systematic comparisons between a large number of states, selected primarily on the basis of their geographical location. In a number of Arab states geographical proximity may be part of a bundle of connected and shared features – historical, cultural, religious, social, economic – which make comparison meaningful. However, comparisons of Turkey with

Yemen, or Israel with Morocco, or Iran with Egypt, or Lebanon with Saudi Arabia need to establish the validity of the exercise more explicitly. Indeed, the more meaningful comparisons, illuminating their polities and significant aspects of their different predicaments, may be with countries outside the Middle East and North African region entirely. Given this methodological difficulty and the dangers of essentialism and easy stereotyping that accompany such comparisons, it is obviously unwise to strain for too comprehensive an approach. Indeed, it is precisely such an approach that lends itself to the kinds of generalization visible in structural-functionalism, wherein the particularities of the political are subsumed within the homogenizing – and in certain contexts hegemonizing – discourse of the 'system'.

Consequently, the intention here is to take the three aspects of the state – as community, as hierarchy and as coercive apparatus – which are universally recognisable, but which can take a variety of forms, both in administrative and in ideational terms. As mentioned above, these features are by no means exhaustive, but they have the advantage of directing attention to three aspects of the states of the Middle East and North Africa which they share with each other, but also with states the world over, whilst not dictating the substance or contents of these three features. It is here that the particularity of each state can be taken into account, as well as its history and the power of its distinctive set of political structures and norms to shape the behaviour of those who command the state's resources. It also leaves open to specific investigation the degree to which assumptions underlying the dominant model of the state produced by Western history, power and preponderance within the international system actually apply in particular cases.

In the states of the Middle East and North Africa, as in states throughout Asia and Africa, histories of European imperialism, of capitalist penetration and of national liberation have created imaginative and material legacies with which the present generation of leaders and citizens or subjects engage. In doing so, they are not simply victims or captives of these legacies, but will be seeking to cope with or profit from the outside world which makes demands upon them. The perception of such demands may be coloured by these legacies and they will be responded to not simply on their own terms (or the terms of those who articulate the demands in question), but also in the terms that are thought appropriate, in a strategic and a normative sense, to the environment in which the decisions are taken.

In the light of the foregoing and looking at the three aspects of the state outlined above, it is worth asking whether developments within these spheres do in fact require us to rethink the state – its capacity and its solidity – in the Middle East and North Africa.

The State as Community

The first aspect – the state as community – is a theme which has been prominent in most, if not all, of the states of the Middle East and North Africa during the past twenty five years or so and relates to the phenomenon of Islamism or the radical restatement of distinctively Islamic objectives in politics. In theory, this is a phenomenon which demands a profound rethinking of the state, both in those countries where Islamists have achieved government power and in those where they are prominent in opposition. Despite the fact that they are organizationally separate, the one aim which can be fairly said to characterise otherwise disparate Islamist groups across the region is their often repeated demand that the state be refounded according to Islamic values as they understand them ('Awda 1988: 67–120; Jaadane 1987: 112–148; and Ayubi 1993: 1–34).

Although implicitly and explicitly an indictment of the governments of those states which they regard as insufficiently marked by the 'true' Islamic ethos, and lukewarm in their commitment to the realization of the *Shari'a* in public law, the main articulated thrust of the Islamist critique is against the current dominant understanding and practice of the state. Islamist parties across the region dismiss the notion of sovereignty based on the secular principle of territorial nationalism which underpins the rationale for the modern state's existence as the embodiment of the sovereign will of a distinct community. Instead, they demand state structures more in keeping with distinctively Islamic norms. From this perspective, therefore, the present configuration of territorial states in the Middle East and North Africa can have no moral validity, since the principles which legitimise their existence as separate entities are at odds with the asserted unity of all Muslims. This may not require expression in a unitary state, but it does require, according to many apologists, a rethinking of the nature of the state and of the appropriate form of public power to rule a distinctively Islamic community. At the same time, it is the Islamic nature of this community which is to be decisive.

The reality of Islamist movements and governments has been somewhat at odds with these claims and it becomes apparent that the power of the state as an imaginative construct in the Middle East remains a formidable one. Even when faced by the Islamist challenge, ideas of community, of collective identity and of collective interests based upon the given state structures of the region have demonstrated a remarkable resilience. Indeed, in some cases it is possible to say that the Islamist movements themselves have been variously shaped and affected by the power that derives from the logic of an emerging state-based nationalism, or at the very least from the established interests of those who find the given configuration of states helpful for their interests (Kodmani–Darwish 1997: 11–40).

This has shown itself in a number of ways. In the first place, even in those countries where an apparently secularist course has been pursued by the regime in power, symbols and markers of Islamic identity have been used to help define the community. In some cases the elite thought this to be strategic, in others such values were an integral part of the elite's own perspective. One could argue that even in Ataturkist Turkey the secularizing rhetoric and policies of the state authorities could not disguise the fact that in some contexts the same authorities found it politic to stress the symbiosis between a Turkish and an Islamic identity (Sakallioglu 1996: 231–251; Hale 1998). In other countries, such as Iran under the Pahlavis or Egypt under the regime of Gamal Abd al-Nasir, where the state was secular in effect, although the regimes were only intermittently secularist in intent, the recourse to Islamic symbols and the use of Islamic authority have frequently been part of the strategic repertoire of governments. The elites in power, regardless of their own personal predilections or the strength of their religious beliefs, saw that an Islamic definition of the community was a key element in any appeal to a mass public (Ajami 1983: 12–35; Vatin 1983: 98–121). This mass public may have remained disenfranchised in all important respects, but in an era of mass mobilization, collective identity definition and growing expectations about the role of the state as representative of the community, it has been important to win recognition and to assert the symbolic identity of government and people. The same has been the case in movements of national liberation. Although ostensibly secular in intent, organizations such as the FLN (Front de Libération Nationale) in Algeria or the PLO (Palestine Liberation Organization), which were aspiring to statehood on the basis of a distinct national identity were unable – possibly also unwilling – to separate their definitions of the community from distinctively Islamic aspects of its character.[1]

217

The significance of these developments for the Islamist challenge has been twofold. In the first place, it is clear that the Islamists organise and act within the given frameworks of these same states. Those few movements which have sought a more universal framework for their activities have rapidly been marginalized. As with any political movement, the Islamists have tried to be an effective political force. This has required taking account of their locale, understanding the concerns, aspirations and the identifying values of the ambient society. This has, in turn, encouraged the growth – often assisted materially by elements of the regime in power – of Islamist movements which, although critical in many respects of the government and calling for the enactment of the *Shari'a*, speak more to the concerns of a local public. This public has, in turn, been brought into being through years of interaction with authorities acting within the framework, and in the name, of the state. Whether voiced or not, the emerging – and in some cases very well developed – discourse of 'state-based nationalism' will form a key part of their cognitive environment and of the community of which they see themselves to be members (Kramer 1995: 39–68).

On a theoretical or imaginative level, it is apparent that it is difficult for most of the Islamists to think of public power outside the context of the state and, furthermore, a state constituted very like those in which the movements find themselves acting in the present. Thus, the question of territoriality makes an appearance, as does the idea of citizenship and state-bounded community. Moreover, the administrative arrangement of state power, the use of coercion and the intervention in the economy are not questioned, but rather echo the current forms of the modern bureaucratic state. The crucial difference, it is claimed, lies in the distinctively Islamic purposes for which this state exists and the content of its laws. However, it has been argued by some of the critics of the Islamists – and by some Islamists themselves – that the wholesale adoption of what is effectively the present dominant model of the state not only makes the Islamic enterprise uncomfortably indebted to the secular and Western inheritance from the outset, but also has distorting effects on the understanding of Islamic obligation. In essence, it is claimed that the Islamists, by seizing on the state as the chief instrument of the transformation of society, will succumb to a logic inherent in its use. The state, as presently conceived and instituted, is not a neutral instrument, but rather one that enhances certain patterns of behaviour and ways of looking at the world that cannot leave identities or aspirations – Islamic or otherwise untouched (Al-'Ashmawi 1989: 29–47; Amin 1987: 185–211; Tripp 1996: 51–70).

The upshot of this is that the Islamist challenge is not a challenge to the state as such, despite claims about the need to institute a new domestic and regional order. In countries where the Islamists are challenging the holders of power, the state becomes the site of contestation, shaping strategies, vocabularies and practices on both sides. Capture of power at the centre becomes the Islamists' goal, whilst the energies of the ruling elite are spent in defending the same. In struggling for control of the state, both sides deploy strategies which are simultaneously meant to mobilise society and to foreclose their opponents' options. For the Islamists, this has generally meant taking careful account of local conditions, operating within the territorial confines of the given state and advancing a notion of the public that may or may not undermine the hold of the regime, but which strengthens the hold of the dominant model of the state on the imaginations of all concerned.

At the same time, the regimes have proved themselves adept not simply at repression, but also at adaptation, cooption and incorporation of Islamists and sometimes Islamist movements, ensuring that they engage on ground determined by the regime itself. This in turn has led in some cases to fragmentation and confusion among the Islamist groupings, but it has also served to implicate them in the distinctive patrimonial structures of most Middle Eastern states. Even in those cases where the Islamists have found themselves in a position of power, such as Iran or Sudan, or in positions that allow them to influence and shape public life, such as in Jordan at least in the early 1990s, there was a logic to state behaviour. This had both a domestic character in its societal relations and its administrative capacity as well an international one, which could not be ignored and which has come to shape government policies in these countries as well, although not without contestation from those who believed that this was an unacceptable compromise with the very forces which the Islamist movement may have initially set out to combat. Here lies the testimony to the power of the state as an imaginative construct, shaping ideas of community and the means whereby collective identities can be protected and interests furthered (Milton-Edwards 1996: 123–142; Ehteshami 1996: 143–162; Sidahmed 1996: 179–198; Abu-Amr 1997: 125–144).

The State as Hierarchy

Analytically distinct from, although often connected in reality to the idea of state as community, is the hierarchical aspect of the state. All states embody distinctive ideas of social order, of the proper relationships between the individuals and groups which constitute the society or societies bounded by the state. As a system of power through which rulers seek to organise social reality the state is, therefore, also a hierarchy of status differences, implying differential access to power. There may be any number of rationales for such hierarchies and indeed world history has thrown up a bewildering diversity of reasons for maintaining status difference and for allocating power accordingly. Consequently, the hierarchical aspect of the state is not something which is tied to any particular cultural manifestation of the form – it is as much in evidence, although based on understandably different grounds, in pre-modern states and empires as it is in the states modelled on the distinctive forms of Western European power that became the arbiter and norm of state existence in the twentieth century.

The significance of hierarchy in the context of the state in the Middle East and North Africa is that it introduces the phenomenon of neo-patrimonialism – a feature of the majority of states throughout the region which nevertheless assumes different forms in different locations, depending upon the cultural and historical configuration of the society in question. The significance of this phenomenon in the light of the present discussion is twofold. In the first place, it has been a pre-eminent instrument of elite maintenance and also a way in which a certain kind of rule reproduces itself, regardless of the changing personnel of the government itself. It thus has a claim to be an intrinsic feature of the state in the Middle East and North Africa which persists not through any cultural atavism, but because its mechanisms serve both the immediate purposes and the sense of propriety of those who are in a position to gain most from it. At the same time, it has the capacity to implicate large numbers of other individuals and communities since it holds out the possibility of reward and privileged access to resources for those who find themselves included in its circle of beneficiaries. Destructive as this may be for certain kinds of collective political endeavour and for certain conceptions of community, it has become deeply entwined with the very structure of the state as an organizing principle and, at the same time, it has helped to structure the expectations and demands of both clients and patrons within the system (Ayubi 1995: 164–174; Richards and Waterbury 1990: 330–352; Waterbury 1970).

It is arguable that every society contains within it its own networks of trust, prejudice and favour which materially affect the life chances of its members. These are not necessarily explicitly acknowledged and indeed in some cases considerable efforts are made to conceal them or to downplay their significance. In other cases, there may be more or less successful efforts to legislate against their operation or to replace them with institutions which operate on different, more egalitarian principles. In relatively open, democratic polities the struggle to curb the influence and power of these networks and exclusions has been a constant cause of concern and theme of contestation. In more authoritarian systems they can form the decisive factor in deciding who gets what when and how, with little opportunity offered for alternative ways of proceeding. Indeed the ideas and practices associated with them may constitute a kind of hegemony whereby it becomes virtually inconceivable to proceed in any other way. Not only do these methods produce concrete results for a limited, but significant, number of individuals and groups, but they may also be set within a moral context in which they are seen as fitting and proper forms of conduct (Al-Hasso 1976).

Across the Near and Middle East distinct histories and cultures have generated their own categories and languages of approval that sustain these practices, without which public life and sociability would be unimaginable and through the mediation of which the distinctive characteristics of the neo-patrimonial state take shape. In Egypt, the direct powers of patronage associated with the presidency filter down through and are in many ways sustained by the cooptation and reward system built into the ruling National Democratic Party, the mutual help generated among professional and educational *shilal*, the structures of rural and urban neighbourhood authority and the networks of familial ties and interconnections that constitute the 'power map' of Egyptian society (Springborg 1982). In Iraq, a more tightly controlled authoritarian system and a differently structured society ensure that the powers of patronage and reward at the disposal of Saddam Hussein operate in a different idiom, following channels that make sense to many in Iraq, whatever their opinion of the president himself (Baram 1997: 1–31). In Syria, the *jama'a* around Hafiz al-Asad is expected to deliver an acquiescent Syrian society and state institutions through the licence granted to them by the president, in part because of his belief in their capacity to 'deliver' their subordinate client-followings throughout Syria (Van Dam 1996: 118–135). Examples such as these could be found across the Middle East and North Africa (and indeed far beyond this region), following lines appropriate to the society in question and thriving on the authoritarian patterns of politics that are so deeply implicated in the reproduction of neo-patrimonialism. In the context of the present discussion, the nature of these lines of patronage demonstrates a more organic link between the ruling oligarchies and the social foundations of the state than has often been assumed. They have also demonstrated a resilience which has helped to sustain the state itself when many of its other formal attributes have fallen away. The very different experiences of Lebanon and of Iraq, respectively, would tend to indicate that the state, understood as a particular constellation of power, a sanctioned hierarchy of power and patronage, has a resilience which should not be underestimated.

Consequently, in thinking about the state in the Middle East and North Africa it would be unwise to divorce it from the various forms of patrimonialism which have sustained it as an organization of power and which have played so crucial a part in the calculations and strategies of diverse elites. It is of particular significance when seeking to understand the part played by such policy initiatives as economic liberalization, the opening up of the economy to private and foreign capital and the privatization of hitherto state-owned assets – in other words, the range of policies associated with the structural adjustment programmes advocated by international organizations during the past couple of decades as the most effective means of increasing productivity and of integrating local economies with the global economy. By placing such initiatives in the context of the state as it is in the Middle East, rather than as it may have been imagined to be or as it is projected to be in idealized form, it should be possible to understand the degree to which these policies are due to a genuine crisis of the state – or form part of a continuing but changing elite strategy of survival and advantage which belies the notion of a crisis of the state as such.

Two features of economic liberalization or *infitah* in the Middle East and North Africa become immediately apparent. The first is the continuing preponderance of the state in the economy, despite some years, even decades of economic restructuring. In some countries this is due to the overwhelming position of state-owned oil and gas sectors in the economy and a revenue generating capacity that is unmatched by any other sector. However, even in those countries where oil and gas production plays a more modest, or even negligible, role, the notion that the driving force of the economy should be beyond the scope of government control has been a difficult one to accept. This has led to the second feature of note: the degree to which the liberalization and privatization measures have been embedded in networks of influence and patronage which derive their ultimate, and sometimes their immediate, sanction from the elite which rules the state and which uses the instruments of state licensing to its own advantage and to the advantage of all those who have been privileged enough to be included within the guarded circle of close regime collaborators, their clients and their kin (Ayubi 1995: 339–67).

In light of this, it is hard to argue that liberalization and privatization in the economic sphere are symptoms of the malaise or bankruptcy of the state. On the contrary, they could be said to testify to the resilience of the state as an organization maintaining a particular kind of hierarchy through the use of patronage and incorporation in various forms by ruling elites which see these measures as helping to extend their own power. Crucially, also they could be said to maintain the blurred distinction between private and public which has been so much a part of elite strategy and in which the very notion of 'privatization' or the selling off of 'public' assets has a curious ring when the realities behind these labels become apparent. It is, of course, in the interest of the ruling elites that these realities should not be overly apparent. However, the opportunities for profit that they may offer those who are willing to become part of the network of obligation and favour standing behind the apparent commitment to the 'new economic orthodoxy' must be sufficiently known to exercise a hold on the imagination and to shape the aspirations of those who need to be implicated in state projects of this restrictive kind.

This very ambiguity, of course, characterized the system before the present wave of 'structural adjustment'. The state bureaucracies that sprang up to administer the nationalized industries and the assets taken under 'public' ownership soon after independence or following the wave of broadly social-developmentalist revolutions that characterized the first few decades of independence in many Middle Eastern countries provided a fertile field for the exercise of patronage and the placing and reward of clients (al-Khafaji 1986: 4–9; Sadowski 1988: 160–84; Waterbury 1983: 57–122). In many important respects, these structures still survive and although the personnel may have changed, the principle remains intact. Indeed, it is a testimony to the resilience of the political that the economic rationale and system may change to some degree, but the political structures remain untouched. This is scarcely surprising since the economic management systems, whether 'public' or 'private', and their associated rhetorical justifications may simply be devices or strategies designed to ensure that elites maintain their ability to reproduce the system of privilege that has served them, their kin and their associates so well. To read it simply as an attempt to cope with an apparent fiscal crisis is to miss the political continuities between one phase and another.

These developments, if read in this way, can be seen to bear witness to the power and resilience of the state as a hierarchy in which neo-patrimonialism in its various guises sustains elite privilege and effectively strengthens the state even when the government appears to be dismantling state assets or reducing state direction of the economy. In the absence of any clear and enforceable set of boundaries between the 'private' and the 'public', it is difficult to argue that one or other economic strategy is more or less conducive to enhancing state capacity. On the contrary, the state in the Middle East and North Africa, understood as the network of unequal relationships that sustains a hierarchy which in turn underpins a particular ruling elite, could be said to thrive as much in the culture of licensed entrepreneurs, dependent capitalists and politically indebted cliques and cronies of the rulers as it ever did in the equally congenial environment of state capitalism and bureaucratic proliferation. The fact that the latter is still preponderant in the great majority of Middle Eastern states demonstrates the degree to which these same elites are aware of the political need to retain a wide array of instruments of patronage to ensure social control through clientelist competition. There are, after all, many ways of rewarding conformity and of reinforcing the prejudices and markers of discrimination on which elite rule is based. Of course, in all of this control is necessary. Without the ultimate sanction at the disposal of those who rule, the patrimonial system would fall apart, however rewarding it might be for particular individuals. It is in this connection that it is worth considering a third aspect of the state: its capacity as a coercive apparatus.

The State as Coercive Apparatus

Deeply implicated in the sometimes familial patronage structure of Middle Eastern regimes or enjoying privileged access to resources

224

where such structures are less in evidence, the armed security forces have been key players in Middle Eastern politics. Whether through direct interventions, through the emergence of military personnel to positions of political command, or through the role that force plays in the strategies of governments throughout the region, the armed forces have helped to shape the states of the Middle East and North Africa in a variety of ways. At the same time, they have performed a range of vital tasks in the maintenance of the hierarchies that sustain rule and certain conceptions of rule within the bounded arena of the state. The continued prominence of the armed forces in the politics of the region bears testimony to unresolved conflicts both within and between the states of the Middle East.

It is this which has given rise to the notion of the 'national security state' in the Middle East – a state, in other words, whose existence is justified largely with reference to the physical elimination or deterrence of threats to the ruling regime and to the state over which it presides (Korany, Brynen and Noble 1993: 1–25; Sayigh 1993; Ayubi 1995: 256–88). These threats are alleged to be synonymous, in the sense that the ruling elite is determined to project its own interests as those of the state as community and vice versa. Thus, any threat to the regime is claimed to be a threat to the state, further blurring the distinctions between the 'private' interests of those who actually rule, their kinsmen and clients, and the 'public' interests of all those inhabitants who are technically if in no other sense citizens of the state in question. As a reflection of the patronage system that lies at the heart of power in the majority of Middle Eastern states, this is a logical development. Associated with this, the structural forms which have emerged from and have also encouraged these ideas and rationales of power have taken distinctive forms which further implicate the military apparatus in the formation of the state.

In a number of Middle Eastern countries, the duality finds institutional expression in the existence of two separate armies: one to guard the regime and one to guard the state more generally conceived. The latter has the longer pedigree and the wider recruiting ground, based as it usually is on general conscription. Historically, it has also been from these formations that the present rulers emerged to overthrow their predecessors by force of arms. Aware of this danger and yet also aware of the need to maintain a convincing military force identified with the state in the region and also within the local society, the ruling elites have often developed smaller, but heavily armed organizations whose prime task is to deter or to defeat conspiracies whether from within the regular state armed forces or elsewhere. Recruited very often from particular social communities which have some pre-existing link with the ruling group, these units have helped in some measure to get round the difficulty of having to place the coercive power of the state in the hands of those who are beyond the circle of trust as defined by the ruling elite.[2]

In other countries of the region, such as Turkey, Egypt and Israel, where the institutional configuration of the state is very different, there may be elite formations within the armed forces, but they do not serve the same purposes as the 'army to guard the army' of so many of their neighbours. Nevertheless, in these countries the role and attitude of the armed forces not only within the structure of the state, but also in its very conception, has been of prime importance, although in different ways. This has had various implications for the organization of power, the definition of state purpose and the allocation of economic resources. In Turkey, the distinctive position of the officer corps within the ideational and power structures has clearly had an effect on issues that go far beyond purely military or defence related concerns (Hale 1994: 303–36; Harris 1988: 177–200). In Egypt, much the same applies, generating a particular culture in which state rulers can be assured of continuing support for broadly authoritarian rule in which the officer corps feels it has a corporate interest. Egyptian presidents are by no means unwilling authoritarians, but the peculiarly intimate relationship with the security services limits the ruling elite's imagination both of what is desirable and of what is possible (Springborg 1982: 19–44; Kienle 1998: 219–235). In Israel, the history of the state, its continuing predicament vis-à-vis the Palestinians and its neighbours, as well as the background of many of the senior personnel in government, give the military a formidable, although not unchallenged, claim on budgets. In addition, the armed forces occupy a distinctive, and in some senses privileged, place in national political life which has shaped the ambitions and strategies, both regional and domestic, of many Israeli politicians (Peri 1983).

These features are testimony to the continuing power of the state as a coercive apparatus. For many elites in the Middle East, the coercive resources of the state are key elements in their calculations of political survival and advantage. They have worked hard to reinforce them in a variety of ways, claiming with greater or lesser degrees of plausibility that in doing so they are reinforcing the state itself. They are generally reinforcing the particular regime that sustains them, but in doing so they could also be said to be maintaining and reproducing a particular kind of state in the region. In the absence of effective challenge, the claim may lead to the general belief that the state itself is better maintained in this way.

Some of the still fragile opposition forces in these states point out that such a deployment of military resources is effectively helping to create a certain kind of state and not, as the regimes would have their subjects believe, the only possible or desirable one. Nevertheless, the 'national security state' with all its rationales and in the various forms it has taken in the Middle East is still the dominant model for the Middle Eastern state. There is little sign that it is in crisis. In many cases it is quite clearly closely connected to the structures of the society and the economy that allow a certain kind of patrimonialism to reproduce itself. This gives it a resilience as a method of organizing which may leave particular regimes vulnerable (depending upon their competence and other events or developments which may be beyond their control), but which does not invalidate it as a system of order. It suggests particular relationships that may have important economic aspects, but which are also intimately connected to the structures of association and privilege within the given society. They are also testimony to the potential violence of the multitude of unresolved inter and intra-state conflicts in the region and thus cannot be reformed or wished away in the absence of more comprehensive, substantive rather than formal, resolutions of key power imbalances in the Middle East.

CONCLUSIONS

The politics of the countries of the Middle East and North Africa bear testimony not to the enfeeblement or the crisis of the state, but rather to its resilience as a form of organization and as an imaginative field. Particular regimes and elites may face challenges, but the state retains a powerful hold on the imagination of those who might challenge them, as well as remaining for many the chief instrument of power. It is in competition for the power conferred by control of the resources of the state that the struggle is at its fiercest and where the logic of state maintenance has its tightest grip. This is not to say that the form of the state is identical across the region, despite apparent conformity to certain dominant international criteria of statehood. Similar histories and societies have produced broadly similar ways of organizing power, but there are also marked and significant differences in the constitution of the state between countries which appear to have much in common. These are the result of struggles specific to those territories and to the communities inhabiting them. They have produced state structures of differing appearance, leading some to be characterized as 'weak' and others 'strong'. However, this assumes that there is only one way of 'properly' being a state, of qualifying for the epithet of 'un pays sérieux'. It also assumes that the ruling elites which determine the direction of state resources are unproblematically engaged in a broadly similar project, voluntarily or otherwise.

Yet it is precisely these assumptions which have been put to the question in this chapter. Whilst it seems clear that elite concerns in the Middle East and North Africa revolve around a number of common themes, the content of these themes is often quite country specific and, across the region, can result in very different kinds of policies, with correspondingly varied results for the nature of the state. Indeed, the ways in which the powerful have maintained systems of blurred distinction between the public and the private, between what would – from the perspective of the dominant Western discourse of political analysis – be seen as the realm of the state and the realm of the private individual confounds many of the assumptions on which these dominant understandings of the state are based. For the elites concerned, however, this is an integral and well understood strategy which has allowed them to keep in place systems of privilege and exclusion necessary for the defeat or cooptation of challengers, whether these are challenging their vision of the political community, their hierarchies of privilege or their hold on armed force.

In these strategies, economic resources and the structures which allow for their exploitation and distribution play a role – sometimes a very important one. However, they do not necessarily constitute either the primary or the underlying concern of those who are seeking to preserve and extend their power. It is consequently in the context of struggles for political survival, for political identity, for status and recognition that programmes of economic reform must be situated. The underlying premises may be wholly at variance with those of the reforms conceived by external agencies, yet paradoxically these very programmes may only be viable because of the systems of power which, in theory, they should be helping to dismantle. Just as the initiation of the reforms implied by economic restructuring may only be possible because of the ambitions of elites who see this as a manageable strategic asset in their struggle for survival, so the consequences may be sealed by the unforeseen outcome of those struggles. Consequently, 'rethinking the state' may involve thinking less about the question of the state's role in the economy, and more about how the struggles outlined above have shaped and continue to shape the structures of the state and the actions of those who rule, as well as the aspirations of their challengers.

NOTES:

1 In part this has been because they were or are locked in struggles with non-Muslims, making the question of self-definition more likely to have Islamic resonance. But in these two cases, at least, the influence of the Islamic strand within the larger discourse of Arab nationalism, especially at a popular level, has also played a role (see Abu-Amr 1994: 23–52; Spencer 1996: 93–107 and Colonna 1983: 106–126).

2 For instance, in Iraq the key divisions of the expanded Republican Guard are officered and manned by soldiers recruited exclusively from the al-Bu Nasir (Saddam Husscin's tribal grouping) and allied clans from the region around Takrit; in Libya the Qadhdhafa Battalions are similarly recruited from Mu'ammar al-Qadhdhafi's fellow tribesmen and their traditional allies; in Saudi Arabia the National Guard, commanded by Crown Prince Abdallah bin Abd al-Aziz is recruited from tribes long associated with the Al Sa'ud.

REFERENCES

Abu-Amr, Ziad (1994) *Islamic Fundamentalism in the West Bank and Gaza*, Bloomington and Indianapolis: Indiana University Press.

—— (1997) 'La Monarchie Jordanienne et les Frères Musulmans ou les Modalités d'Endiguement d'une Opposition Loyaliste', in Kodmani-Darwish, B. and M. Chartouni (eds) *Les Etats Arabes Face à la Contestation Islamiste*, Paris: Armand Colin for Institut Francais des Relations Internationales.

Ajami, F. (1983) 'In the Pharaoh's Shadow: Religion and Authority in Egypt' in J. Piscatori (ed.) *Islam in the Political Process*, Cambridge: C.U.P. for R.I.I.A.

Al-'Ashmawi, Muhammad Sa'id (1989) *Al-Islam al-Siyasi*, Cairo: Sina' li-l-Nashr.

Al-Hasso, N.T. (1976) *Administrative Politics in the Middle East: the Case of Monarchical Iraq 1920–1958*, University of Texas at Austin, PhD 1976, Ann Arbor, Michigan, UMI.

al-Khafaji, I. (1986) 'State Incubation of Iraqi Capitalism', *MERIP Reports*, no. 142, (September).

Amin, Husayn Ahmad (1987) *Hawl al-Da'wa ila Tatbiq al-Shari'a al-Islamiyya*, Cairo: Maktaba Madbuli.

Ayubi, N. (1993) *Political Islam*, London: Routledge.

Ayubi, N. (1995) *Overstating the Arab State*, London: I.B. Tauris.

'Awda, 'Abd al-Qadir (1988) *Al-Islam wa-'Awda'na al-Siyasiyya*, Beirut: Mu'assasa al-Risala.

Baram, A. (1997) 'Neo-Tribalism in Iraq: Saddam Hussein's Tribal Policies, 1991–1996', *International Journal of Middle Eastern Studies* 29.

Colonna, F. (1983) 'Cultural Resistance and Religious Legitimacy in Colonial Algeria', in Ahmed, A.S. and D.M. Hart (eds) *Islam in Tribal Societies*, London: Routledge and Kegan Paul.

Ehteshami, A. (1996) 'Islamic Governance in Post-Khomeini Iran', in Ehteshami, A. and A.S. Sidahmed, (eds) *Islamic Fundamentalism*, Boulder, Co.: Westview Press.

Foucault, M. (1986) *The Archaeology of Knowledge*, (tr. A.M. Sheridan Smith), London and New York: Tavistock Publications.

Hale, W. (1994) *Turkish Politics and the Military*, London: Routledge.

—— (1998) 'Identities and Politics in Turkey', unpublished paper.

Harris, G. (1988) 'The Role of the Military in Turkey: Guardians or Decision-Makers?', in Heper, M. and A. Evin (eds) *State, Democracy and the Military – Turkey in the 1980s*, Berlin: Walter de Gruyter and Co.

Hirst, P. (1997) *From Statism to Pluralism*, London: UCL Press.

Jaadane, F. (1987) 'Notions of the State in Contemporary Arab-Islamic Writings', ch. 5 in Salamé, G. (ed.) *The Foundations of the Arab State*, London: Croom Helm.

Kienle, E. (1998) 'More than a Response to Islamism: the Political Deliberalization of Egypt in the 1990s', *Middle East Journal* 52/2 (Spring).

Kodmani-Darwish, Bassma (1997) 'Introduction', in Kodmani-Darwish, B. and M. Chartouni (eds), *Les Etats Arabes Face à la Contestation Islamiste*, Paris: Armand Colin for Institut Francais des Relations Internationales.

Korany, B., R. Brynen and P. Noble (1993) 'The Analysis of National Security in the Arab Context: Restating the State of the Art', in Korany, B., R. Brynen and P. Noble (eds) *The Many Faces of National Security in the Arab World*, Basingstoke: Macmillan Press.

Kramer, G. (1995) 'Cross-Links and Double Talk? Islamist Movements in the Political Process' in L. Guazzone (ed.) *The Islamist Dilemma*, Reading: Ithaca Press.

Milton-Edwards, B. (1996) 'Climate of Change in Jordan's Islamist Movement', in Ehteshami, A. and A.S. Sidahmed (eds) *Islamic Fundamentalism*, Boulder, Co.: Westview Press.

Peri, Y. (1983) *Between Battles and Ballots – the Israeli Military in Politics*, Cambridge: Cambridge University Press.

Richards, A. and J. Waterbury (1990) *A Political Economy of the Middle East*, Boulder, Co.: Westview Press.

Sadowski, Y. (1988) 'Ba'thist Ethics and the Spirit of State Capitalism: Patronage and Party in Contemporary Syria', in Chelkowski, P. and R.J. Pranger (eds) *Ideology and Power in the Middle East*, Durham, NC and London: Duke University Press.

Sakallioglu, U.C. (1996) 'Parameters and Strategies of Islam-State Interaction in Republican Turkey', *International Journal of Middle East Studies* 28.

Sayigh, Yezid (1993) 'Arab Military Industrialization: Security Incentives and the Economic Impact', in Korany, B., P. Noble and R. Brynen (eds), *The*

Many Faces of National Security in the Arab World, Basingstoke: Macmillan.

Sidahmed, A.S. (1996) 'Sudan: Ideology and Pragmatism', in Ehteshami, A. and A.S. Sidahmed, (eds) *Islamic Fundamentalism*, Boulder, Co.: Westview Press.

Spencer, C. (1996) 'The Roots and Future of Islamism in Algeria', in Ehteshami, A. and A.S. Sidahmed, (eds) *Islamic Fundamentalism*, Boulder, Co.: Westview Press.

Springborg, R. (1982) *Family, Power and Politics in Egypt*, Philadelphia: University of Pennsylvania Press.

—— (1989) *Mubarak's Egypt*, Boulder, Co.: Westview Press.

Tribe, K. (1978) *Land, Labour and Economic Discourse*, London: Routledge and Kegan Paul.

Tripp, C. (1996) 'Islam and the Secular Logic of the State', in Ehteshami, A. and A.S. Sidahmed (eds) *Islamic Fundamentalism*, Boulder, Co.: Westview Press.

Van Dam, N. (1996) *The Struggle for Power in Syria*, London: I.B. Tauris.

Vatin, J-C. (1983) 'Popular Puritanism versus State Reformism: Islam in Algeria', in J. Piscatori (ed.) *Islam in the Political Process*, Cambridge: Cambridge University Press for R.I.I.A.

Waterbury, J. (1970) *The Commander of the Faithful: the Moroccan Political Elite*, New York: Columbia University Press

—— (1983) *The Egypt of Nasser and Sadat*, Princeton: Princeton University Press.

—— (1998) 'The State and Economic Transition in the Middle East and North Africa' in Shafik, N. (ed.) *Prospects for Middle Eastern and North African Economies*, Basingstoke: Macmillan Press Ltd. in association with the Economic Research Forum for the Arab Countries, Iran and Turkey.

World Bank (1997) *World Development Report 1997 – The State in a Changing World*, New York: Oxford University Press for World Bank.

Chapter Ten

The Middle Eastern State: Repositioning not Retreat?

Roger Owen

INTRODUCTION

There are three interconnected discussions concerning the role of the state in the globalizing, post-Cold War world. The first focuses on the impact of globalization itself and the effect of the huge increase in cross-border flows of capital, information, people and ideas on the ability of governments to manage their own economies. To this must be added the accumulation of promises and commitments (these same) governments have made to international organizations such as the World Trade Organization, to cut tariff and non-tariff controls on trade and to open up local markets for goods and services in stages over the next ten to fifteen years. A second, slightly older discussion, addresses the question of whether the state itself is in retreat as a result of both market forces and its inability to finance or sustain its previous levels of health, educational and welfare services. The third discussion concerns the ability of states to maintain their monopoly over the creation of values and the definition of citizenship in the face of new forces of pluralism, decentralization or local, ethnic and religious nationalism.

Perhaps somewhat inevitably, these discussions have mainly taken place in the context of European and North American experience. It was there that a pressing need for state retrenchment was first proclaimed during the early Reagan/Thatcher years. And it is there that the most evidence exists about the process of privatization and economic liberalization, as well of the impact of the new supra-national institutions and trade arrangements like the European Union and the North American Free Trade Area (*The Economist* 1997).

Given the political sensitivities involved, it is not surprising that a large part of the public debate about the future of the European state involves such highly emotional issues as the loss of jobs, loss of national sovereignty and the virtues, or otherwise, of an international currency like the Euro. However, there are also the beginnings of a new consensus among economists and political scientists, that, according to certain quantitative indicators, the state is not in retreat at all but is spending a greater proportion of the national product than ever, taking new regulatory powers upon itself and, in important areas, dealing with a much less cohesive set of opponents, for example a weakened trade union movement.

Patchy evidence supports those who argue that some of these same tendencies may be apparent in the non-European world as well. Even before the Asian crisis began in 1997, it was clear that the introduction of market reforms involved a process, not of de-regulation alone, but of re-regulation which, in some cases, simply replaced one form of statist controls and official monopolies with another. Privatization often left the state with a majority share holding in a notionally private company. More generally, there was also much evidence from the Middle East and some parts of the ex-communist world that economic liberalization was not necessarily associated directly with political liberalization, leaving many regimes with just as much power to control as they had before. Then came the economic crisis and the perception that some countries at least might well be forced into a re-play of the 1930s with the re-imposition of the old batteries of barriers and controls designed to protect local economies from world economic forces. As Mahathir Mohamed, the Prime Minister of Malaysia, put it forcefully in early September 1988: 'The free market system has failed and failed disastrously... The only way we can manage the economy is to insulate us ... from speculators' (McNulty 1998).

Regardless of their merit, what all such discussions have in common is the assumption that what is referred to as the 'state' is a single entity, that it is knowable (at least in the sense of being relatively easy to define) and that the term itself forms part of a set of binary opposites – state/society, public/private, politics/economics, etc. – which have been a basic part of the social science vocabulary since the end of the eighteenth century. This assumption has obvious advantages. There are many significant points which can be made in such a way, using such a vocabulary. Just as important, most international discussions would be impossible without the shared assumption that what everybody is talking about is, in fact, more or less the same thing. However, I will argue that these same binary opposites are often too crude to capture the highly complex realities they are supposed to describe and that, all too often, they end up by predicting, or even advocating, such movements as the retreat of the state or the advance of society, simply because this is all that the use of these particular terms allows.

In what follows I will try to elaborate these arguments a little further before going on to introduce a somewhat more disaggregated notion of the state in order to suggest that what is taking place is not a simple retreat but a much more varied and contradictory process of reorganization leading to a re-positioning in relation to other social and economic actors.

SEEING THE STATE AS A SINGLE ENTITY

Criticism of the notion of the state as a single entity has quite a long and well-established academic history (Abrams 1988; Mitchell 1991; Ayubi 1995: ch. 1; Migdal 1988: ch. 1). One such tradition, which goes back at least as far as Marx, argues that what is called the state is in fact no more than a smoke screen to hide the self-interested activities of a ruling class. A more recent formulation which seems to sum up this perspective is associated with the work of the late Philip Abrams: 'The state is not the reality which stands behind the mask of political practice. It is itself the mask which prevents us from seeing political practice as it really is' (Abrams 1977: 58). Among its many important implications is the suggestion that the conventional use of the notion of the state as single entity seems deliberately to exclude politics (Kumar 1998: 7).

Another perspective, associated with the work of Tim Mitchell and others, concerned the fact that use of the state-society distinction is based, in part, on a spatial metaphor in which both entities exist within a single field with a boundary between them (Mitchell 1991: 80–81). But where exactly is this boundary? Or, to put it another way, how do we know what constitutes one and what the other? This is important because it goes right to the heart of the question of how are we going to start to think about the retreat or, in my formulation, the repositioning of the state. For it would seem logical that such an inquiry must begin with some sense of what the state *is*, as well as where it is in relation to the other entities which surround it, before we can move towards an understanding of whether these relationships have, in fact, significantly changed.

Making use of these insights, I would like to proceed along another tack. This takes as its starting point Talal Asad's observation that 'there are many different ways of talking about the state and they exist for many different purposes – to legitimate, to further the exercise of power, etc. etc.' He goes on to suggest that while, in certain vocabularies and for certain purposes, the state is best thought of as a single entity, in other vocabularies and for other purposes, it needs taking apart so as to examine its components (Mitchell and Owen 1991: 25–26). This provides a useful licence to pursue our analysis of the changing role of the state from a number of different perspectives without committing ourselves to any instant conclusion one way or the other. I now propose to take advantage of it myself by looking, firstly, at what we can reasonably say about the state as a single entity in its Middle Eastern context and then, secondly, how we might disaggregate it to look at what is happening to some of its component parts. As always in such discussions, the enquiry will be guided by the following set of philosophical questions: What is it we want to know? What can we know? And, how can we reconcile these two positions?

It is appropriate to begin by saying something about the state in history, for it is here that its essential characteristics are best seen through an examination of its role and its relationships in the medium to long term. It was in such a manner, after all, that the first theorists of the state proceeded, looking at the several hundred years of European development up to the end of eighteenth century for signs of the emergence of that basic differentiation between state, civil society and the market economy which they took to be characteristic of the modem world. Much of their vocabulary is still in use. However, it is now usually employed to make short-run predictions, something for which it was never originally intended.

Looking at the Middle Eastern state in the modern period, two approaches seem promising. One is simply to look at the statistical aggregates over time, which allow us to plot the growth of the state both as an employer of persons and a controller of national resources. The empirical raw material for this approach can be found in such sources as the World Bank's successive *World Development Reports*, although one has to bear in mind that in many Middle Eastern countries, the value of private sector transactions is hugely under-reported for reasons which I will address later.[1] It may also be that the quality of national statistics produced in many of the Arab countries in the last decade or so is, in many ways, distinctly inferior to that of those which came before. Hence, although the increase in the size of the machinery of government has been well reported by Nazih Ayubi (1995: ch. 9) and others, its possible shrinkage in the 1990s is much less well recorded, perhaps because it is much more immediately, controversial as far as both domestic and foreign critics are concerned.

With regards to the balance between public and private consumption as a proportion of total gross domestic product, the only Middle Eastern country to show a substantial shift in the direction of the private between 1980 and 1994 is Israel, where government consumption dropped from 38 to 26 per cent, largely due to reduced military expenditure. Elsewhere, Turkey showed a small drop, from 13 to 11 per cent, while in Egypt the fall was from 16 to 14 per cent, and in Morocco from 18 to 17 per cent. In Tunisia, however, there was a small rise (World Bank 1996: 212–213).

In addition, there is also evidence that, in some countries at least, the absolute numbers of persons in government employment are beginning to drop, due to various types of down-sizing, which include voluntary early retirement supported by increased pensions. For example, between 1993 and 1997, Egypt reduced its public sector work force of just over 1 million by 200,000 (Essam El-din 1997). Such trends obviously result in a smaller state. But this does not necessarily mean that the state has lost any real power. Indeed, as Michael Shalev has argued in an Israeli context: 'While the scope of the state has declined, it has freed itself from obligations that limited political and bureaucratic discretion and brought state and society to the brink of a serious crisis in the early 1980s. Rule changes and the dominance of a free-market ideology in economic discourse have also favoured a leaner, more autonomous state' (Shalev 1988: 33).

A second approach stems from the argument that states are best perceived as single entities when they are engaged in some large national project, nation-building being one, statist economic development being another. Note that these are, of course, the same terms which are utilized by the local elites themselves, as well as by political scientists and others looking for the defining characteristics of modernity in the second half of the twentieth century. Let us note, too, that even the most apparently powerful developmentalist state, like that constructed by President Nasser in Egypt, was never anything like as capable of promoting whole-sale economic and social change as its supporters, or critics, used to like to think (Ayubi 1995: ch. 12; Migdal 1988: 23–33). However, the notion of the national project proceeding over time raises a number of questions as to where we might look, in general, for various possible indices of change in the state's role and direction.

One such question concerns the possibility that the introduction of economic liberalization and market reforms have promoted a transition from a 'developmentalist' to a 'managerial' state which, in its latter form, is concerned not with directing economic growth itself but with laying the ground-rules for others, limiting its own immediate role to questions of how quickly to proceed in the interests of general harmony and social peace. A second question involves asking what the implications are of a possible shift in a vital part of the original national-building project: from one of imposing a homogeneous ideology and notion of citizenship to one that is being forced to come to terms with the fact that the people insist on clinging to a variety of different, often over-lapping, identities, now that the old secularist-modernist ideologies are much devalued and that the various fissiparous forces inside are being reinforced by notions of pluralism and multiculturalism coming from the international community outside.

Let us then hypothesize that at least a few Arab countries, notably Egypt and Tunisia, now contain such managerial states, as well as, perhaps, Turkey and Israel. There is certainly a great deal of circumstantial evidence for this. In Egypt, for example, the extent to which the Mubarak regime has any vision of how it is going to direct the economy once marketization and privatization have been achieved has already become a subject for lively political debate. It is also clear that the regime itself is trying to avoid such a discussion where possible, as it is thought to interfere with its larger goal of controlling the pace of change, a process which involves pulling some economic and social groups back and jolting others into proceeding at a faster rate. By the same token, it wishes to side step what it sees as socially divisive debates about culture, identity and so on by putting a lid on them where possible and giving ground grudgingly only when forced to do so. There may even be a clue here to some part of its lack of enthusiasm for a proper multi-party democracy which would provide a platform for the various sectional interests and so, in its own eyes, make its task of managing economic change that much more difficult. While it would be wrong to suggest that all this allows any great degree of certitude when it comes to characterizing a process which has been going on for no more than nine or ten years, it does suggest enough questions to focus our attention on where the important changes are taking place and what the general direction of political and economic development might be.

DISAGGREGATING THE STATE

Another approach to the analysis of the role of the state is to look for methods which take account of the perhaps obvious fact that it contains a whole host of different institutions and practices which act, not in a single interest, but according to a variety of separate logics and dynamics, some compatible, others obviously contradictory and incoherent. Because of limitations of space, I would like to concentrate on just two of these. The first is the role of the state as an arena for the interplay of different political forces. The second addresses the vexed question of the boundaries between state and society, and state and economy, by examining the notion of informality. Justification for such a choice comes from the hypothesis that both methods add necessary extra dimensions to the more general argument about the changing role of the state.

Regarding the first method, the starting point should be a recognition of the fact that one of the essential features of globalization is its direct impact on the domestic political process. It is, at one and the same time, an extraordinarily complex process consisting of interlocking circles of economic, cultural and international institutional factors, and an ideology which, for the purposes of local debate, is usually simplified and distorted in support of particular political arguments. Broadly speaking, there are those who present it as a threat and those who present it as an opportunity. However, talk of globalization also has any number of other different uses and can be addressed at any number of different levels. Hence, for example, regimes can present it both as an unfortunate necessity – as in 'we don't like having to do this but global markets dictate it' – and as a challenge requiring the wholesale reorganization of administrative, legal and other arrangements. In other words, the world has reached a stage where it is globalization, both in fact and as interpreted by local actors, that largely dictates the domestic political agenda.

How does this impact on particular areas of debate? For the purposes of exposition, let me look at four interconnected sets of issues which I will call the politics of privatization, the politics of re-regulation, the politics of global competition and the politics of national efficiency.

Privatization is, of course, still taken to be the main index of the regime's sincerity concerning the creation of a market economy, something of which all the significant local and international actors are all well aware. It is also being seen as a much more difficult and drawn-out process than was originally believed. As such, it offers any number of openings for those who wish to exert influence over it, whether administrators, potential purchasers or those with vested interests to defend, such as the existing state sector managers and workers. The result, very often, has not been a simple sell-off to private investors in the interests of competition and greater efficiency, but the creation of new monopolies (as in Israel) or of companies in which the government retains either a controlling interest or an ability to impose all kinds of rules and regulations limiting future managerial freedom (Egypt). And, whatever the case, the politicians or officials concerned seem to have an enormous, and in many cases unaccountable, freedom to decide how and to whom any public enterprise is to be sold.

The politics of regulation is connected to that of privatization in a number of ways, most notably in the need for new (or amended) laws governing property, investment, companies and labour relations, thought necessary to provide the framework for a market economy. These too are the subject of intense debate by the various parties concerned and, not surprisingly, their drafting often seems to reflect the local balance of political interest. For example, in Egypt, this is represented in the proposed Trade Union Law which does not permit the existence of unions independent of the General Union established during the Nasser era and continues to place significant limits on the right to strike. The same point can easily be made with regard to the new Egyptian laws removing limitations on rents which can be charged for rural land and new houses and flats.

All this is linked again to the politics of competition. Well aware of their weakness once the economy is opened up to outside forces, local entrepreneurs are naturally anxious to try to protect their own position in any way they can. This may involve reinforcing local monopoly positions, sometimes with strategic assistance from foreign partners, or seeking loopholes in the new foreign trade regime to protect themselves from 'dumping, or else demanding subsidies and other forms of state assistance to ease the transition. And all this in a business climate of great uncertainty, with no one quite sure how the new rules will be interpreted, what level of protection they will actually receive, or how exactly to take advantage of international opportunities such as those offered by the European Union through membership of its Euro-Mediterranean Free Trade scheme.

Lastly, there is what I have called the politics of national efficiency in which, at various levels, different interests debate and then try to suggest new policies concerning such vital matters as the future of higher education, technical education, infrastructural investment, laws and legal procedures or anything else which impinges on the role of the country in a global economy. Here, a sense of urgency and a sense of threat meet hard-headed reality in the form of institutions, seekers after profit and the personnel in the ministries, in an effort to chart policy by identifying opportunity and national need.

The novelty of the situation cannot be disguised. Although it bears some resemblance to the challenges faced in Europe and North America, there are many aspects for which neither those in the Middle East nor ourselves have any guidance from history. Rarely before the 1990s has it been necessary to try to create new markets so quickly and never, I would argue, under such international pressure and control. For this, and many other reasons, its actual outcome in any particular country is highly unpredictable, not only to outsiders but, more importantly, to the domestic actors themselves. It follows, too, that the full enormity of the changes involved creep up on the businesses and organizations concerned without them really knowing what it means, how the new regulations are going to be enforced and what leeway they may have either to amend or to avoid them. For those seeking to promote such changes, this relative ignorance may well turn out to be one of their most powerful weapons. But it makes the task of those seeking to understand them that much more difficult.

Some tentative conclusions follow. One is that the state itself, whether in aggregate as manager, or as the site of an intense debate about future policy and national and sectional interest, is the central actor in the process of interpreting, and then trying to shape the pressures of globalization as they interact with local forces. How this works out in practice depends on a whole host of variables, some of the most important of which would seem to be the presence (or absence) of a pluralist popular participation, the amount of reliable information available about present and future trends and the speed at which institutions can change their procedures and vision of their own role to meet the new demands being placed upon them. Another such conclusion is that, on the evidence so far, the creation of an open market via structural adjustment policies is not a once-for-all activity but an on-going process including, as in Europe and the United States, a never-ending debate about the proper balance between the public and the private, about which sector has the resources and the motives to undertake particular activities most efficiently, most fairly or most in keeping with some generalized notion of fairness and the national interest.

Let me turn now to my second perspective on the state, that provided by the concept of informality. This operates in at least two areas, the political and the economic, although it is only the latter which features extensively in the literature. I will look at this first.

Analysts of the informal sector of the economy tend to use a number of different terms to describe it: 'parallel', 'unobserved', 'black', 'grey', 'underground', etc. However, what they seem to have in common is the notion of a binary opposition between something controlled and supervized by the state (the formal) and something just beyond its reach. This has the virtue of focusing directly on the question of the relationship (or lack of it) with the state but misses many of the complex reciprocities which normally obtain in this area. It also tends to ignore certain obvious characteristics of the informal. To begin with, it is not just one sector, as usually described, but a collection of a whole variety of usually discrete activities, and the incomes, production and services which derive from them. These take place in any number of separate sites: in towns, villages and shanty-towns, and in households, workshops or simply out on the streets. Furthermore, each activity, whether legal or illegal, observed or unobserved, permanent or transitory, stands in a different relationship to various local agents of the state. Some are simply unrecorded because they fall under no category employed by either the national income accountants or the ministry of finance for purposes of tax collection (Thomas 1992). Others are unreported in order to avoid taxation or regulation. Others again are officially unobserved by agents of the state who are perfectly aware of what is going on but choose to turn a blind eye for some reason or another, perhaps because of a bribe. And a large number are technically criminal, however that may be defined in any particular circumstances.

In what follows, I will focus just on the unreported and the unobserved because they involve examples of what has been called 'state avoidance' in those grey areas where all concerned – whether the local state officials or private citizens – are complicit in whatever is going on. Hence, studying them can throw light on the processes by which the state, in terms both of its regulations and its agents, coexists with a variety of non-state actors to contest, negotiate and debate many areas of day-to-day economic life, often watched over, or influenced by, other local agencies such as political parties, religious groups, NGOs or, on occasions, international observers representing

241

Human Rights, Women's or similar organizations.[2] It is for this reason that I prefer the use of words like 'grey' or 'informal' to describe this shadowy area as they suggest both a relationship and a sharing of joint space rather than an absolute opposition across well-defined boundaries.

One salient example of grey area activity can be found in Egypt. It involves the collection of taxes on business profits, the state's major source of direct taxation. In its present form, it gives great licence to the collectors themselves in a situation in which there are no officially-recognized accounting standards, no independent appeal if a company's return is challenged and where the inspectors themselves are rewarded in proportion to the sums they are able to collect. In these circumstances, the inspectors usually make their own estimates of the taxes to be paid, after which there is a costly and time-consuming process of bargaining before agreement with the business concerned is finally reached. Alternatively, the businessman and the inspector may come to an informal understanding between themselves as a way of settling the matter as quickly as possible. According to a World Bank research paper, this is the course adopted by half the businesses concerned. It speeds things up, but prevents the state from receiving the full amounts to which it is legally entitled (ARE 1995: 4–7; 31).

Egyptian businesses practice a more direct form of avoidance when it comes to the establishment of new plants. Due to Cairo's complex zoning laws, there is now virtually no opportunity to obtain any legal space. In addition, anyone given official permission must also agree to observe a whole range of other regulations, for example payment of the employer's share of the workers' social security payments. The result, once again, is that an incoherent, poorly-administered system simply invites businessmen to ignore its provisions while often forcing them to pay bribes to state officials in order to secure their implicit co-operation and tolerance.

A final set of examples concerns the ways in which people wishing to build houses do so illegally and then try to bargain with state officials not only to allow them to remain but also to allow the new structure to be hooked up to neighbourhood supplies of water and electricity (Razzaz 1994). In Turkey this process assumed a regularity and predictability which was helped by the fact that municipal politicians saw new shantytown dwellers as potential voters for whatever party they might represent. However, it obviously allowed the new owners to ignore existing property rights to the land they occupied while often throwing them into the hands of whatever local mafia might control the allocation of land and the provision of building equipment in that particular area.

What I conclude from examples such as these is that there are many areas of economic life in which activities are shaped only indirectly by the state and where laws and practices encourage avoidance or negotiation. Much the same can be said of the informal political activity in which people come together to form networks to promote their interests. These can exist at all levels of society but have been best studied at the grassroots, where neighbourhood networks use the resources of a locally-based NGO or religious organization either to resist state regulation or to obtain some form of state benefit (Singerman 1995: chs 4 & 6; Sullivan 1994; White 1994). The importance of such activities is, of course, magnified by the poverty of most of the participants, the absence of most types of social security and the general uncertainty which surrounds their relationship to the state, with rules and regulations subject to constant change and amendment and their enforcement unpredictable. From the state's own point of view, they are not regarded as particularly threatening, unless linked to some larger religious or political agenda which poses a challenge at the national level. But they often make a negative critique of its ability to deliver the services which the poor require in terms of jobs, health care and a usable legal system.

Just above the local level is a variety of NGOs, run by local (generally English-speaking) nationals but often funded by international agencies of one kind or another. These organizations are usually skilled at using the language of empowerment to find a niche for themselves in programmes designed to alleviate poverty by generating income from such activities as handicrafts while offering a rudimentary training in legal rights. Once again, none of this is particularly threatening to the state itself. It fits generally into the government's own agenda while avoiding anything which might challenge the basic political and socio-economic structures which generate poverty in the first place. It also makes such organizations relatively easy to co-opt, thus reducing their power to challenge state policy even further.

Various conclusions follow. One is that the mere existence of so much informal political and economic activity does not suggest, *per se*, the presence of the kind of vibrant civil society which could be used to challenge the very existence of current Middle Eastern regimes, as it is said to have done in Eastern Europe at the end of the communist era. It is much too caught up in its day-to-day confrontations, negotiations and accommodations with the state to act as an independent source of challenge and resistance, at least in the short ran. Only in Turkey and Israel can we begin to see the emergence of groups with access to resources which are entirely beyond the power of the state. A second conclusion suggests that the mere call for better governance, as a way of tidying up the interface between the formal and the informal, is unlikely to prove an immediate antidote to all the inefficiencies and petty corruption which the existence of so many grey areas tends to promote. Indeed, given the proven ability of policies of structural adjustment to increase poverty, unemployment and inequality, at least in the short run, it is likely that the intensity of grey area activities will have to increase and expand before, hopefully, becoming fully regularized within some new politico-economic dispensation. And yet, even then, some doubts must remain: considering the extent of tax-avoidance inside the European Union or certain North American cities, it is not immediately clear that market economies are any better regulated in this respect than their communist or command rivals.[3]

RE-ASSEMBLING THE STATE

How does one best make sense of the notion of change when it comes to the role of the Middle Eastern state? Is it best described in terms of a unilinear movement from somewhere to somewhere else? Or is it better seen in terms of a process of internal reorganization and adaptation in the face of an intensified number of new challenges and constraints?

As I have tried to suggest, the answer to these questions is bound up with the vocabulary one wishes to use. Change, in terms of unilinear movement, is best captured via the notion of the state as a single entity changing its direction as a result of its becoming involved in a new national project. This, as I argued, has some descriptive power – suggesting, for example, recent movement in the direction of a smaller (although not necessarily less powerful) Middle Eastern state – but leaves many important questions unanswered. How, using this vocabulary, can one account for the initial shift in state direction, the changing relationship with other large entities like the economy and society and, above all, the play of internal politics which dictated its course? Use of the alternative vocabulary of a disaggregated state will not only help us answer at least some of these questions but will also provide insight into a process which is best understood as one of repositioning, of reshaping vis-à-vis the society, and of taking on some new tasks while abandoning some old ones.

Having made this initial argument, a note of caution is immediately necessary. The processes we want to illuminate have not been going on long enough for their outline to be at all clear. They are also taking place in what for all the actors concerned is pretty much *terra incognito* with the uncertain present made even more uncertain by the difficult task of weighing the pros and cons of existing commitments to open up markets and to introduce new regulatory mechanisms in the future. And, whether they concern the activities of well-to-do entrepreneurs or the very poor, they involve compromises and negotiations which are too ambiguous and incoherent to suggest how the process might settle down if and when a functioning market economy is achieved. To this should be added the possibility that a world economic crisis might de-rail the whole process or, as seems likely in a Middle Eastern context, cause regimes to proceed even more slowly than they have done up to now.

Nevertheless, I would not want to end by coming down too far on the side of caution. The process of change taking place in the Middle East, as well as in other parts of the non-European world, is far too fascinating to be ignored. They also pose an exciting challenge to find the intellectual resources needed to capture some part of their essential features and basic momentum. In my opinion, we should concentrate our attention on two features which go right to the heart of the matter. One is the tension between monopoly and competition, played out in the political as well as the economic realm. There are interests which wish either to retain their present high level of control or to re-create it in new forms. There are others which see benefit in a more competitive atmosphere, not just in terms of their own particular interests but also as a way of breaking up some of those formidable centres of economic and political power which ensure that the playing field is never quite level.

A second feature is the tension between the public and the private, with neither sphere well defined at the moment and the boundary between them fuzzy and difficult to maintain. An example of this was provided by President Mubarak when he criticized Egypt's rich private sector entrepreneurs on the grounds that they had failed to use their new wealth to support his voluntary school-building programme. He clearly thought it was time for them to be cajoled into using some of their profits to the benefit of those parts of educational system which the state itself could no longer provide with adequate funds. But, equally clearly, such attacks are accompanied by the none too subtle threat that the rich should remember how they made their money in the first place. Hence the distinction between private and public is first opened, to allow the accusation of private greed to be made, and then closed again to remind everyone that the creation of new wealth still depends heavily on the activities of the state itself.

To conclude: we will get a better idea of the changing role of the state by examining its internal tensions and incoherence than by treating it as a single entity consciously moving from one role, one distinctive set of relationships, to another.

NOTES

1 To give just one example, Ibrahim Oweiss suggests that Egypt's GNP may have been twice as large as the figure appearing in the national income statistics for the early 1990s, (Oweiss 1994).

2 Critics of government policies and practices, for example the failure to provide proper accounts for public sector enterprises, are usually better protected in the Arab countries by Human Rights organizations than they are by the existing political parties.

3 For example, a 1995 report suggests that the poorest 20 percent of Britain's population financed about a third of their spending from unreported income while the average household funded an eighth of their spending and saving from work in the 'black' economy (*Financial Times*, 10/11 June, 1995). A US estimate for the same year suggests that the American 'black economy' was seven to eight times larger (Feige 1989).

REFERENCES

Abrams, P. (1977) 'Notes on the Difficulty of Studying the State', British Sociological Association, annual conference paper.

Abrams, P. (1988) 'Note on the Difficulty of Studying the State', *The Journal of Historical Sociology*, I/1 (March 1988).

ARE (19 March 1995) *Economic Policies for Private Sector Development*, 'A Policy Action Plan For Private Sector Development' and 'Background Analysis'.

Ayubi, N.M. (1995) *Over-stating the State: Politics and Society in the Middle East*, London and New York: I.B. Tauris.

The Economist (1997) 'A Survey of the World Economy: The Future of the State', (20 September), London.

Feige, E.L. (1989) *The Under-ground Economics: Tax Evasion and Information Distortion*, Cambridge: Cambridge University Press.

Financial Times (1995) '"Black Economy" Believed to Exceed $100bn', 10/11 June, London.

Essam El-Din, G. (1997) 'Privatization at the Crossroads', *Al-Ahram Weekly*, (23–29 October), Cairo.

Kumar, D. (1998) 'A Critique of the 1997 World Development Report', Weatherhead Center for International Affairs, *Working Papers*, 98–2, Harvard University.

McNulty, S. (1998) 'Mahathir Declares Markets Have Failed', *Financial Times*, (2 September).

Migdal, J. (1988) *Strong Societies and Weak States: State-Society Relations and State Capabilities in the Third World*, Princeton, NJ: Princeton University Press.

Mitchell, T. (1991) 'The Limits of the State: Beyond Statist Approaches and Their Critics', *American Political Science Review*, 85/1, (March).

Mitchell, T. and R. Owen (1991) 'Defining the State in the Middle East: A Report on the Second of Three Workshops Organized by the SSRC's Joint Committee on the Near and Middle East', *MESA Bulletin*, 25.

Oweiss, I. (1994) 'The Underground Economy with Special Reference to the Case of Egypt', Cairo: National Bank of Egypt, Commemoration Lecture Programme, (19 December).

Razzaz, O.M. (1994) 'Contestation and Mutual Adjustment: The Process of Controlling Land in Yajouz, Jordan', *Law and Society Review*, 28/1.

Singerman, D. (1995) *Avenues of Participation: Family, Politics and Networks in Urban Quarters of Cairo*, Princeton: Princeton University Press.

Sullivan, D.J. (1994) *Private Voluntary Organizations in Egypt: Islamic Development, Private Initiative and State Control*, Gainsville: University Press of Florida.

Shalev, M. (1998) 'The Contradictions of Economic Reform in Israel', *Middle East Report*, (28/2, 207 Summer).

Thomas, J.J. (1992) *Informal Economic Activity*, Ann Arbor, MI: University of Michigan Press.

White, J.B. (1994) *Money Makes Us Relatives: Women's Labor in Urban Turkey*, Austin, Texas: University of Texas Press.

World Bank (1996) *World Development Report*, New York: Oxford University Press for World Bank.

Chapter Eleven

Global Change, Interdependence and State Autonomy: A View from the MENA Region

Ziba Moshaver

INTRODUCTION

The state is being challenged by globalization processes, forcing it to retreat from the centre of economic and political activities.[1] This view, based on the neo-liberal paradigm, postulates that structural forces, mainly economic, push other agencies, specifically the state, to withdraw from its position of centrality within the international and domestic arenas. The growth and diffusion of the power of non-state actors, global market and international economic institutions in particular, have contributed to this transformation. Accordingly, the autonomy of governments, whether in small or large states, is being increasingly undermined.

Several key questions arise from these assumptions in relation to the impact of global changes on the position of states. The main question addressed in this chapter is how global changes, or what is known as the 'globalization' process, influence state autonomy and state capacity in developing regions in general and in the MENA region in particular. Do these processes influence states in developed and developing areas in the same way, or do differences among states, in terms of their capacity, influence the nature of challenges and possibilities? How does the global process of change affect the state and its autonomy in the MENA countries in particular?

The main assumption here is that the impact of global forces, largely economic in origin, is related to the location and capabilities of the state within its domestic environment. Global forces interact with domestic patterns of authority, institutions and structures to produce an outcome. As such, it cannot be assumed that the globalization process necessarily benefits all along the way. The impact of globalization on the state depends on the prevailing conditions within the state, or the 'inside', in interaction with the 'outside'.[2] In other words, the way states benefit from globalization and adjust to global forces for change depends greatly on the pattern of power, authority and interests within their domestic political and economic environment.[3]

Therefore, considering the inside-outside interdependence, it is argued that many less developed countries (LDCs) are likely to retain their location within the domestic environment, but will suffer a loss of capability and autonomy within the international environment.[4] The main reason is that their resources and structures are less flexible, making adjustment to global forces for change more difficult. It is also argued that the less developed countries, including MENA countries, no longer have the strategic position they once had to be effective players in the new international environment and are thus increasingly marginalized. This is influenced by a shift away from the bi-polar world order, dominated by political/strategic calculations, to another, guided primarily by international political/economic considerations. Accordingly, a large part of the developing world that mattered to the bi-polar order for political/strategic reasons is no longer important in a global environment dominated by economic parameters set by global economic relations. Finally, it is argued that there is an invigorated North-South gap, in both the political and economic areas, as the poorest and least competitive parts of the South are becoming increasingly isolated within the international political economy.

The MENA states have a relative advantage compared to some other states in the less developed regions. Despite pressure from global changes, these states have a degree of autonomy vis-à-vis the 'inside' because of their functional location in relation to society. Their geographical position and oil resources, too, give them a clear advantage. But, like many other developing states, they are being increasingly marginalized vis-à-vis the 'outside' because of their weaknesses in relation to the international political economy.

This chapter begins by analysing the current globalization process in the context of the evolution of the international system of state. Placed within this framework, the impact of the globalization process on the 'South' or developing world will be analysed in order to explore how the process challenges the MENA region.

GLOBAL CHANGE AND THE WESTPHALIAN STATE SYSTEM

The globalization process is undoubtedly challenging the state in many serious ways. Territorial sovereignty is being diminished on a wide range of issues, undermining the capacity of the state to control and protect its land and its people from outside influences. Equally important is that non-state actors hold an increasing proportion of power and influence in shaping the global order. This phase is sometimes referred to as a post-Westphalian age.

While the intensity and extent of the current wave of global change is greater than at any time in the past, the phenomenon itself is not new. The Westphalian model of the state has had to operate under pressure from other competitors since its inception after the Peace of Westphalia in 1648. Introduced in Europe in the form of an autonomous geographical entity, the state was to replace previous forms of authority. By positioning this superstructure at the centre of international politics, the state was to organize interaction between the community and the external environment (for a more recent analysis of the origin and causes of the system, see Bussmann and Schilling 1998). As such, it was meant to fulfil rather limited functions. The central role of this model of the state was to act as a venue for negotiating and allocating resources for war. State capabilities were primarily confined to defending national territory and accumulating resources to meet this function. This state system was not meant to be either impenetrable or free from external challenges. In other words, there was nothing to prevent the system from surviving under pressure, which it did for so long before the current wave of globalization.[5]

The resilience of the state has had less to do with the extent of global pressure for change and more to do with the state's ability to accommodate this pressure and to benefit from the possibilities created by external changes. The question, therefore, should be not only what kind of pressure this latest process of global change puts on the state, but rather how states, especially those in developing regions including MENA, accommodate and adjust to this pressure. Furthermore, as the trajectory of change is as yet unclear, the phenomenon itself may not necessarily prove to be more challenging than previous phases of global change. In this century alone, the international system of states saw great challenges with two radical developments: change in the state's location within the domestic arena, and change in the international system, resulting from rapid expansion of the system into non-European areas.

Domestically, modern societies have been placing diverse demands on their states. The introduction of the welfare state was an important challenge that substantially altered the location of the Westphalian state as originally devised. This transformed the state into a functional actor within the domestic environment. Internationally, the state as a form of authority rapidly expanded into other regions, substantially adding to the number of independent states. With colonial engagement, Europeans transplanted into a wide range of regions, many of which had very different experiences of authority, an already transformed model of the state. In other words, the 'post-Westphalian state' came into being much earlier than the current discourse on globalization seems to suggest.

Viewed in this context, the debate over the impact of the present wave of global change on the state and its autonomy becomes a paradigmatic debate, depending on how one defines the autonomous state system, its location and capacity within the domestic and international environments. The realist paradigm in International Relations (IR) with its focus on the power and the autonomy of the territorial state – the main intellectual current during most of the post-War period – helped to perpetuate the notion of the impenetrable sovereign state. This view of IR takes key concepts such as state, power, sovereignty or security as given. It also associates these concepts with fixed physical and functional boundaries. Therefore, while comparative politics tends to consider horizontal and vertical patterns of authority in tackling the *problematique* of change, international politics long remained indifferent to these issues. In a sense, the state-centric perspective regards the society-centric as a reductionist theory of the state. It considers the state to derive its power not from the society but from the international arena. The 'inside-outside' dichotomy is equally upheld by the society-centric theories as they, too, tend to ignore the international dimension of the state.

Therefore, for the Realists, state and state borders were assumed to be resilient to outside penetration, and thus they focused on the external as their topic of enquiry. This allowed them to overlook even changes that had an impact far beyond their territorial borders. Forces such as revolutions – like the Chinese, Cuban or Iranian – were regarded primarily as internal developments believed not to alter international power relationships, thus not challenging their basic premises. Other important topics of enquiry neglected by this paradigm included: a feminist perspective on international relations,

251

human rights, or international public opinion.[6] The post-WWII bi-polar system has helped the realist's intellectual stance and the centrality of war and the capacity to execute war as the main functions of the state.

But increasing diversity in global patterns of authority, coming to the fore by the end of the Cold War, forced the IR discipline to tackle the issue of change and its impact on both horizontal and vertical levels of state authority. Analysing change, its direction or its impact on other topics of analysis – the state, in this instance – has become an increasingly important topic of enquiry. Some view the direction of change as 'back to the future' postulating that global changes do not alter the fundamental system of states based on power relationships (Mearsheimer 1990: 5–56; 1994/95: 5–49). There are also those who promise the 'end of history', postulating the triumph of liberal democracy and free market economy over alternative models (Fukuyama 1992).

This post-Cold War analytical shift and the relative decline of the realist paradigm have helped the neo-liberal institutionalist paradigm to gain greater prominence and popularity (Keohane and Martin 1995: 39–51; and Keohane 1997). Global changes in favour of diverse sources of authority question the traditional location of the state and its autonomy in relation to other actors, both 'inside and outside'.[7] It is increasingly clear that the nature of 'within-state and state-to-state relations'[8] is more complex than the realist paradigm has allowed. Whereas the state-centrist view denies the importance of global forces challenging the authority and centrality of the state, the neo-liberal paradigm attempts to offer explanatory possibilities. This shift of paradigm thus allows International Relations to analyse the 'outside' in conjunction with the 'inside', instead of focusing on the state as a unified monolithic actor in international politics. Such a shift also allows issues belonging to the 'inside', like demography, technological and ideological changes, or the power of groups in civil society such as ethnic minorities, religious groups and women, to be considered when analysing the impact of global forces for change. Equally, analysis of the 'outside' includes state as well as non-state actors, such as the International Monetary Fund, the World Bank, and the European Union, non-governmental organizations (NGOs), international public opinion and so on.

This could be a useful analytical approach helping to identify the impact of the globalization process on the state's location and capacity, both as a domestic and as an international actor. This perspective also conforms with the structural reforms advocated by international economic institutions and taken up by many developing states including several in the MENA region.

INSIDE–OUTSIDE: THE IMPACT OF GLOBAL CHANGES ON DEVELOPING STATES

While the current globalization process affects all states and regions, the extent and nature of its impact thus vary, depending on two fundamental criteria. The first is the location of the state within the domestic and international political and economic environments. The second is the ability of the state to benefit from possibilities created by global processes of change and to adjust to the challenges posed by them with minimum cost to its autonomy.

Based on these two criteria – location of the state and its capabilities – many developing areas are likely to benefit less than the developed countries from the possibilities created by the globalization process and to suffer more from the challenges posed by global changes. This is due to the characteristics associated with globalization, on the one hand, and the different levels of capabilities that states and regions have, on the other.

An important characteristic of the globalization process is its identification with free market economic rationality and multiple sources of authority. As such, the process is closely associated with an Anglo-American ideological premise of liberal capitalist origin. This ideological premise has a somewhat limited application in terms of being a predominantly one-way exchange: from the developed to the developing region, or from the North to the South. At times, the term globalization could be re-labelled 'Westernization'.

The difficulty with this project – being promoted globally by the international financial institutions – is that it overlooks North-South and South-South differentiation. The project seems to assume a degree of homogeneity and similar capability between the two. Faced with global forces for change, states with advanced economies are both more flexible in adjusting to global pressures, and better positioned to influence global changes. By contrast, most developing areas, the MENA region being a prominent example, are far less flexible in adjusting to the demands of the globalization process and its project for change.

Their central location vis-à-vis the 'inside' makes the developing states less flexible in adjusting to change. The state in the MENA region, in particular, tends to assume a central location in society. Like those in many other parts of the Third World, MENA states have become the functions of their capacity to generate, collect and distribute resources. The state provides public goods, individual and national defence, law and order and, at times, the cultural preferences of the society. In other words, the developing state as an organizational agency has played a central hegemonic role in relation to society and, for reasons to be discussed later, has emerged somewhat independent of other domestic sources of authority.[9]

The hegemonic model of the state dominating political, socio-economic and cultural spaces has come to the fore in the MENA region irrespective of regime type or resource availability. This model, adopted by conservative monarchies, revolutionary military leaderships or one-party regimes, or by oil-rich as well as oil-poor countries, needed elaborate state machinery. Therefore, institution-building, the introduction of bureaucratic capability, and the creation of norms and values were all functions that the state needed to fulfil in order to legitimize its hegemonic location within the domestic arena (for a useful analysis of the state building process in the Middle East, see Ayubi 1995). The state thus went beyond not only the Westphalian model, but also beyond the state in advanced regions in terms of location as a domestic actor.

This level of domestic hegemony, however, reduces the MENA states' ability to accommodate globalization pressures and to adjust to diverse sources of authority. This, in turn, creates tensions with the global project for change that requires the state to alter its hegemonic location. Altering this control might create difficulties for the state and its leadership as it has been a response to certain structural conditions, none of which seem to have been eroded. The structural conditions that helped the MENA states to gain a hegemonic location at the centre of the political economy revolved around several important areas:

1. To satisfy the needs of the development programme adopted by most MENA regimes, which in turn require control over two important mechanisms: bureaucratic and financial resources.
2. The need of the political elite to undermine traditional and competing sources of authority, and to win loyalty for the state and its leadership.
3. Oil-rent and its dominant place in national economy.

Since none of these conditions have been eroded, the state continues to retain its autonomous location which cannot be occupied by other forces nor can the society live without it. It should be noted, however, that this hegemonic control has little to do with being a strong state, as most MENA states remain predominantly weak.[10]

Another tension is related to the incompatibility between what society expects of the state and what the new globalization orthodoxy recommends. States in the MENA region are still required by society to fulfil their function as 'providers'. Whatever system of 'pseudo-welfare' exists is a result of the state's function as provider of welfare (this aspect of globalization is usefully elaborated in Ruggie 1995: 507–26). The state on the whole absorbs and distributes, directly or indirectly, a large part of the total domestic product. One outcome of this is that the state occupies spaces that would otherwise be taken by other actors, either in parallel to, or in cooperation with the state. In most MENA states, the state effectively encourages disconnection with society, and adversely affects cooperative and autonomous state-society relationships. By contrast, the globalization project requires the state to accept forces from the civil society as independent 'partners'.

Therefore, given its location as provider, it is difficult for the state to withdraw from the centre without creating socio-economic difficulties and their attendant political risks. The short term impact of reform has been largely that of economic stagnation – even regression – with reduced wages. This aggravates existing social tensions by increasing pressure on the least privileged sections of the population and effectively helping the more privileged ones. These uncertainties obviously go against the kind of political stability and continuity that successful and sustained economic liberalization would require. In view of these tensions, the question is whether the global project for change would be followed if the ruling elite believes it threatens its position. Past experience shows that the ruling elites in the MENA states have never volunteered to withdraw from the centre of the political and economic stage by allowing competitors from civil society to emerge.

The currency of global change also proposes the introduction of a 'civil state' differentiated as a guarantor, rather than as an interested party. Again, in the case of the MENA region, the state leadership is the interested party and its attempt to initiate political or economic reforms tends to be a function of survival strategy and of the desire to secure financial opportunities for itself and its supporters. One of the main reasons for the leadership to favour reforms is to increase the possibilities of co-option, negotiation, and corporatist arrangements with those societal elements that are more likely to follow, rather than to compete.

Reforms carried out so far in most MENA states show a close connection between the growing private groups of entrepreneurial classes and the political elite. This suggests a further tension between the requirements of global forces and those of the local decision-makers. The paradox is that global forces rely on the political elite to introduce the reforms that they recommend, whereas the elite's prime goal is to preserve its own central location. What seems to have emerged in most MENA states is the enlargement of the financial elite, not as independent actors, but as part of the political leadership.

This links up with the political implications of the global project for change. The implicit liberal assumption behind the current economic orthodoxy is that it would encourage the enlargement of the political space to include other actors, i.e., move toward democratization of the political system. It is thought that the erosion of the state's monolithic centrality in the economy will help to undermine its political centrality. But, as Callaghy puts it, 'the mutually reinforcing character of political and economic reform in the Third and Second Worlds relies on an extension of neo-classical economic logic'. This logic does not appear to hold very often, 'even under authoritarian conditions, much less democratic ones'. Instead, he suggests a rather 'perverse relationship' between political liberalization and economic reform (Callaghy 1993: 241–42; see also 1997).

In view of these uncertainties, globalization pressures might weaken the state as a functional organization. A general problem with this is that the international system has not conceived of an alternative to the state as the main source of authority. The closest to that alternative model is the European Union, which is less of an alternative to state authority, and more of a parallel source of authority. For better or worse, the state is still the only legally and functionally recognized source of authority in the international system.

A further problem connected with the weakening or possible disintegration of the state in developing regions is that it does not necessarily lead to the empowerment of other, or more dynamic, actors from within.[11] Withdrawal from the centre could instead risk the developing state's authority as the central political and economic actor. Here again, differences among the developed and the developing states influence the outcome in terms of the level of *stateness* (Callaghy 1993: 165). The globalization process has in many ways reinforced statehood by increasing the prospect of growth and development and, in turn, the welfare and security functions of the state. But this is more true of the developed and less of the developing regions. The latter are more likely to suffer from a weakened state and reduced welfare prospects. For example, the 'eclipse' of the state in Africa – not a result of the globalization process but despite it – shows that it does not necessarily lead to the emergence of stronger civil associations as a substitute (Evans 1997: 80–81).

Under pressure from the forces of globalization, coupled with their domestic weaknesses, many developing states including the MENA states could face greater social and political uncertainties at a time when political stability is essential for economic transition. The solution thus seems to be a level of *stateness* that is adequate to accommodate changing global conditions without undermining state capabilities and the ruling elite. But there is no workable blueprint for creating this delicate balance. The Chinese experience up to now shows a degree of mutual empowerment of the state and society (Evans 1997: 80–1). But this mutual empowerment is not because they have followed the liberal global orthodoxy, but because they have done so selectively: relocating the state in the domestic arena, and controlling the process of what could be called 'civilianizing' the state.

MENA REGION AND THE GLOBAL MARGINALIZATION OF THE SOUTH

A major impact of global changes since the 1980s and especially the 1990s has been an increasing international marginalization of the South, or what was traditionally labelled the 'Third World'. This process is, in part, a consequence of the developing states' relative difficulty to adjust to globalization and benefit from its possibilities compared to those of the North. More specifically, the globalization process has been associated with two related changes that adversely influence the position of the developing states in the international arena: 1) The centrality of economic issues, and 2) the decline of the bi-polar system. These changes have helped to re-invigorate the North-South gap that seemed to have declined in the early 1980s and denied the South its traditional response mechanisms.

First, because of the centrality of economic issues, weaknesses in terms of institutional, socio-economic and political structures of the developing countries become more important to their position within the international system. These weaknesses were in part compensated by military/strategic considerations of the bi-polar international order.

Second, the end of the bi-polar order has created a new but ambiguous condition for the Third World. As the prospect for strategic conflict between the two post-war blocs is reduced, so is the strategic importance of the South to the North. The North now selects who to support in terms of economic value to the international political economy rather than strategic importance. Of course, the South is far from homogeneous and diversity within that group is at times greater than that between the First and the Third World. Among the developing regions, MENA states have been relatively privileged because of their continued strategic advantage reinforced by oil resources.

These changes contribute to the marginalization of large parts of the South and reduce its ability to influence the international political and economic system (Krasner 1993; also Keohane's commentary 1997: 150–70). In the past, the developing states used their strategic position in relation to the East–West conflict to demand more favourable terms. They at times successfully used international institutions to their advantage, such as the non-aligned movement, GATT, or OPEC. This was facilitated by the fact that in the past the South enjoyed greater homogeneity among its constituents. More recently, however, the differences within the states of the South have been growing fast, with some moving away from its 'poorer' segment and getting closer to the North in terms of location in the international political economy.

Moreover, the 'eclipse' of the state in the South under pressure from global forces could further weaken the 'inside' in negotiating with the 'outside'. In a new international system where the state is not the only source of authority, the competitiveness of the domestic players becomes more important than when the state is the sole actor. Here again, many developing states, including the MENA states, rarely have domestic players that could improve the state's international negotiating position.

Another impact of the globalization process on the international position of the developing states is linked to the level of transnational activities. Generally, state power comes from its resources in relation to other states, and from its capacity to negotiate favourably as an intermediary with the 'outside'. But, as a large part of this capacity is derived from the activities of non-state actors, the developing or late-emerging states score less favourably than the advanced capitalist states, as their transnational activities are far less elaborate. Their more limited share in world trade and investment limits their influence in international economic issues. In the MENA states, like many other developing or late-capitalist states, the size, capacity and growth of transnational activities of non-state actors has little significance. Moreover, as argued before, the influence of independent actors is very limited and closely linked to the state.

Therefore, the state in the South has a very limited function as an intermediary to facilitate transnational activities. Here again, the developed world is better positioned to benefit from the possibilities provided by the globalization process. As Stephen Krasner puts it:

'Large, highly developed states with diversified economies, multiple trading partners, sophisticated domestic markets, and well-trained state bureaucracies can mitigate or adjust to pressures emanating from the international environment. Small underdeveloped states, however, remain extremely vulnerable; they are closer to the European states of the seventeenth and the eighteen centuries than they are to their more powerful and industrialized contemporaries' (Krasner 1993: 303).

As a result, the globalization process has helped to widen the North-South division by increasingly marginalizing parts of the South that are not regarded economically valuable. Obviously, no two regions of the South have responded in identical ways to global changes. Some states have had considerable success, and the ascendancy of globalization has forced the North to cooperate and negotiate with them on the basis of greater equality and commonality of interest. But many others, among them the MENA states, have so far shown less political and economic capability to adjust and benefit from the globalization process. Global changes have helped the North to make a selection by shifting away from the traditional South and towards states where the economic interests of the North dictate, i.e., Newly Industrializing Countries (NICs) in regions such as Latin America, Asia and some European/Asian components of the former Soviet Union. Despite problems with many of these states, the North is forced to stay engaged because of their position in relation to the international political economy. But the picture is different for the less dynamic cases within the Third and Fourth World states, which risk being pushed to the margins of the global system.

Finally, today's globalization process seems to require a degree of ideological homogenization in order for a state to benefit from the possibilities which it provides. Here, too, some stand better chances than others in terms of economic, social and cultural affinity to the North. NICs in regions such as Latin America, South-East Asia or parts of the former Soviet Union are more eligible to benefit from global processes by integrating into the international system and following the neo-liberal economic and structural orthodoxy. In a sense, in the same way that the UN and its Charter accepted the principle of equality among states after World War II but promoted a particular vision of state behaviour, international financial institutions, too, assume equality while promoting a particular economic ideology.

Therefore, unlike in the post-WWII period, the post-Cold War world, dominated by global economic forces, gives less value to the control of territory or large population or even military capability. Instead, access to capital investment, technology, markets and proximity to those powers that control the 'global production network' is what contributes to their negotiating position as actors in international relations. This is where the South in general, and its least privileged members in particular, stay in the margins in relation to the international political economy.[12]

CONCLUSION

The current globalization debate, postulating multiple sources of authority and economic restructuring, has two shortcomings when viewed from the developing areas. The debate does not adequately consider the importance of the 'inside' in examining the way in which global forces influence the developing states. Morever, it fails to recognize the importance of regional differentiation, North-South as well as South-South.

Viewed in this context, global processes of change put considerable pressure on developing areas and provide opportunities that parts of the South would not be able to exploit. Pressures of global forces are not necessarily at the expense of the state, but rather, parallel to it. The state system, as discussed earlier, has proved resilient by way of developing the capacity to adjust to challenges presented to it. With some exceptions, the states in the Third World, especially in the MENA region, have so far held on and are not becoming, in Krasner's words, a 'residual category or empty shell' (Krasner 1993: 302).

Although resilience has been a permanent characteristic of the territorial state, not all states adjust to change in the same way. Some have shown greater capacity to adjust to forces for change and to benefit from it while others have not. It is argued that in most cases the developing states' autonomy and centrality vis-à-vis the 'inside' is not much reduced since the capacity of other actors within the domestic environment is still quite limited. But their location in the international system, 'outside', is increasingly marginal in relation to the international economic system.

The end result is that the gap, both socio-economic as well as political, between the North and South is not likely to decrease. It seems that a relationship is growing: the poorer and the less economically significant a state, the more marginalized it is as an actor in international politics. The Middle East still has greater possibilities than many others within the South. Its geo-strategic location and financial resources relative to its population continue to give the region a comparative advantage, but the future might present a different picture.

NOTES

1 Susan Strange (1996); see also Keohane (1989) positing dominance of the international institutions. For a different perspective, see Skocpol (1985) and Clark (1997).
2 'Inside', as against terms such as 'internal', is used to indicate the *ensemble* of what is within the spatial confines of the territorial state rather than the clean lines of 'state sovereignty'. It is also used to indicate that demarcation of the 'internal' and 'external' is not always possible, nor can the two be easily distinguished from one another. As such, the term could more easily embrace issues associated with international political economy.
3 The focus here is on objective political and economic processes and interests that shape the less developed countries as a whole. While recognizing objective differences between the developed and the developing areas in terms of the processes at work, it differs radically from the essentialist position as these capacities are believed to go through a continued process of change and transformation.
4 State autonomy is defined in terms of the capacity to formulate and pursue the state's own goals.
5 Miller refers to the flexibility of the model as, '"Westphalia's genius" that derives capabilities from "fragmentation" rather than "centralisation".' (1990: 27).
6 On revolution and IR, see Armstrong (1993); also Fred Halliday (1994). On human rights and IR, see the pioneering work of Vincent (1986) and Donnelly (1993). On feminism and IR, Sylvester (1994) offers a good analysis.

7 Rosenau elaborates on vertical, such as territorially defined, entities and horizontal, such as religion or class (1997: 360–69).
8 This is developed in Higgott (1991: 102).
9 The criterion is not the size of the state in relation to the national economy but the extent of the state power in shaping socio-economic policies. See Evans (1997: 62–82).
10 Here a distinction is being made between 'strong' and 'weak' states and states with strong or weak bureaucracies. Bureaucratic expansion does not necessarily translate into strong state. For a useful discussion, see Migdal (1988).
11 The World Bank sketches a bright future with increased capacity and effectiveness for the state with the release and empowerment of dynamic economic forces from within the society. According to its 'state friendly, market friendly' proposal, the State remains central to economic and social development not as a direct provider of growth but as a partner, catalyst, and facilitator. The World Development Report, 1997 suggests two strategies: state's activities to match its capability; and focus to build additional capability by reinvigorating institutional capacity. See World Bank Annual Reports 1997 and 1998.
12 Falk (1997 and 1999). This is also referred to as 'the dictatorship of international financial markets' (Evans 1997: 67).

REFERENCES

Armstrong, David (1993) *Revolution and World Order*, Oxford: Clarendon Press.
Ayubi, Nazih (1995) *Over-Stating the Arab State, Politics and Society in the Middle East*, London: I.B. Tauris.
Bussmann, K. and H. Schilling (eds, 1998) *Pax Europa: Westphalia and After: A Continental Divide*, volume I: *Politics, Religion, Law And Society*, Munich: Bruckmann.
Callaghy, Thomas (1993) 'Vision and Politics in the Transformation of the Global Political Economy', in Slater, R. O., B. M. Schulz and S. R. Dorr (eds, 1993), *Global Transformation and the Third World*, Boulder, CO: Lynne Rienner.
—— (1997) 'Globalisation and Marginalisation: Debt and the International Underclass', in *Current History*, (November).
Clark, Ian (1997) *Globalisation and Fragmentation*, Oxford: OUP.
Donnelly, J. (1993) *International Human Rights*, Boulder, CO: Westview Press.
Evans, P. (1997) 'The Eclipse of the State? Reflections on Stateness in an Era of Globalisation', *World Politics*, (October): 62–82.
Falk, R. (1993) 'Democratising, Internationalising, and Globalising: a Collage of Blurred Images', *Third World Quarterly*, vol. 13, no. 4.
—— (1997) 'State of Siege: Will Globalisation Win Out?', *International Affairs*, vol. 73, no. 1.
—— (1999) 'World Prisms: the Future of Sovereign States in International Order', *Harvard International Review*, vol. 21, no. 3.

Fukuyama, F. (1992) *The End of the History*, New York: Free Press.
Halliday, Fred (1994) *Rethinking International Relations*, London: Macmillan Press.
Higgott, R. (1991) 'Toward a Nonhegemonic IPE: An Antipodean Perspective', in Murphy, C. and R. Tooze (eds), *The New International Political Economy*, Boulder, CO: Lynne Rienner.
Jackson, R. (1990) *Quasi State: Sovereignty, International Relations and the Third World*, Cambridge: CUP.
Keohane, R. (1989) *International Institutions and State Power*, Boulder, CO: Westview Press
—— (1997) 'Problematic Lucidity: Stephen Krasner's "State Power and the Structure of International Trade"', in *World Politics*, vol. 50, no. 1, (October).
Keohane, R. and L. Martin (1995) 'The Promise of Institutionalist Theory', in *International Security*, vol. 20, no. 1, (Summer).
Krasner, S. (1993) 'Economic Interdependence and Independent Statehood', in Jackson, R. and A. James (eds, 1993), Oxford: Clarendon Press.
Mearsheimer, J. (1990) 'Back to the Future' *International Security*, vol. 15, no. 1, (Summer).
—— (1994/95) 'The False Premise of International Institutions', *International Security*, vol. 19, no. 3, (Winter).
Migdal, J. (1988) *Strong Societies and Weak States: State-Society Relations and State Capabilities in the Third World*, Princeton, NJ: Princeton University Press.
Miller, L. (1990) *Global Power: Values and Power in International Politics*, Boulder, CO: Westview Press.
Rosenau, J. N. (1990) *Turbulence in World Politics*, Princeton, NJ: Princeton University Press.
—— (1997) 'The Complexities and Contradictions of Globalisation', *Current History*, (November).
Ruggie, J. G. (1995) 'At Home Abroad: International Liberalisation & Domestic Stability in the New World Economy', *Millennium*, vol. 24, no. 3, (Winter).
Skocpol, Theda (1985) 'Bringing the State Back in', in Skocpol, Theda, Peter Evans and Dietrich Rueschemeyer (eds, 1985), *Bringing the State Back in*, New York: CUP.
Strange, S. (1996) *The Retreat of the State: the Diffusion of Power in the Global Economy*, Cambridge: CUP.
Sylvester, C. (1994) 'Feminist Theory and International Relations in a Postmodern Era', *Cambridge Studies in IR*, 32, Cambridge: CUP.
Vincent, R. J. (1986) *Human Rights and International Relations*, Cambridge: CUP.
World Bank (1997) *The World Development Report*, New York: OUP for World Bank.
World Bank *Annual Report, 1997 & 1998*, Washington D.C.: The World Bank.

Index

Index

Index

state: as arena of differenct political forces 238–41; armed forces 225–6; autonomy 132–3; avoidance 241–3; changing role 160–3; as coercive apparatus 214, 224–7; as community 214, 216–19; conformity/collapse 212–13; debate concerning 232–4; developmentalist/managerial shift 237; differences 227–8; disaggregating 238–44; economic role 156–8, 211–12; and elite concerns 228; external influences on 157; formation 115–16; growth of 235–6; as hierarchy 214, 220–4; impact of globalization 232; and informality 238, 241–4; inside/outside interdependence 249, 252, 253–7; interventions 158–60; monopoly/competition tension 232, 245; national efficiency 239–40; as national project 236–7; political aspects 214–27; privatization 238–9; public/private balance 223, 225, 236, 245–6; re-assembling 244–6; Realist stance 251–2; reforms 256; and regulation 239; resilience 227, 250; rethinking 211–28; as in retreat 232; role of 1; shift in policies 156–7; as single entity 234–7; and society 115–16, 234, 251, 254–5; strategies 228–9; structural-functionalist approach 212–14; as transformed 163–5; weakening of 236–7, 262; Westphalian system 250–3
State Owned Enterprises (SOEs) 139, 179, 186–92, 205–6
statism 85–6, 112
Stiglitz, J.E. 93, 96
Strange, S. 261
Structural Adjustment Programmes (SAPs) 141, 142–3, 148, 149, 173; role of state 144–51
Sukkar, N. 129
Sullivan, D.J. 128, 169, 170, 243
Sylvester, C. 261
Syria: assessing reform strategies 132–3; elite interests/strategies 129–30; evolution of political economy 120–1; explaining economic liberalization differences with Egypt 130–2; political systems 124–6; and international system 122; reconstruction/incorporation of bourgeoisie 126–7; state formation 124–5

technos 130
telecommunications 192–3, 206–7
Tendler, J. 23
Thailand 91–2, 94–5, 103–4, 105
Thomas, J.J. 241
Togan, S. 73, 178
total factor productivity (TFP) 21, 40–2, 45
trade: cooperation/coordination 100; openness/liberalization 43, 54, 60, 102; regulation 124; verticalization of 99
transformation: assessment 3; chapter outlines 4–11; and economic liberalization 111–33; and economic reform 135–53; globalization, crisis, economic reform 80–102; and international/regional environments 156–74; logic for/strategies 3, 15–102; missing links 15–52; processes/outcomes 2–3, 111–204; rationale for 2–3; restructuring public setor 178–204; structural obstacles 59–77
Tripp, C. 219
Tunisia 136–7, 153, 158, 174; abandonment of socialism 139; Association Agreement with EU 143, 149–50; comparative perspective 151–3; economic crisis 139–40; from corporatism to reform 138–41; international environmental effects 169; as managerial state 237; old corporatist state 137–8; onset of reform in 142–3; patronage 150–1; persecution of Islamists 141; political challenges 140–1;